Global Masculinities

Series Editors
Michael Kimmel
Department of Sociology
Stony Brook University
Stony Brook
New York, USA

Judith Kegan Gardiner
University of Illinois at Chicago
Chicago
Illinois, USA

The dramatic success of Gender Studies has rested on three developments: (1) making women's lives visible, which has also come to mean making all genders more visible; (2) insisting on intersectionality and so complicating the category of gender; (3) analyzing the tensions among global and local iterations of gender. Through textual analyses and humanities-based studies of cultural representations, as well as cultural studies of attitudes and behaviors, we have come to see the centrality of gender in the structure of modern life. This series embraces these advances in scholarship, and applies them to men's lives: gendering men's lives, exploring the rich diversity of men's lives—globally and locally, textually and practically—as well as the differences among men by class, race, sexuality, and age.

More information about this series at
http://www.springer.com/series/15013

James D. Bloom

Reading the Male Gaze in Literature and Culture

Studies in Erotic Epistemology

James D. Bloom
Center for the Arts
Muhlenberg College
Allentown, PA, USA

Global Masculinities
ISBN 978-3-319-59944-1   ISBN 978-3-319-59945-8   (eBook)
DOI 10.1007/978-3-319-59945-8

Library of Congress Control Number: 2017947169

Cover illustration: Supapixx/Alamy Stock Photo

Printed on acid-free paper

This Palgrave Macmillan imprint is published by Springer Nature
The registered company is Springer International Publishing AG
The registered company address is: Gewerbestrasse 11, 6330 Cham, Switzerland

Let him gaze
—*Virginia Woolf, To The Lighthouse*

ACKNOWLEDGEMENTS

Thanks to Tom Cartelli, Mark Edmundson, James Kaplan, and Alan Nadel for their counsel and encouragement over the course of this project.

Thanks to Muhlenberg College's Provost's Office and my colleagues on the Faculty Development and Scholarship Committee for their support over the years.

Thanks to Muhlenberg's Trexler Library and IT staff for their expertise, patience, and timely eagerness to help.

Thanks to Tom René, Brigitte Shull, April James, Sridevi Purushothaman and their associates at Palgrave Macmillan/Springer Nature for getting *Reading the Male Gaze* to its readers.

Thanks to Jim Barszcz at *College Hill Review* and John Wills at the *European Journal of American Culture* for giving the ideas in *Reading the Male Gaze* an early hearing.

CONTENTS

CHAPTER 1

Introduction: The Shelf Life of a Meme

THE TITLE

Since the 1960s the phrase "the male gaze" has migrated beyond academe and become a commonplace in works of fiction, art exhibits, and movie reviews. "The male gaze" now reverberates throughout cultural conversations across disciplinary and national boundaries. Coincidentally, I completed the first draft of *Reading the Male Gaze* only weeks before the *Chronicle of Higher Education* ran a special section titled "The Male Gaze in Retrospect," commemorating this meme's fortieth anniversary. During the same week, an interviewer in the *New Yorker*, Ariel Levy, quoted Jill Soloway, the creator of the controversial Amazon TV hit *Transparent*, claiming "complete access to the male gaze" for women as well as for men. By this time, male gazing had become commonplace enough among the culturati for another *New Yorker* writer to refer knowingly to what he called simply "the stereotypical male gaze" (Brody). This reviewer's use of the definite article serves to remind, even to reassure, readers that "being in the know" now entails recognizing male gazing as a ubiquitous meme, essential in any diversified portfolio of cultural capital. *Reading the Male Gaze* documents this diffusion and explores its implications.

When I first read and heard the phrase "the male gaze," it struck me immediately as aptly—and embarrassingly—applicable to the way I had been observing and exploring the world around me at least since my age hit double digits. I say embarrassingly because when I began

© The Author(s) 2017

J.D. Bloom, *Reading the Male Gaze in Literature and Culture*, Global Masculinities, DOI 10.1007/978-3-319-59945-8_1 looking over the scholarship I was obliged to read during my professional apprenticeship, I learned that the phrase was being used critically, polemically, and even disparagingly. Wherever the phrase appeared, male gazers were being stigmatized, vilified as complicit in "the crime" that novelist Yiyun Li describes in a 2008 *New Yorker* story as a transgression that "amounted to nothing more than a few moments of gazing." Li illustrates the extent to which, as Linda Williams observes, the male gaze now functions as a "totalizing concept," as a "largely unchallenged ... orthodoxy ... something akin to a popular villain whose specter has haunted the field of visual representation ever since" the 1970s (2–3).

As both an effort to resolve these tensions between this concept's clarifying richness and its stupefying hegemony and as a plea for exoneration, *Reading the Male Gaze* represents an effort to legitimate at least one aspect of male gazing by demonstrating how it operates as an epistemological practice integral to the conceptual sophistication I've aspired to cultivate as a teacher and writer and to reconcile this practice with political and ethical imperatives customarily treated as antagonistic to the "objectifying" impetus associated with male gazing. Throughout what follows I'll be arguing that this impetus is too complex, its effect too variable, for it simply to be dismissed and disparaged. In 1975, the same year that Laura Mulvey coined and launched the phrase "the male gaze," Helen Bishop, less influentially, introduced a collection of pioneering photographs by Garry Winogrand ("Winogrand's"). Writing from the perspective of a gaze object, Bishop praised male gazing, at least Winogrand's male gaze, as the work of an "artist [who] has caught the conflict ... the body as object vying with the self as person" and goes on to voice an aspiration "to enter the world of the Winogrand women." My argument for probing rather than censuring "the male gaze" builds on Bishop's heterodox understanding of the relationship between gaze objects and gazers.

Even the opprobrium typically aimed at male gazers can suggest, however scathingly, intellectual or at least cognitive development as a possible motive for gazing. In Paul Laurence Dunbar's 1902 novel *The Sport of the Gods*, for example, Dunbar's narrator observes a southern barber newly arrived in Manhattan. During his first visit to the theater, a cultural rite of passage, he "gazed steadily across the aisle at a girl" and convinces himself that "he had made a decided advance in knowledge." My argument on behalf of male gazing rests on the hope that readers will at least consider the possibility that Dunbar—however sardonically—acknowledged over a century ago.

Considering male gazing in this light, that is, as an intellectually engaging, cognitively demanding reading practice, aligns it with the legacy of Dunbar's contemporary and pioneering *female* gazer, the Victorian photographer Julia Margaret Cameron, who described "the history of the human face [as] a book we don't tire of, if we can get its grand truths, & learn them by heart" (Lane, "Names"). Over a century later, the Irish novelist Deirdre Madden renewed Cameron's legacy by showing the male protagonist of *Time Present and Time Past* realizing how a woman "fascinating to both men and women" can exhibit a "beauty [that] can suggest more than what she is." In the wake of this realization, he turns to a photograph reminiscent of Cameron's work: "a post card-sepia ... studio portrait of a young woman from the early years of the twentieth century or the end of the nineteenth." Though Madden notes this gazer's predictable attention to the portrait subject's "full mouth ... and abundant hair," she shifts his attention from these hereditary or cosmetic attributes to the cultivated, perhaps hard-earned traits her beauty, particularly her "strange smile" expresses: "knowledge, complexity ... a sort of power" (48–49). In this spirit, *Reading the Male Gaze* will look to bodies, faces included, and the ways in which writers, moviemakers, and other artists and theorizers have represented bodies and faces over the centuries for the kinds of truths and lessons that Cameron extolled and Madden has more recently has promoted.

In draft form, *Reading the Male Gaze* bore the title *The Male Gaze Reader*. The change in title aimed to forestall some anticipated confusion over where to shelve and how to sell *Reading the Male Gaze*, yet the completed version retains the spirit of the wordplay of my initial title phrase, at least to the extent that the noun "reader" can refer to both a person and a kind of book. (Perhaps most familiar to Americans or at least among Americanists is William Holmes McGuffey's pedagogically oriented *McGuffey's Reader*, ubiquitous in American schoolrooms beginning with its first edition in 1836.)

Like anthologies, books designated "readers" strive for representativeness and focus on defined topics or widely acknowledged questions. But in contrast to anthologies, the books we call readers favor ad hoc selection choice over coverage. Considered either as a reader or as an anthology, *Reading the Male Gaze* was written in the hope that my reflections and analyses will matter less than the words of the writers quoted and in the belief that often, as Ralph Waldo Emerson assured his readers, "a writer appears more to advantage in the page of another book than in his own" ("Quotation").

In assembling the work of the writers and other artists included in *Reading the Male Gaze* I have set out to do the work of what we now call aggregators as well as the more traditional work of annotators. Cumulatively, these writers, along with the image-makers whose work *Reading the Male Gaze* addresses, speak to the cultural practices that Denis Donoghue calls attention to in observing that, inevitably, all "cultural practices are anthologies" (18), including male gazing. I occasionally turn in the following pages to recount how I came of age as a male gazer and how during the years in which I grew increasingly conscious, as a consumer and a critic, of the narratives, tropes, and images that surrounded me, my own male gazing, as an idiosyncratic, individual practice, came to converge with male gazing as an age-old, trans-genre, multimedia legacy.

PAST MASTERY: CHOICES AND IMPEDIMENTS

For anthologizers, the simple act of choosing becomes an argument in favor of particular "cultural practices"—at least an argument for studying, though not necessarily emulating, such practices. Thus, *Reading the Male Gaze* also functions as a discursive commonplace book that always amplifies, sometimes dissents from, and sometimes treasures influential accounts of male gazing and memorable critiques of male gazing. This amplifying, criticizing, and cherishing necessarily eclipses my curatorial project. For all my eagerness to share male-gaze material gathered over years of reading and reflection, the primary motive at play in these pages rests on an argument—or counterargument—over what we mean and what we might mean in using the very phrase "the male gaze."

A more practical reason for restraining my anthologizing impulses will be familiar to fellow scholars and writers who have edited anthologies or readers and to anyone who has published an evidence-based study of copyrighted texts and images. Like me, they've labored under the constraint to quote and illustrate parsimoniously so as not to run afoul of intellectual property laws and misnamed "fair use" guidelines.

In order to work around these institutional constraints and to make my occasional autobiographical turns integral to my conceptual argument, I have sought throughout *Reading the Male Gaze* reader to follow anthropologist Michael Taussig's recommendation to practice what he calls "Nervous System" writing. Taussig disparagingly contrasts this with conventional academic writing, or "agribusiness writing," which he defines as writing that "wants mastery," that operates as "a mode of

production," and at the same time "conceals the means of production."
Agribusiness writing reflects a purely "communicative" view of "writing
as information to be set aside from writing that has poetry, humor, luck,
sarcasm, leg pulling, the art of the storyteller" and functions as "a source
of experience for reader and writer alike." Nervous System writing also

> finds itself implicated in the play of institutionalized power as a play of
> feints and bluffs and as-ifs taken as real in which you are expected to play
> by the rules only to find there are none and then, like a fish dangling on
> the hook, you are jerked into a spine-breaking recognition that yes! after
> all, there are rules. (31)

Therefore, according to Taussig, Nervous System writers keep feinting
and bluffing, quixotically, to stay "one jump ahead of the rules." My
most transparent "feint" is a reaction to the realization that accounting
for the experience of a male-gaze reader necessitates detailed consideration of images that have long shaped, inspired, and disciplined male
gazing. Hence, readers will notice my use of URLs instead of actual
illustrations, indicating where readers might find the images that museums and media conglomerates have priced above nearly every individual
writer's and even many publishers' means.

Beyond this economizing tactical feint, my adoption of Nervous System
writing speaks more conceptually to Taussig's prohibition against "mastery" and his corresponding endorsement of "the mastery of nonmastery."
As an intervention in the now-ubiquitous male-gaze conversation, my
reflections aim to advance an understanding of gazing as an expression of
curiosity and a bid for reciprocity. While at the beginning of this conversation Laura Mulvey introduced gazers as invariably playing a commanding
or mastering role in images of and narratives about women, my evidence
and reflections on this evidence complement this prevailing view with
accounts of male gazing as often entailing acts of submission and accounts
of male gazers relinquishing, surrendering, or simply lacking the mastery
Mulvey and the conversations she spawned ascribe to male gazing.

THE POST-MULVEY CONVERSATION

Questions raised throughout *The Male Gaze Reader* about whether the
actual experience of male gazing as well as numberless accounts of and
remarks on male gazing correspond to Mulvey's critique—the argument

that produced the phrase—target two very different kinds of reader. Readers accustomed to the phrase "the male gaze" typically treat it as a critical judgment, even an expression of indignation, and are likely to have a political, moral investment in what Stuart Hall, writing a generation after Mulvey introduced academia to "the male gaze," designated as "the displacement of the masculine gaze" (201).

Beyond academia, curious lay readers may be familiar with the phrase "the male gaze" without knowing about its 1975 coinage in Mulvey's groundbreaking essay "Visual Pleasure and Narrative Cinema." Now, however, that both lay and academic readers have been long accustomed to encountering the phase, the time may have come to record and explore its durable impact and ubiquitous iterations, its status as a conversational commonplace. My imagined audience as I composed *Reading the Male Gaze* included everyone ever touched by this conversation—anyone who has used, heard, or read the phrase "the male gaze."

The way this conversation has unfolded over the past five decades shows that what started out as a narrowly focused, arguably esoteric academic insight has apparently come speak to an abiding preoccupation. Simply to utter the phrase "the male gaze" now entails at least alluding to and often betraying a fascination with sexual desire, both reciprocal and unidirectional, opposite-sex as well as same-sex. In her recent review of the controversial French movie *Blue is the Warmest Color*, the novelist Lorrie Moore argued that the time has come to reconsider what we mean when we refer to "the male gaze." Moore's call for reconsideration acknowledges the rich complexity of Mulvey's concept while exposing what has, too often, become its "antique" polemical, pseudo-explanatory convenience:

Can a moviegoer set academic theory aside and still ask, What is the cinematic male gaze, and is it so very different from the female one? Is the camera inherently masculine, a powerful instrument of anxiety, and lust, forever casting women as objects? (The phallic pen has never once deterred a woman writer.) And when is a gaze not a gaze but something else—something prurient or false or constructed as if through a rifle sight, or, as one filmmaker friend of mine has said, "as something to be viewed in the safety of a dark theater"? Moreover, is "gazing," with its fraught exile and exiling, what a camera should be doing anyway? Shouldn't the camera instead be trying to get past the gazeness of its gaze—that is, its condition of exclusion—and engage with the observed, knitting together an alliance between viewer and viewed? Is looking necessarily a form of desire? Of covetousness or envy? Was not the ultimate male gazer Hans Christian Andersen's poor Little Match Girl? ... 1970s film theory (Laura Mulvey, John Berger, and others) sometimes had it that the male gaze is directed at a woman, and the female gaze is directed at the male gazing at the woman (Hitchcock's *Vertigo* builds its entire plot on this dialectic between viewer and viewed). Yet from the current vantage point, in this somewhat antique model, the female gaze may consist of a composite vision and be the more complex and authoritative, by virtue of containing additional information. Then again, of course, the male gaze may be watching the female gaze as well, which adds an additional layer of power and perception, becoming a tertiary gaze, and then the female may gaze back, ad nauseam, in the nature of a hand-slapping game or the infinite regression of a Quaker Oats box or the badinage of Abbott and Costello. (Moore, "Gazing")

The Male Gaze Reader aims to continue the conversation Mulvey inaugurated while integrating into this conversation the rethinking that Moore advocates.

THE APPRENTICE

The world is full of renunciations and apprenticeships, and this is thine: thou must pass for a fool and a churl for a long season. Ralph Waldo Emerson

This hope for sustaining and transforming the male-gaze conversation grows out of several decades spent living as both an amateur, occasionally amatory, "male gazer" and as a professional reader. During my half-century as a professional reader, beginning soon after "the end of the *Chatterley* ban and the Beatles' first LP" that Philip Larkin so famously commemorated (34), sexual desire became an approved and even essential subject in literary study (see Chaps. 4 and 5). Arriving on US campuses as a French import labeled *desir* and often tied to Roland Barthes' supposedly not-quite-translatable synonym for orgasm, *jouissance* (Gallop 566), this liberating approach to reading developed, perhaps paradoxically, into a subdiscipline: "an anti-normative, anti-institutional erotics," in Jane Gallop's phrase (565). This subdiscipline bore both the cultural prestige and the whiff of scandal that made it catnip to an intellectually aspiring, incurably horny twenty-something academic wannabe just beginning an apprenticeship as a literary scholar.

A conceptually appealing English import, Mulvey's phrase "the male gaze" stood out; her "male gaze" argument held its own among all this seductive Francophone *richesse*. "The male gaze" quickly became, in spite of its censorious edge, part of every apprentice critic's must-know conceptual repertory. Unlike much of the "theory" in which I immersed myself as an apprentice, Mulvey's coinage has proven durable enough to continue at once to inspire and antagonize this male-gaze reader.

I knew as soon as I first saw the phrase "the male gaze" that it applied to me. I also realized that, at least as Mulvey framed the concept, male-gazing as customarily practiced was wrong or at least retrograde and perhaps even unfair to many of the women who drew my gaze. After decades of gazing and almost as many years of knowing myself as a gazer, the time seems ripe for a reckoning with these contradictions, for sorting out and holding myself and my fellow gazers accountable.

The Material and the Setup

Conversations about accountability run the risk of sounding bureaucratic and grimly legalistic. But they needn't be. In the hope of keeping the conversation lively, my argument and my reflections throughout *Reading the Male Gaze* encompass a diverse selection of quotations and images that I hope readers will savor and ponder while challenging and questioning my own inferences and the analyses on which they rest. Much of the material cited has provoked both lust and, often, more gradually and more durably, reflection. Therefore, making inferences and drawing conclusions from what I quote has entailed reliving the pains and pleasures of these provocations and revisiting the writers and artists who have over the years played the all-important role Walt Whitman ascribed, in "Song of Myself," to the "prurient provokers" who "stiffen[ed his] limbs" and "strained the udder of [his] heart." About a century later another poet of the American city, LeRoi Jones (soon to become Amiri Baraka), in his perennially provocative drama *Dutchman*, conferred intellectual legitimacy on gazing or at least attributed to it some cognitive merit by characterizing this ubiquitous activity as the disposition to "run your *mind* over other people's flesh" (7; emphasis added). With such precedents in mind, my argument in *Reading the Male Gaze* will proceed by treating gazing as a mindful activity belonging to the multitude of minds whose work I've aggregated in the following pages.

This diverse array of writers, artists, and performers includes James Baldwin, Titian, Rembrandt, Bob Dylan, Theodore Dreiser, Emily

Dickinson, Italo Calvino, Charles Chesnutt, Jeffrey Eugenides, Søren Kierkegaard, Jules Feiffer and Mike Nichols, John Berryman, Shulamith Firestone, Philip Roth, Sarah Silverman, Henry James, Robert Stone, Gary Shteyngart, W.B. Yeats, Flannery O'Connor, J.M. Coetzee, John Dos Passos, D. H. Lawrence, Nathaniel Hawthorne, Washington Irving, John Schlesinger, F. Scott Fitzgerald, Edith Wharton, Willa Cather, Andrew Wyeth, Colm Tóibín, Tim O'Brien, Elif Batuman, James Joyce, Zora Neale Hurston, Geoff Dyer, Elizabeth Bowen, Aleksandr Solzhenitsyn, Don DeLillo, William Golding, Chester Himes, Gertrude Stein, Nell Zink, Ernest Hemingway, Joyce Carol Oates, Sinclair Lewis, Ingmar Bergman, and Dana Spiotta, among others who come and go throughout the following chapters, with several making encore appearances.

Reading the Male Gaze consists of six chapters including this introductory first chapter. Chapter 2, "Coming Clean: Readings, Confessions, Shortcuts," recounts the convergence between my own unintended and often unwanted career as a viscerally driven male-gazer, from adolescence on, and my interests as a literary critic and cultural inquirer. Chapter 3, "American Fiction: Gaze Canon," surveys American fiction since the incubation of a distinctive American literary culture early in the nineteenth century. Chapter 4, "Scopes on Trial," reflects on a selection of male-gazing poets and novelists and their relationships to technologies of seeing and framing beginning with Galileo's telescope and extending to the role of kaleidoscopes, microscopes, and astronomical observatories in literary representations of gazing. Building on the broad survey of American literature in Chap. 3 and on brief readings of contemporary novels by Eugenides and Calvino in Chap. 4, the more narrowly focused approach to American fiction in Chap. 5, "American Fiction After Mulvey," examines work by two eminent novelists, one recently retired and the other recently deceased: Philip Roth and Robert Stone. This chapter treats both novelists' oeuvres as responses to feminist criticism in general and to "male gaze" theorizing in particular. Chapter 6, "British Invasions: Post-Bar Mitzvah," revisits the autobiographical narrative with which Chap. 2 opens and looks to the 1960s and the cultural ferment that gave rise to Mulvey's theorizing. The contextual coordinates in this chapter include this decade's twin British invasions: popular songs by the Zombies, the Beatles, and the Rolling Stones and the controversial movies by John Schlesinger and Lindsay Anderson that once shaped my own coming of age as a male gazer.

CHAPTER 2

Coming Clean: Readings, Confessions, Shortcuts

During first decade of our millennium memoirs filled bestseller lists. Readers were apparently counting on the memoir writers' therapeutic good faith and trusted them not to be *in denial*—or at least to avoid appearing so. The spirit of the age seems to demand that even an intellectual inquiry like *Reading the Male Gaze* ought to open with a soul-cleansing revelation. Even if what's confessed couldn't have happened, what I'm about to confess needs to have happened so that readers know what's at stake in the following inquiry.

Marianne Moore memorably insisted that poetry should show a "real toad in an imaginary garden." However, the "real toad's" reflections that follow never managed to find a home genre or home shelf like those that libraries and book retailers afford poems and novels, biographies and cookbooks. Moreover, my Christian–Jewish heritage revoked my garden privileges about 6000 years ago (at least according to some pious accounts). Therefore what follows begins as the account of a real toad (not even a kiss-redeemable frog prince) neither in a bookstore nor in a garden—and certainly not in *the* garden—but in another kind of sanctuary. It begins in a suburban church basement.

I stood up as if stepping from my grave, nursing a Styrofoam cup of cold black coffee. It was my first time inside the Treat Avenue Methodist Church, a suburban landmark I'd passed a thousand times. Struck by its Romanesque Revival gravity—its limestone masonry, its cobalt-bright stained glass, its rounded, pillared portico—I'd also imagined it as more eclectic than architectural historians would allow. In contrast to all this

© The Author(s) 2017
J.D. Bloom, *Reading the Male Gaze in Literature and Culture*, Global Masculinities, DOI 10.1007/978-3-319-59945-8_2

intriguing busyness, Treat Avenue Methodist's basement "social room", all plywood, sheet-rock and linoleum, seemed to boast of its charmlessness. This difference between what I saw on the outside of Treat Methodist and what I felt on the inside was apt preparation for joining my new community, the community for whom this book aims to speak.

The organization, unknown to even my best-informed readers, resembles the many organizations we all know about, organizations based on regular meetings and candid anonymous sharing: groups committed to healing the millions overwhelmed by addictions, dependencies, ungovernable compulsions to seek pleasure whatever the consequences. Following the familiar protocol, I made my ritual declaration:

My name is Jim and I'm a male gazer.

No catharsis followed. My soul—or psyche, or whatever intangible organ I was supposed to be fixing—would remain uncleansed. Confessing my compulsion and enlisting in this community of regretters would oblige me to make amends to anyone my gazing had harmed. I couldn't shake my conviction that my gazing has always been pure or at least innocuous, untainted by consequence.

Had I shared these protestations with my fellow addicts they would have called me out for being in a place familiar to all catharsis-seeking therapeutic self-cleansers: *in denial* about "objectifying" and therefore harming the women I've gazed at. Objections that a lifetime of restrained behavior doesn't let me off the hook would have reverberated from the sheetrock to the linoleum and back. Though steering clear of equating explaining with excusing, what follows addresses these objections, even if it fails to quell them.

These explanations rest on the midlife realization that the compulsion to gaze grew apace with another less stigmatized compulsion, another besetting and besotting obsession: reading. Both obsessions date back at least to puberty and to the onset of the accompanying endocrinal dysfunction from which I'm still convalescing. Medical science, we can only hope, will some day learn to diagnose and treat what we sufferers recognize as early onset testosterone poisoning. Though the nursing chart makes no mention of the ailment, this condition contributed to at least one of my several hospital stays.

During the third of several lifetime hospitalizations, the week I turned sixteen, my testosterone poisoning was probably at its most lacerating.

Oblivious and cruelly insensitive to what most ailed me, an orthopedic surgeon was treating me for a sports injury. Lest readers get the impression that I had any athletic talent or successes, I should hasten to add that for teenage boys at the time, in the 1950s and 1960s, sport was a fate, not a choice. No computers, no videogames, no Fenders (couldn't carry a tune to save my ears), Cold War virility and normality anxieties dinning in my ears, JFK's reverberating insistence on moving forward with great vigor resulted in countless hours devoted to such baseball variations as hardball, wiffle ball, softball as well as to tennis, wrestling, basketball, and football (English and American)—and always playing badly.

In only one sport did I come close to excelling, probably because it took place hundreds of miles from home, because it was unconscionably expensive and required no teamwork, and I could do it with girls: skiing. Unlike all my other sports, skiing also afforded an elevated, permissible perch for male gazing. From a ski lift I could follow my gaze object plummeting down the mountain. During that run, on an Easter morning some fifty years ago, my gaze fixed on Lauren Willow as she managed, all at the same time, to sway and plummet headlong, more recklessly than I dared, about a foot of thick yarn-like black hair flying behind her tangling with a Valencia orange scarf in the wind tunnel she opened before her. What my gaze couldn't catch from the lift, including dark eyes sunk so deep as to make her look precociously dissolute, necessitated keeping up with her fleet schuss back down to the lift line.

Finally, in my eagerness for a close-up view daring to ski in front of Lauren, I lost control of my left ski's inside edge against a mogul. Hard on my tail sped the dark-lady-in-training. One of her ski's steel edges sliced through my Levi's and into the side of my left calf. Bound as I was by (male) peer pressure and compromised as I was by testosterone toxic shock, I secured some peroxide and a large gauze bandage and skied on. A week later another of my chronic adolescent maladies complicated my condition: weekend binge drinking. After I slipped in the dark down a steep dusty, root-snared bluff while stumbling home, the difference in the sizes of my two shins became unconcealable. My diagnosis the reader in me heard as a clumsy coupling of Greek and Latin facilitated by an unassuming Saxon preposition: *hematoma with contusions.* Hospitalized for a couple of days as a surgically inserted drain sucked out my puss, I turned to the only consolation I knew: to my only absolutely reliable friend, the printed word. The words belonged to 35-cent Mentor paperback I had probably filched from a sibling's bedroom titled *A Primer of Freudian Psychology* from the hand of a WASP-y sounding eminence named Calvin S. Hall. Hall's explanations both mesmerized and agitated me. Back to the hormone-infested world of a huge public high school, I brought the hope that, by means of what Freud (with as much optimism as he could ever muster) called sublimation, I might someday find release from gazing and the cravings that spurred and that it in turn fed.

I'm still waiting.

Instead of looking to find cold comfort in Hall's distillations of Freud's insights, my reader's gaze would have done me more good had I aimed it toward work by some of the decade's darker novelists. They would have thrown needed ice water on my fantasy that I could read my way out of my addling compulsion to gaze. In a 1961 essay by William Golding, now renowned for such provocative novels as *Darkness Visible* and *Lord of the Flies*, Golding reminisces about the schoolmaster who taught him a lasting lesson about the incurability of male gazing.

> Mr. Houghton was given to high-minded monologues about the good life, sexless and full of duty. Yet in the middle of one of these monologues, if a girl passed the window, tapping along on her neat little feet, he would interrupt his discourse, his neck would turn of itself and he would watch her out of sight. In this instance, he seemed to me ruled not by thought but by an invisible and irresistible spring in his nape.

Golding introduced Houghton's tic derisively, as illustrating the most primitive kind of thinking in Golding's hierarchy of thought processes, topped apparently by practices that fall under the heading "discourse," most notably "high-minded monologues." While this remembrance begins by seeming to uphold higher order "discursive" intellection, at Mr. Houghton's expense, Golding ultimately came to honor this distractible mentor as a kindred spirit, conceding that his own gaze reflex turned out to be as incurable as Mr. Houghton's: "I was growing toward adolescence and had to admit that Mr. Houghton was not the only one with an irresistible spring in his neck." Luckily, Golding also realizes that his gaze can be harnessed to the higher-order thinking needed to contend with life's cognitive challenges and moral quandaries, with "contradiction" and "hypocrisy." Golding's reminiscence held out at least the possibility that, once on the lookout for liaisons, male gazers might also look forward to discovering relationships between male-gazing as mindlessly visceral and impulsive and the opportunities male gazing provides for cognitive-enhancement and conceptual enrichment.

In a far darker vein, in his monumental 1960s narrative *The Gulag Archipelago* Aleksandr Solzhenitsyn recalls making such a discovery from within the depths of the Soviet prison-camp system. Dire as their circumstances were, Solzhenitsyn and his fellow *zeks* also found themselves in the grip of the same mechanism Golding recollected. Despite their diametrically opposite material and emotional circumstances, these *zeks*, in Solzhenitsyn's account, bear a pronounced resemblance to the pampered socialites of yore whom Cole Porter once playfully rebuked for the frisson they enjoyed from a mere "glimpse of stocking." That few twentieth-century legends could differ more than Porter and Solzhenitsyn, with respect to what they accomplished and what they represented, underscores the value of male gazing as an artistic and intellectual resource. Identifying himself with Porter's glimpsers, Solzhenitsyn recounts the brief, serendipitously thrilling *frisson* he experienced when a "jailer was fussing with a lock" and routine discipline lapsed, allowing male prisoners an unprecedented opportunity: thirty seconds to peer out of part of a "corridor window":

>...we suddenly saw, down below, in the
>little green garden on a corner of asphalt ... women's shoes and
>ankles!
>All we could see was shoes and ankles,
>but on high heels! And it was like a
>Wagnerian blast from *Tristan and
>Isolde*....the jailer was already
>driving us into the cell, and once
>inside we raved there, illumined
>at the same time beclouded,
>and we pictured all the rest to ourselves, imagining them as heavenly
>beings .... (II, 227).

The horrors he endured notwithstanding, Solzhenitsyn even found an opportunity to particularize such idealizing and place one "young girl—a real genuine heroine of labor" on a proverbial "pedestal" where she "stood like the queen of the shop," and where "she moved at the speed of fast gymnastics ... like a beauty queen" so that "everyone could see her strong, bare legs below her hitched-up skirt and the ballet-like elasticity of her waist" (III, 191). During his post-Gulag exile in Kazakhstan, Solzhenitsyn was grateful and felt lucky in getting a well-paid office job, but saved his most rapturous hyperbole for the clerk who bestowed this blessing, "the exiled Greek girl of cinematic beauty" who processed this reassignment (III, 424).

This passionate idealizing of gaze objects contrasts painfully with Solzhenitsyn's depiction of his jailers, men and women alike, as gazers (I, 105) who stripped a prisoner "locked her in a 'box' [cell] naked" so they could "peer through the peephole and appraise her female attributes with loud laughs ... with but a single purpose" in mind: "to dishearten and humiliate" (I, 105). This recurring attention to gazing throughout a decade of prison-camp labor and nearly 2000 pages reveals the extent to which both the motives for gazing and consequences of gazing can differ as much as jailers differ from prisoners or as much as torturers differ from their victims. What motivates gazing and the thinking it produces, as Solzhenitsyn and Golding illustrate, may be more varied than the current penchant for discrediting the male gaze allows.

AFTER AND BEFORE

Such reflexive disparagement seems to have become a corollary of the very ubiquity of the phrase "the male gaze." Consider, for example, the reception of Joe Treasure's 2007 novel, which bears the Mulveyeque title *The Male Gaze*. In reviewing the novel Nicola Smyth fretted that "it is very difficult to write a book about the male gaze without female readers (or perhaps just readers) finding it just a little bit creepy." This complaint comes at the very end of the review, so the reader never learns whether this admission constitutes an aesthetic judgment or a representative objection on behalf of gaze objects. Wise gazers expect such objections and prepare for the likelihood of seeming "creepy." Alice Munro, for example, recalls "the men who made me sick" with "the looks they gave me, of proper disapproval and sneaky appraisal ... as the level of sludge rose in their heads" (202). James Salter numbered himself among these sludged-headed "creeps" when he complained that he "could not look at" an arresting gaze object without feeling "embarrassed" and "dismayed" by his "long[ing] to stare at her" (48–49).

Advertising, perhaps the business traditionally most dependent on male gazing and most complicit in sustaining male gazing as a

2 COMING CLEAN: READINGS, CONFESSIONS, SHORTCUTS   17

male-subject-to-female-object transaction, has been increasingly held accountable for its complicity in confirming familiar aspersions against male gazing. As depicted on AMC's now canonic TV series *Mad Men* (a series lavishly praised for its documentary accuracy), advertising began in the twentieth century to challenge the prevailing, constraining understanding of gazing as a male-subject-to-female-object transaction. Thus in *Mad Men*'s fourth season one of the series' few inspiring main characters, the glass-ceiling-shattering copywriter and later copy-supervisor Peggy Olson, enters a room full of male "creatives" and turns to a colleague whom she spots perusing a copy of *Playboy*. Peggy then asks confrontationally "Are you gonna work or just stare at pictures of women who can't stare back?" ("Waldorf"). As both *Mad Men* creator Matthew Weiner and James Salter demonstrate, for all its ubiquity as a phrase and a concept "the male gaze" seems disturbing—"creepy," "embarrassing," "dismaying"—both to women and men in ways that its glib familiarity seems to belie.

This disparity between the current status of "the male gaze" as a readily handy stock phrase, as a mindlessly adaptable received idea, and its disturbing, provocative charge may parallel a conflict between its *au courant* availability as a phrase and its boundless legacy as a concept. As a conversational staple, "the male gaze" has been around for about forty years. It has become such a commonplace that its uses now extend far beyond its origin and its initially limited scope as a tool early in the evolution of Film Studies as an academic discipline. When Laura Mulvey introduced the concept in 1975 as a "political weapon," she aimed to expose the oppressive "freedom exhibited by" male protagonists in narrative movies "to command the stage," "control events," and "create the action." Mulvey set out to challenge the power of the male spectators whom conventional movies encouraged to identify with these protagonists. The male gazer's "contact with the female form displayed" onscreen "for his enjoyment," in Mulvey's account, not only fosters exclusively "male fantas[ies]"—it also enables gazers to "gain control and possession of" women. Mulvey's core argument, that this male gaze sustained an exclusively male freedom "to command the stage," envisions a "stage of spatial illusion in which" the gazer's desire "creates the action" on screen. Though Mulvey's male-gaze argument treats a quintessentially twentieth-century form of cultural production and though it came to be regarded as making daring, pioneering contributions to a powerful cultural insurgency, it also seems to rest on a Victorian view of gender relationships. Mulvey's polemic seems to assume that despite the movies and modernism, the suffragists, Roe vs. Wade, the integration of higher education, "women's liberation" in the 1960s, sexual politics had changed little since the 1860s when the male gaze was as imperious as she claims. In his 1869 novel *Phineas Finn*, Anthony Trollope portrayed this imperiousness, describing a commanding, self-seeking, overprivileged British lord as "looking at her still with the same gaze, and there seemed to be a power in his eye from which she could not escape." More often than not this Trollopian gazer seems to be the character or caricature contemporary commentators have in mind whenever the male gaze is mentioned.

First appearing in the UK journal *Screen*, Mulvey's formulation marked a watershed in Film Studies, literary theory, and art history (Kipnis, *Ecstasy* 8). Its indelible imprint continues to be felt throughout academe and beyond (Walters 53; Lane, "Lady"; Butterfield 14). This discursive diffusion extends beyond naming and describing the male gaze. Mulvey's argument and analysis aimed to make both heuristic and "political use" of her concept to explain and resist the impact of male gazing. Some critics now argue that as an instrument of both resistance and explanation Mulvey's 1975 case for an "alternative cinema" still functions as a manifesto for a more encompassing movement, a rallying cry for the nebulous sensibility that Laura Kipnis has characterized as an ideologically contradictory "left aesthetic vanguardism" (*Ecstasy* 108). As a result, refreshing and provocative as it once was, the phrase "the male gaze" now confounds at least as often as it clarifies.

Therefore acknowledging my debt to Mulvey and voicing my appreciation of her work's significance as both a student and practitioner of the male gaze, my fascination with the male gaze has little to do with my views about the accuracy of her analysis or rigor of her argument. Fifteen years after its publication, even Mulvey reconsidered her argument, describing it as "ephemeral … polemic … not likely to last." She had aimed primarily to introduce a "line of thought" (*Visual* vii) and thus offer the opportunity, which I'm taking here, to sustain a conversation. Mulvey's reconsideration frees us from treating her concept, as first envisioned, as "a weapon." Her reconsideration also sundered her argument from its initial "proselytizing mission" and thus freed readers to treat her concept as an "interpretive" goad, a chance "to arbitrate controversies" rather than as a "legislative" and adjudicative critical instrument (Bauman 5, 108).

Mulvey seems to have disappeared from this endlessly renewable conversation that she inaugurated. In the wake of her disappearance, the "the male gaze" now seems to operate not only as shared cultural capital in the public domain, but often as merely a floating signifier. An art dealer writing in the *New York Review of Books in* 2009 observed, matter of factly and intransitively, that "in recent decades there has been considerable discussion of the male gaze" (Butterfield 13). No longer do male-gaze conversations even need to acknowledge women as the assumed object of male gazing. In 2007 the *New York Times* registered this escape of male gazing from Mulvey's invidious heterosexual binary when its review of a Brooklyn art exhibit celebrated "a burgeoning of gay male art" in an exhibit titled "The Male Gaze" (Trebay).

After the millennium, in fact, the *Times* became a prime mover in promoting this escape of male gazing from Mulvey's polemic. According to another *New York Times* writer, the male-gaze conversation has reached a self-negating inflection point. Thus Daphne Merkin, also neglecting to credit Mulvey for "inventing" "the male gaze," proclaimed the obsolescence of male gazing as a notable controversy and treated the problem Mulvey's essay addressed as solved. Merkin's profile of the Hollywood director Nancy Meyers touts Meyers' achievement, the way her movies portray men, as being "as subject to critical scrutiny via the female gaze as women are subject to the male gaze." On behalf of male gazers everywhere, Scheherazade-like, the conversation I'm orchestrating here represents a plea for a reprieve from Merkin's "end-of-conversation" death sentence.

Writing in the same year as Merkin, yet another *Times* reviewer, Roberta Smith, at least acknowledged Mulvey when she tracked changes in these ongoing male-gaze conversations, reflecting that "a lot has happened since 1975, when Laura Mulvey's groundbreaking essay 'Visual Pleasure and Narrative Cinema' made the 'male gaze' an art theory staple." Accounting for both the impact and the elusive malleability of Mulvey's concept, Smith elaborates that what "happened" has prompted a realization that "who is looking at whom with what kind of gaze at any given moment is not always easily pinned down."

Avant La Lettre

"A lot" had also happened in and to this conversation *before* 1975 and before the *Times* certified the concept as "groundbreaking." So much gazing and so much discussion of gazing occurred that the French phrase *avant-la-lettre* seems in order in accounting for the overwhelming appeal of Mulvey's concept since its introduction. The French phrase *avant-la-lettre* (literally "before the letter") refers to ideas and practices widely known well before they've been conveniently named, let alone thoroughly "theorized"—and then often neutralized and co-opted upon reaching a horizon of ubiquity. My own experience as a male gazer, who began gazing before Mulvey's *Screen* article appeared and has continued to do so since its publication, has prompted me to wonder how much better (or worse) off I am now, cognitively and conceptually, *apres la lettre*, secure in the knowledge that I'm an inveterate male gazer.

Without ever being decisively answered, this question can help clarify the relationship that, the very phrase "the male gaze reader" insists, is central to sustaining the male-gaze conversation: the relationship between gazing and reading. In her second novel, the coming-of-age narrative *Bitter in the Mouth*, Monique Truong raised—and left open—this question with her narrator's realization that, once introduced, "the word" can't contain "the entire body of" the "experiences" it's meant to hold (257). Reading as a male-gaze reader means looking incessantly and so far never finding whatever "word" or "words" Truong had in mind. Nevertheless, questions about the uncontainable experiences Truong cites inform my own seemingly endless recognition of myself as an archgazer and my goal of searching out such elusive "words" has inspired the inquiry I'm pursuing in these pages.

INVOKERS AND PROVOKERS

Joyce Carol Oates' 2013 short story "Lovely, Dark and Deep," another first-person coming-of-age retrospect, depicts an *a-clef* Robert Frost as at once a boorish lech and as an astute, cultivated observer of beauty and value "whose gaze moved up and down" the narrator's "body with the finesse of a practiced gem appraiser." This discomfiting balance between the "finesse" Oates' narrator can't avoid noticing and the threat of exploitation this cultivation abets belongs to the contradictory heritage linking the erudition much male gazing rests on and has produced with the threat male gazing has often—and often accurately—been accused of posing. Therefore recognizing this legacy and weighing its intellectual richness against the harm it has done and has threatened to do entails untethering male-gaze conversations from facile polemics and familiar controversies and articulating instead the aesthetic and heuristic legitimacy of male gazing as a long-lived, multifaceted cultural practice, a practice that men and boys have by no means monopolized. In *The Apparitional Lesbian*, for instance, Terry Castle voices the very claims of command, control and even possession that Mulvey ascribed to male gazers in 1975. Castle's description of her own "transfiguring" female "gaze" focuses on Castle's discovery of her converging identities as both a gazer and a gaze object, a discovery integrating submission, new knowledge, and intellectual humility. Her partner in gazing, she recalls, "had become ... less than herself ... her eyes seemed to say I own you now. And I realized, too, though I had no words for it at the time, how much I adored her, and what tumult lay ahead" (26).

Castle's reminiscence exposes one too-obvious-to-mention blind spot in Mulvey's theorizing. As the texts I've been citing illustrate, glib invokers of "the male gaze" seldom consider the implications and limitations of the concept's origin: Mulvey's narrow focus on the movies as the primal scene of male gazing. Since Mulvey confined her argument to cinema, to second-hand *mediated* gazing at images on a flat screen, it seems ahistorical and myopic to treat her account of gazing (as we often do now) as all-encompassing or paradigmatic, as unequivocally applicable to gazing at printed and painted images of women and to unmediated, direct, three-dimensional, "real-time," *in the flesh* gazing. Nowadays one needn't be a pedantic "postmodernist" to concede that all perception is mediated and that gaze objects are mediated not only by the movie and TV screens, the picture frames, shunga boxes, and vitrines we pay to view and own, but also, willy-nilly, by ubiquitous windows, and, with more consistent calculation, by the positioning of fixtures and furniture in institutional spaces like malls, museums, classrooms, theaters, offices, restaurants, and sanctuaries.

HUMANITIES GAZER

The most durable account of European or "Western" literature looks back to the ancient Mediterranean traditions that, in 1869, Matthew Arnold memorably named Hellenism and Hebraism. Almost a century later, Erich Auerbach illustrated this pairing by contrasting Homer's style with that of the Hebrew Bible. Such contrasts notwithstanding, narratives in both traditions famously pivot on scenes of male gazing. The most memorable example may be the reaction to what Christopher

Marlowe calls "the face that launched a thousand ships and burnt the topless towers of Ilium": Paris's sighting and subsequent abduction of Helen, the gaze that provoked the Trojan war. Adherents of Abrahamic creeds, though, may be more readily familiar with Isaac's genealogically pivotal sighting of Rebecca at her father's well in Genesis or King David's fatal sighting in second Samuel of Bathsheba bathing on her Jerusalem rooftop.

During the Renaissance and the Enlightenment, such images became staples of European painting. Rembrandt's 1654 portrait *Bathsheba at Her Bath* shows the king's gaze object not merely naked "at her bath" but as a naked reader, apparently having just perused her summons from her king, even though scripture (2 Samuel 11:4) neither specifies whether the summons borne by the king's messenger was oral or written nor whether Bathsheba was clothed or bare when the summons arrived. By showing Bathsheba as a reader, Rembrandt moves to turn this gaze object into a subject and not simply an exploited object. This literate Bathsheba, Simon Schama argues, appears to be a "meditative ... self-interrogatory" thought-burdened agent (551–552). Imputing agency to Bathsheba, by showing her reading and therefore considering—even judging—the royal summons, Rembrandt suggests the possibility of resistance to or at least compromise with her monarch's absolute sovereignty. In portraying Bathsheba as a deliberating agent, Rembrandt also raised questions about his relationship with his model, perhaps even inviting viewers to regard *her* not simply as an object but as a collaborator in the production of what Mulvey calls "visual pleasure." By allowing for these ambiguities, *Bathsheba at Her Bath* may represent male gazing dialectically. as both "crudely sensual" (551) and as intent on liberating its object.

In his art history classic *The Nude*, Kenneth Clark explains this dialectic. Clark reads this portrait of Rembrandt's mistress (his "whore," according to Amsterdam officials), Hendrickje Stouffels, as an instance of non-objectifying male gazing. Clark argues that the subject's "thoughts" appear as "indissolubly part of her body," and that Rembrandt was conducting a respectful inquiry rather than producing a reductive objectification (441). Rembrandt's "full-frontal nude," in Clark's view, shows "an expression of reverie so complex that we follow her thoughts far beyond the moment depicted." Even though Rembrandt "was painting in a period when hierarchical gender and sex roles were understood as ... divinely ordained," Mary Winkler argues, he "succeeded in according

2 COMING CLEAN: READINGS, CONFESSIONS, SHORTCUTS   23

respect to this woman by acknowledging the limits of observation and objectivity." In Rembrandt's work, according to Clark's and Winkler's accounts, the gazer renounces the authority and power that "objectivity" confers. Hence Rembrandt's male-gazing aims, modestly, at once to complicate the gaze-object and chasten the gazer himself, perhaps to humble rather than empower him. Though challenging Clark, John Berger has argued that Rembrandt, along with Rubens, resisted becoming typically objectifying gazers because they achieve a "particularity" that "transcends" objectification by embracing the "banality" of their own desire for the women they paint (53–54; Williams 3).[1]

Instead of circumspectly chastening gazers, eighteenth-century paintings of Paris and Helen by Jacques-Louis David and Benjamin West treat gazing more punitively. These works show Helen clothed (but not fully covered) instead of fully naked like Rembrandt's Bathsheba. David and West both show the gazer, Paris, *inside* the frame gripping Helen as he beholds her.[2] Apparently lacking the wherewithal to "command" his gaze object, which Mulvey imputed to male gazers, both David's Paris and West's Paris grip their gaze object loosely as if waiting for a cue from Helen. David, moreover, depicts the man in the picture rather than Helen in the nude and therefore, as John Berger argues, as diminished in status (54–60): Thus Paris appears in David's painting wearing only sandals, a crimson cap and a cloak thrown over his shoulders. The nudity of the gazer rather than of his gaze object might arguably reflect absolute confidence in his power to seduce or subdue. But Paris's nudity may also intimate anxiety over the limits of a gazer's control. By highlighting Bathsheba's intellectual competence, as a reader, Rembrandt seems to have allowed for a degree of equality between the gazer and the gaze object and thus dispensed with the need for such assertions of mastery.

One needn't be a Classicist to recall that Paris earned his preeminent role as a male gazer prior to his catastrophic abduction of Helen. When Zeus authorized Paris to extend his gaze far beyond that of any other mortal, Paris became perhaps the only divinely authorized male gazer in

---

[1] Rembrandt, *Bathsheba at Her Bath*. https://mydailyartdisplay.files.wordpress.com/2011/04/bathsheba-by-rembrandt.jpg.

[2] Jacques-Louis David, *The Love of Paris and Helen*. http://upload.wikimedia.org/wikipedia/commons/8/8d/Helene_Paris_David.jpg. Benjamin West, *Helen Brought to Paris*. http://uploads4.wikiart.org/images/benjamin-west/helen-brought-from-paris-1776.jpg.

legend or in history. Judging him superlatively impartial or "objective," Zeus delegated Paris to judge a beauty contest among three goddesses: Aphrodite (sex), Athena (wisdom), and Zeus's own consort, Hera. Paris's choice of Aphrodite and his preference for her promise of the life of a voluptuary fueled his obsession with another man's wife, Helen of Sparta, and so precipitated the Trojan war. The Judgment of Paris also implicitly established Paris as "Western Civilization's" Ur-gazer and set a precedent, nearly three thousand years before Mulvey's essay, for male gazing as a staple of European mimesis.

Though Paris and Zeus seemed, in Mulvey's phrase, to command the stage, a closer look at these foundational narratives exposes this command to be more precarious than Mulvey and her influential lock-step followers have supposed. The three goddesses whom Paris judged, along with a fourth Olympian, Eris (goddess of discord), controlled the action by shaping the narrative outcome of the judgment of Paris. Notwithstanding our understanding of three millennia of European folk and elite culture as largely men's work, at least in these Hellenic Paris narratives, these goddesses determined both the identity and position of the gazer, as well as the consequences of his gaze.

Thus Paris, the gazer-turned-supreme judge, can serve as a convenient stand-in for generations of painters and their patrons. But even work by painters famous or infamous as connoisseurs of women's bodies, like Botticelli, Ingres or Modigliani, sometimes betrays the difficulty of maintaining this supremacy, the sense of omniscience it entails, and the sovereignty Mulvey associates with male gazing. In such work, the gazer's mastery collides with the painter's dependency on the gaze object as a muse and as a source of frustrated curiosity—as desired but unattainable. In 1876 Edmond de Goncourt identified this transformation of gazers into dependents or supplicants as a commonplace response among painters, novelists, and other gazers. Apparently striving to sublimate his own drawing-room lechery and to identify a muse, Goncorut turned to two masters of European painting, Anthony Van Dyck and Titian to validate his own connoisseurship as a gazer:

> The Jews retain, from their oriental origin, a peculiar nonchalance. Today I was I was charmed as I observed Mme. Louise Cahen ... she moved like a lazy cat ... when they are blonde—these Jews—there is, at the heart of their blondness, something golden, like [Van Dyck's] painting of The Mistress of Titian ... the Jewess dropped onto a chaise longue, her head

flung back to one side ... revealing ... a coil of hair that resembled a nest of snakes. Pulling various amused, questioning expressions, and wrinkling her nose, she complained of the unreasonableness of men and of novelists expecting women not to be human creatures and not to have, in love, the same disgust as men. (DeWaal 45)

Goncourt's sublimation begins with what Freud called over-intellectualization, and his art-history musings begin as an endorsement of his century's pseudo-anthropological "race science." When he cites the seventeenth-century Van Dyck's engraving of a cinquecento predecessor's mistress, Goncourt aligns his perspective with a venerable artistic and ideological legacy. Goncourt is reaffirming the power of gazers in general and the power of artists in particular over their gaze objects, since "mistresses"—like models—can be readily treated as silent and subservient gaze-objects. Titian, the painter whom Van Dyck pictured, moreover, stands out not only as an art-historical legend but as an influential pioneer in the annals of male gazing who became "famous across Europe for the overt sensuality with which he portrayed the female nude" and as the first artist "known to use living, breathing women as models" (Wullschlager). But when Goncourt recognizes his gaze object as a subject rather than an object he swerves from this tradition. Goncourt identifies his gaze object as the member of a group long oppressed and despised by most Europeans and then identifies her as entitled, arresting, insouciant, and even threatening. Finally, after what begins as a put-down, a snarky move to objectify the blonde feline and ophidian Jewess, Goncourt yields to Mme. Cahen's authority as an arbiter of literary convention.

Van Dyck's etching inverts the customary relationship between a gazer and his gaze object.[3] The portrait shows Titian looking *up* at his mistress, who appears conspicuously larger than him, while soliciting *her* gaze. Like many of his Renaissance contemporaries Titian often painted scenes from classical mythology, the tradition from which European writers and painters derived their lasting faith in muses as a source of inspiration. Therefore *Titian and His Mistress* might arguably be read as an account of the artist soliciting his muse and as an up-close evocation of the gazer's dependence on, perhaps even his subservience to, his gaze

---

[3] Attributed to Van Dyck, *Titian and His Mistress*. http://everypainterpaintshimself.com/article_images_new/Ttmis.jpg.

object, thus offering a cautionary object lesson about the self-subjugating perils of male gazing.

A generation after Goncourt called upon Van Dyck and Titian to transform Mme. Cahen from a gaze object into an influential subject, Henry James turned to exploring male gazing in another Renaissance master: Hans Holbein. At this point in his career, James had already established himself as an attentive student of male gazing. His best-known "tale," the 1878 "Daisy Miller," features a viewpoint character who epitomizes the post-Mulvey understanding of male gazing that *Reading the Male Gaze* illustrates: male gazing as a cognitively demanding, conceptually sophisticated intellectual practice. James introduces this understanding by attributing to Winterbourne, the viewpoint character in "Daisy Miller", such a "great relish for feminine beauty" that "he was addicted to observing and analyzing it." A generation later, in 1903, in another first-person narrative "The Beldonald Holbein," James shows a similarly attentive and "analytic" gazer overpowered by his gaze object.

The painter who narrates "The Beldonald Holbein" and whom a colleague compares to Titian introduces himself as inclined to "collect all the beauty I could." Upon receiving a commission to paint a friend's elderly sister-in-law, sight-unseen, he hears his patron, Mrs. Munden, rank her sister-in law, Lady Beldonald, among the "great beauties." Mrs. Munden adds, metaphorically, that her beauty has been "only preserved—oh but preserved, like bottled fruit, in syrup." Soon after closing the deal, Lady Beldonald hires a distant cousin, "a certain Mrs. Brash," as a companion. Mrs. Brash's primary qualification for the "special service" she can provide Lady Beldonald is that "she was ... ugly enough ... consistently, cheerfully, loyally plain ... unfortunately ... dreadfully plain." James's narrator, however, dares to speak to Mrs. Munden and Lady Beldonald of "the esteem in which [he] held Mrs. Brash's appearance," and even "of her beauty." Overwhelmed by his "æsthetic need of giving life to my idea," he shocks Mrs. Munden and Lady Beldonald by proposing that Mrs. Brash also "sit for" him because, he recalls,

> She was a good, hard, sixteenth-century figure, not withered with innocence, bleached rather by life in the open ... in short, just what we had made of her, a Holbein for a great museum; and our position ... rapidly became that of persons having such a treasure to dispose of. The world—I speak of course mainly of the art-world—flocked to see it.

As James's narrator envisions the possibility of enhancing his gaze object's prospects and of improving her state of mind the anticipated popularity of this portrait—along with the profits it promises—expands the range of male gazing beyond simple domination. At least James's narrator imagines such a possibility in speculating that Mrs. Brash's

> nature had been pitched in the key of her supposed plainness. She had known how to be ugly—it was the only thing she had learnt save, if possible, how not to mind it. Being beautiful took in any case a new set of muscles.

As envisaged by James, male artists who promote male gazing can pose the kind of threat to traditional male gazing that Goncourt found in *Titian and his Mistress*. In favoring an appearance that flouts the conventions of gazing and the role of commissioned portrait painting as an instrument for sustaining conventional understandings of female beauty, James seems to be allowing for both the self-aggrandizement—money, fame, reassurance—that artistic male gazing has customarily yielded and for open-ended mutually beneficial give-and-take between gazers and gaze objects.

Flannery O'Connor's 1952 novel *Wise Blood* encapsulates and perhaps even provides a model for such give and take between the gazer and his object. With her genius for dialect and wordplay, O'Connor coins a formula for pushing back against what the gaze object in the following exchange calls, in an unwitting pun, "looker indignation" (104). (As dialect, of course, "looker indignation" reads as "look of indignation"; read literally, though, it allows for the gaze object, often a "looker" in the slang of the era, to gaze back, fiercely, at the male gazer, who is also, literally and transitively, a *looker*.)

> 'What I gave you the other night,' she said, 'was a looker indignation for what I seen you do. It was you give me the eye. You should have seen him papa,' she said, 'looked me up and down.' (56)

So authoritative is the voice of this gaze object, a wayward teen named Sabbath Lily Hawks, that Hazel Motes, the gazer who bills himself as the founder of the "Church Without Christ" and consequently had "expected a secret welcome," ends up instead finding the Hawks' household's "door shut in his face." While Sabbath Lily gazes on him through a crack in the shade, she confesses to her father that she's "just crazy about him" and aims to "get him" (105–106) on her own terms, as a gatekeeper inside rather than as the supplicant on the outside.

THE UPHILL *CUL-DE-SAC*—PARDON MY FRENCH

Bosky Hollow Court rose to a dead end. Fifty years ago, when the late-lamented elms that helped make the area so bosky and gave the town its name still loomed over the curb that closed off this "dead end," Bosky Hollow Court lost its official designation as a dead end. By posting a new sign, thanatophobic municipal officials transformed Bosky Hollow Court from a "dead end" into a NO OUTLET byway. For a teenage boy, the very phrase "no outlet" proved all too apt at the time. Years after this rechristening, I learned that in the US cognoscenti call these roads "cul-de-sacs." Well into midlife, though, I learned from a Parisian street sign that actual French-speakers less metaphorically refer to a road leading nowhere simply as an *impasse*. The more fancifully named impasses we call cul-de-sacs widen circularly where they stop, having once-upon-a-time reminded some long-ago trendsetter of the bottom of French bags or *culs-de sac*.

Facing this cul-de-sac stood the last house on the south side of Bosky Hollow Court. A three-story colonial with a stone chimney, it looked west through two living-room windows into a shadowy copse. All second-growth hardwoods, the expanse was leafless—providing long sightlines—for most of the September-to-June school year, during which it served as one of my homeward shortcuts and met our unspoken routing rule: never travel along streets when you can cut across backyards, where more secrets and mysteries are likely to appear.[4] Decades later, thanks to the *New York Times*, I learned what makes the backyard so much more compelling than the street side and how routinely, with my shortcutting, I was plumbing the heart of darkness:

> while the front lawns of suburbia reflect how residents choose to present themselves to the outside world, their backyards are Freudian maps of their unconscious lives. (Holden)

---

[4] New Jersey Backyard. http://4.bp.blogspot.com/_OBcBbXOBT-Y/S8ElRLJMqsI/AAAAAAAABEQ/Pwv1e_QYUOA/s1600/Crooked47.jpg.

Late fall's early twilights often found me crossing these yards and passing the windows that looked out on the hillcrest where Bosky Court
Hollow dead-ended. Here I was tempted and here I succumbed to
temptation, lapsing into a condition Freud called scopophilia (*Three* 58).
On the other side of the window sat a girl I knew from school. Her
name was Ginny. Or maybe it was Jenny, since there were even fewer
Virginias than Jennifers in our mostly Jewish neighborhood. (I speak
as a member of a Jennifer-deficient generation, with dozens of Susans,
Carols, and Ellens filling the rosters of the schools I attended.) To this
day I don't know for sure whether I had in my sights a Ginny or Jenny,
since I had never had anything to do with her except maybe to wave
"hi." Maybe I only knew *about* her. I knew she was one of a group of
similar-looking sisters because, inevitably, my mother of "knew the family." My parents seemed to have gone to high school with or done business or served on the PTA or the UJA with someone from every family
(at least with every Jewish family) in the neighborhood and decades
avant la lettre (the letter being *Z* for Zuckerberg) my mother was the
consummate social networker.

Did my parents' and my community's influence, my meta-erotic frame
of reference, compromise or enrich my experience as a gazer? Did leav-
ening my lust with some homespun sociology make me less of creep or
simply less of an aesthete? About a decade later, soon after completing
college, I took a test to become a pornographer. Answering an ad in
a Manhattan weekly called the *Village Voice*, I found myself in a huge
sunlit office overlooking Sheridan Square facing an industrial-strength
manual typewriter and the landmark Village Cigar store—a source of
TE AMOs at the time—across Christopher Street, hunting and pecking
while concocting a character named Maria. Though I had eloquently blazoned the tiny gold cross nesting in her cleavage, her irresistibly rolled
contralto Rs, the rough weave of her Dodger blue denim skirt, I wasn't
hired. My incorrigible habit of adulterating gazing with religion, linguis-
tics, cotton-consciousness, etc.—an inclination dating back at least to my
Bosky Hollow Court reveries—seems to have tripped me up and nipped
in the bud a promising career. My dreams of such a career had been
fueled when a few years earlier a friend gave a copy of Kenneth Patchen's
Memoirs of a Shy Pornographer. This 1945 novel's eponymous narrator
serendipitously succeeds (24) by publishing a book, which he titled *Spool
of Destiny* and his publisher retitled *Spill of Desire* (23), assigning the
work genre heretofore unknown to the novelist:

'What do you do?' the young lady asked.
I tried hard to remember what type of book My Agent told me my
book was. The word wasn't in my dictionary—sort of a long one ...
Then I remembered.
I write pornography. (Patchen 27)

His pornography proves so successful, both commercially and critically,
that Patchen's pornographer realizes "Now I can do anything in the
world I want to do" (24). In the wake of his success, he meets a Vassar
woman who calls *The Spill of Desire* a book about which she dreams and
extols it as "the most beautiful innocent story I've ever heard" (31).
Patchen's hero notwithstanding, pornographers may never be innocent.
But questions about whether male-gazers, Mulvey notwithstanding, can
gaze innocently remains open for debate.

ROMANTIC GESTURES?

I can't remember for sure if watching Ginny—or Jenny—strum was a one-
off transgression or became a regular stop on my daily homeward trek.
In either case, watching Ginny has come to have, at least in retrospect, a
greater impact than most of the more documented, more public rituals I was
obliged to engage in growing up. As a grownup, as a parent, as a teacher,
and presumably as some kind of "role model," I'm probably obliged to look
back on my window-gazing as a misdemeanor or at least as an unneighborly
breach of propriety. As a nearly mindless teenage ritual, though, my gazing
has a canonic imprimatur and qualifies as more of a Romantic gesture. As
a developmental watershed this window reverie carries the endorsement of
the eminently gentlemanly Romantic gazer William Wordsworth. Himself
a habitual beholder of arresting peasant girls, like the one he extolled as a
"highland lass," and an anatomizer of a "sportive" grace-molded "maiden's
form," Wordsworth designated such solitary reflective occasions as "spots of
time" (see Chaps. 3 and 5). Mind-nourishing and spirit-renovating, these
moments of "distinct preeminence" serve at once to disrupt the round of
ordinary intercourse and to stretch the range of our sympathies, all the while
pleasurably sensitizing us to our surroundings.

From the perspective of a later Romantic, D.H. Lawrence, "my spot of
time" became part of a series of moments that Lawrence described in his
1920 novel *The Lost Girl*. In a characteristically Lawrentian move, introducing voices ranging from priestly to pastoral to scriptural, Lawrence's

narrator recalls watching a stranger "as if she were Woman itself" and characterizes his own "gazing" as "the sort of je-sais-tout look of a private swain." This phrase, "the sort of je-sais-tout look," seems to ascribe omniscience and therefore a position of command to this gazer, a position of authority, which Lawrence confirms when this gazing ends with the gazer approaching his gaze object "like a policeman." Throughout the novel Lawrence subjects the heroine, Alvina Houghton, to various forms of male gazing, not all of which prove effective at subduing her. For example, a subsequent gazer—and lover—endows Alvina with Eve's power to do harm by looking upon her "the same way he might have watched a serpent." My neighbor Ginny or Jenny, or one of her sisters, might have moved me to such Lawrentian mythography had I known fifty years ago that such opportunities existed. Unlike Lawrence's, though, my gaze was more prone to idealizing than to subduing or "policing."

The object of my idealizing gaze sat by the window playing a gilded two-yard-high harp. It never occurred to me to seize on the harp and to make the customarily transcendent leap, to associate what I saw with what I'd later learn to call a seraph. Some thirty-five years on, this formative, viscerally unsettling watershed moment as a tyro male gazer found a narrative correlative, a conceptual anchor, in my lifelong education as a male gazer and especially in my eventual transformation into a "mature" male-gaze reader. I reached this watershed while reading Philip Roth's 1998 novel *I Married a Communist* (see Chap. 5) in which Roth's narrator recalls how he once believed that "if I looked long enough" at a celebrated stage beauty "a *meaning* might emerge" (53). My faith in such a result and my fascination with the harpist in the window, it turned out, exposed me not simply as a peeper. Worse than a gazer, I was, in Roth's view, a snob. *I Married a Communist* features an acerbic harpist who frames her musical calling as primarily a gaze-enhancing, hyper-feminizing ritual: "Most little girls who start the harp start the harp because Mommy thinks it's such a *lovely* thing for them to do. It looks so pretty and all the music is so damned sweet, and it's played politely in small for polite people who aren't the least interested .... Really refinement" (135–136).[5]

[5] Harpist. https://abstract.desktopnexus.com/get/360301./?t=8c756h4m1nca3mq8d 807sbu7i059009b2c3a0e9.

It never would have occurred to me, fifty years ago, to transform
Jenny or Ginny into a symptom of my refinement or an affirmation of
my *"je-sais-tout"* omniscience. Entirely unfamiliar with D.H. Lawrence
at the time, I would never have thought to see her as Eve either, or to
view my peeping as a reenactment of a primal biblical encounter between
a serpent and an Ur-temptress—as an eternal lesson for all humankind.
Nor would it ever have occurred to me to do the opposite to the gaze
object: intensify her materiality and distill her earthiness. This kind
of anti-idealizing downward gazing, a view of gazing as slumming,
appeared in the same year as Lawrence's *The Lost Girl* in John Dos
Passos' novel *Three Soldiers*. Dos Passos' gazers, World War One dough-
boys, collectively examine a *mademoiselle* who appears before them:

> Several soldiers lounged awkwardly against the counter
> and the jambs of the door, following her movements
> with their eyes as dogs watch *a* plate of meat. (Dos Passos, *Three Soldiers*)

Just as I didn't know enough to idealize or demonize, like Lawrence's gazers, or to demean and belittle, like Dos Passos' gazers, I didn't even know
enough to make the most of my gaze object's props or her *mise-en-scène*:
the harp, the grand piano and the built-in bright white bookshelf flank-
ing it or the plush forest green carpet under it. I didn't know enough, in a
word, to aestheticize what I saw. Fifty years ago, the harpist was simply tall;
now, as a trained aesthete, I'd be obliged to call her "statuesque."

Meat or capital *W* woman? Tall or statuesque? Passing glance or
epiphany? Fifty years after Dos Passos and Lawrence raised these questions, Don DeLillo finally demonstrated for me how a novelist can explicitly introduce his gaze object as prompting a capital *E* "epiphany." In his
1973 novel *Great Jones Street*, DeLillo shows a gaze object as at once
earthy in her demeanor and transcendent in the legacy she incarnates, as
overwhelmingly eroticized and in full command of her surroundings.

> A young black woman stood in the hall, legs well apart, hands on hips. She
> was arrayed in burnishings and pleated streaks, and there was a trim glit-
> ter about her, a commercial grace, evident in the seamless way she shifted
> weight to orches-trate a sort of stylish body violence …
>
> "Who's the nice lady?"
>
> "Security," he said. "Her name's Epiphany Powell." (181)

2 COMING CLEAN: READINGS, CONFESSIONS, SHORTCUTS   33

The very name Epiphany holds out the promise of illumination, even transformation. It nods to the familiar literary tradition, with the promise and
expectation of *epiphany* in fiction and poetry. DeLillo's contemporary, novelist Charles Baxter, has argued that "epiphany" has become most familiar as
a tool used in "marketing and therapy" (76). In Baxter's account, the epiphany tradition rests on the belief "that a character's experiences ... have to
be validated by a conclusive insight ... a visionary stop-time moment" (66).
Epiphanies therefore promise the "security" DeLillo's "glittering" Epiphany
claims as her calling, including the cognitive and emotional security afforded
by "conclusive insights" such as male gazing can sometimes foster.
    This tradition weds James Joyce's famous explanation of epiphany in
Stephen Hero (211) and Wordsworth's "spot of time" ideal with "male gazing" at its most idealizing, its most self referentially poetic. When Joyce's
early alter-ego Stephen Hero spots "a young lady ... standing on the steps,"
this seemingly "trivial incident set him composing some ardent verses which
he entitled a 'Villanelle of the Temptress.'" Joyce's Hero also looks to
epiphany for "security," relief from "the dance of unrest in his brain." More
highmindedly, Stephen seeks sublimation of his carnally prompted unrest
into an emotionally reassuring evanescing spiritual epiphany:

> By an epiphany he meant a sudden spiritual manifestation, whether in the
> vulgarity of speech or of gesture or in a memorable phase of the mind itself.
> He believed that it was for the man of letters to record these epiphanies
> with extreme care, seeing that they themselves are the most delicate and
> evanescent of moments ... all at once I see it and I know at once what it is:
> epiphany ... Your mind to apprehend that object divides the entire universe
> into two parts, the object, and the void which is not the object. To appre-
> hend it you must lift it away from everything else: and then you perceive
> that it is one integral thing, that is a thing. You recognize its integrity. (212)

Separating himself from his hero, Joyce shows Hero repeatedly interrupting his own comforting reflections with undermining questions:
"Isn't that so? ... And then? ... You see?" Likewise, the promise embodied in Delillo's Epiphany falters, even more decisively, disintegrating on
the page into a litany of sentence fragments:

> Hair worn short. Caved face. Slender imperial neck.
> Hurdler's fused body. All in all a well-crafted piece of
> smoked glass and chrome. (184)

Instead of looking to transcend her condition as an object, DeLillo's narrator revels in Epiphany's status as an object—"a well-crafted piece." Instead of appearing "lift[ed] away from everything else," Epiphany's aesthetic appeal as a gaze object rests on her embeddedness in decidedly material, earthbound processes of design, manufacture, and marketing— processes that encompass marketing herself as a gaze object:

> Epiphany used to sing in supper clubs, according to
> the data on her. Did I tell you that? Supper clubs. I
> didn't know places like that existed anymore.
> Must have been a weird scene. She acted in exploitation movies for
> six or seven months. A real pro-fessional.
> She did some modeling here and there. It's been a hard road. All
> that
> professionalism. It does things to people. Makes them
> hard. (184)

As if intent on discrediting the very facts of Epiphany's life and his own account of her demeaning work experience, especially her "exploita- tion" as a sex object, the "manager" describing Epiphany looks to what "the data on her show" in reaching for a transcendent story or at least a redeeming myth, an experience-validating fable that might establish how her tribulations have made her stronger. Joyce's Stephen Hero, by con- trast, lacked such data. Perhaps because he only overheard the "young lady standing on the steps," without the benefit of any conversation, the reflections she prompted remained scattered and uninterpretable, unlikely to produce any epiphany:

> as he passed on his quest heard the following fragment of
> colloquy out of which he received an impression keen enough to
> afflict his
> sensitiveness very severely.
>
> The Young Lady-(drawling discreetly)... 0, yes... I was... at the...
> cha... pel.... (211)

By contrast, DeLillo delivers an informational cornucopia in *Great Jones Street*. Nevertheless, DeLillo also severs gazing from the epiphanic prom- ises gazers customarily seek. DeLillo's disconnect differs from Joyce's, though, in that the gaze object herself claims and emphatically articulates the last word and not simply some garbled first words. Biding her time, listening to herself being discussed by the two men in the room, the "nice lady" dismisses the manager's seemingly benevolent myth-making:

> 'It don't faze Piiffany,' she said. 'Nothing faze Piffany.'
> Azarian looked at her a while longer, then turned to me. (184)

With this disclaimer Ephiphany frees herself from the gaze to which the men in the room and especially the explanation-hungry manager, Azarian, are subjecting her. By dropping the first syllable of her name, Epiphany has pointedly refused to serve as any man's experience-validating epiphany.

Only when I had been a literature professor for a decade or so and had prepared classes on works such as *The Lost Girl*, *Three Soldiers*, and *Great Jones Street* did I begin to realize what it was that I'd been doing on Bosky Hollow Court, solitary but not knowing enough to be furtive in the gloaming way back in the middle of the twentieth century: I had to learn from wiser minds that I'd been male gazing *avant la lettre*.

ROCK OF GAZES

As crucial as trespassing across suburbia proved in my initiation as a gazer, more consequential was the bombardment from far beyond the neighborhood of mass-manufactured sounds and images. During these years my go-to authority on what was supposedly occurring beyond the backyard shortcuts I trod became a man who "comes on radio telling me more and more" in order to "fire my imagination." Day after day, almost hourly, my radio blared the Rolling Stones' denunciation of this overpowering authority figure in their 1965 breakout hit "Satisfaction."[6] Such bodiless voices from afar spoke to me repeatedly, insistently, in many guises and in hundreds of different announcements and (most influentially) in countless songs. The most memorable song, not surprisingly, harped on the promise and pitfalls of male gazing, on the condition diagnosed in Manfred Mann's eloquently titled 1964 hit "Do-Wah-Diddy."[7] In this epiphany narrative, the singer discovers that

---

[6] "Satisfaction." https://www.youtube.com/watch?v=QgYblVYEldY 'date accessed' [9th May 2017].

[7] "Doo Wah Diddy Diddy." https://www.youtube.com/watch?v=43vOAw2sAFU 'date accessed' [15th August 2017].

the woman to whom he ends up betrothed after three verses "looked good, looked fine." But the singer also recalls, more darkly, with an off-rhyme (with *"fine"*), that before a happy ending (when "wedding-bells" were "gonna *chime"*) could come to pass, he had to endure having "nearly lost my *mind.*" Over a decade before Mulvey conceptualized and indicted male gazing as an instrument of gender inequality, this song's co-writers, Jeff Barry and Ellie Greenwich, ended "Do-Wah-Diddy" with this affirmation of gender equality: "I'm hers. She's mine."

As a ubiquitous source of information and insight, these songs of my boyhood argued, implicitly and incessantly, for an understanding of gazing as reciprocal. This message came from both the elite and lowest-common-denominator ends of my cultural spectrum: from subtitled black-and-white European "art cinema" and from top-40 AM radio, which woke me up each morning, often failed to lull me to sleep each night, and accompanied every car trip I took. One of the more obscure "gold" top-ten hits during 1968—a year full of still-familiar hits by the Beatles, Eric Clapton's "supergroup" Cream, Simon and Garfunkel, The Doors, and Otis Redding—came from a one-hit-wonder band out of North Carolina who called themselves the O'Kaysons. Titled "Girl Watcher,"[8] the song recalled Frank Loesser's Broadway and radio hit from a decade earlier, "Standing on the Corner Watching All the Girls Go By." The O'Kaysons' vocalist, Donnie Weaver, confessed unambig-uously and repeatedly in their song's refrain that "I'm a girl watcher, watching girls go by." While the singer in the antecedent Loesser hit occupies a similar social space, his gaze yields nothing tangible:

> Haven't got a girl, but I can dream
> Haven't got a girl, but I can wish
> So I take me down to Main Street and that's where I select my imaginary
> dish.[9]

"Standing on the Corner" presents gazing entirely as a subject-to-object reciprocity-free encounter. As its defensive last verse insists, "Standing on the Corner" confines the act of gazing to consequence-free male bonding: "Brother, you can't go to jail for what you're thinking." The 1968 "Girl

---

[8] "Girl Watcher." https://www.youtube.com/watch?v=raJWuz7qQVc 'date accessed' [9th May 2017].

[9] "Standing on the Corner." www.youtube.com/watch?v=rlbGQ0xKZbY 'date accessed' [9th May 2017].

Watcher" song, by contrast, allows for the possibility of reciprocity. The lyrics acknowledged that Loesser's "imaginary dish" might actually be an actively complicit, fully conscious participant in the gaze-encounter, with the singer musing "I wonder if you know that you're putting on a show."[10]

At about the same time that the now-obscure O'Kaysons speculated about the desirability of a rebalancing or a concession of power by the traditional male gazer, the legendary "Jersey Boy" Frankie Valli (and his songwriters Bob Gaudio and Bob Crewe) introduced a male gazer in the throes of a crisis of confidence, abjectly surrendering his supposed authority, forswearing manly autonomy, abandoning the commanding position that Mulvey would identify as male gazing's *raison d'être*. In "Can't Take My Eyes off of You," Valli's first (post-Four Seasons) solo hit, which reached number two on the Billboard charts and went gold in 1967, the gazer speaks subjunctively about how his gaze object "*would* be like heaven to touch" (emphasis added). After *begging* "pardon" for "the way that I stare," the singer concedes that "the sight of you makes me weak" and has silenced him so much that "there are no words left to speak."

The durable popularity of "Can't Take My Eyes off of You," in numerous cover versions and as a soundtrack favorite, illustrates the extent to which, at least in one widely popular view, male gazing may be as much an occasion for renunciation and surrender as it is an instrument of command. This anguished account of male gazing became especially pronounced about a decade later with the inclusion of Valli's hit in Michael Cimino's acclaimed Vietnam trauma spectacle *The Deer Hunter*. A barroom shot showing only young men—no women in the frame— cuts between a group around pool table and actor John Cazale standing up at the bar trying to sing along with "Can't Take My Eyes off of You" as the bar's jukebox vies with the noise of his friends. As a memorable set piece in what arguably became Hollywood's most harrowing account of the traumatic impact of the Vietnam war, this scene links the impotence of the single gazer to an entire nation's geopolitical debacle and to the thousands of private traumas that became that war's most lasting legacy.

Whether celebrating men's power or lamenting its absence, male gazing permeated the most durable hit songs of the twentieth century from "Ain't She Sweet (See Her Walking Down the Street)" to "Do-Wah-Diddy." Norman Gimbel, lyricist for the US version of "The Girl from Ipanema," singled out male gazing as "the oldest story in the

---

[10] "Girl Watcher." http://www.youtube.com/watch?v=raJWuz7qQVc 'date accessed' [9th May 2017].

world," arguing that "the beautiful girl goes by, and men pop out of manholes and fall out of trees and are whistling and going nuts, and she just keeps going by. That's universal" (Vinciguerra). Even as the 1960s stretched the boundaries of the permissible with hits like the Rolling Stones' "Let's Spend the Night Together" and the Trogs' "Wild Thing," I had to turn to the big screen for the starkest and most candid answers to the girl-watcher song's question: "I wonder if you know that you're putting a show." Ingmar Bergman's 1966 *Persona* addressed this question relentlessly by "playing with the paradoxical nature of film", characterized by Susan Sontag as "the illusion of having a voyeuristic access to an untempered reality" ("Persona"). This homage to Bergman followed Sontag's call, in her landmark 1966 essay "Against Interpretation," for "an erotics of art" instead of a "hermeneutics" (*Against* 14) and for treating responses elicited by all cultural work—texts, sounds, images (moving and still), every product accepted as art or "merely" as entertainment—as invitations to sexual if not exclusively "male" gazing.

As a sustained invitation to gaze, *Persona* illustrated how "an erotics of art" might work. One scene in particular struck me as especially apt in illuminating the implications of the O'Kaysons' conjecture—or fantasy—about reciprocal gazing and in pressing their question about gaze objects' awareness of their impact as performers. A nighttime conversation between a reminiscing, convalescing actress named Elisabet (Liv Ullman) and her psychiatric nurse, Alma (Bibi Andersson), turns Alma into a performer and turns her nearly catatonic patient into an audience of one. Alma's performance consists of recounting her deliberate, arguably heedless decision some years back to revel in and exploit her position as a gaze object. Contrary to Mulvey's static scenario, instead of passively accepting her status as the object of male gazing, Alma recalls seizing "command" of the scene in which she found herself and "creating the action." Describing a day at the beach with "another girl" she recalls how

> We lay there
> completely naked and sunbathed…
> Suddenly I saw two figures on the rocks above us.
> They hid and peeped out occasionally.
> "Two boys are looking at us,"

I said to the girl ...
"Let them look," she said,
and turned over on her back.
I wanted to jump up
and put my suit on,
but I just lay there on my stomach
with my bottom in the air,
unembarrassed, totally calm ... next to me with her breasts and big
thighs.
She was just giggling.
The boys were coming closer.
They just stood there looking at us ...

In response to the gazing boys' mute stillness, the "other girl," Katarina, begins scripting her own scenario:

Suddenly Katarina said ... "Hey, you, why don't you
come over here?"
Then she took his hand and helped him
take off his jeans and shirt.
Suddenly he was on top of her.
She guided him in ...
The other boy ... sat and watched ...

In response to this additional instance of gazing, the actress follows suit and begins to collaborate with Katrina:

Suddenly I turned and said,
"Aren't you coming to me, too?"
... Katarina said,
"Go to her now."
He pulled out of her and...
then fell on top of me,
completely hard ...
I was overwhelmed and came almost immediately ...
I came over and over.

This encounter leaves the boy and two women not only sated but entertained, "laughing," as the two women affirm their command of the scene by "calling over to" and summoning "the other boy" for a second act.

The lighting and camerawork serve as adjuncts to the male gazers for whom, theoretically at least, narrative movies are produced. These filmic elements accentuate the two gaze objects' "command" of the scene as well as Alma's burgeoning sense of control over her choices. The camera's gaze follows her around the dark bedroom, as she passes back and forth in front of a shadeless night-table lamp that functions intermittently as a spotlight. As she speaks, she occupies multiple vantage points. Appearing in a close-up, in a few medium-shots, and in a long shot, she moves away from the camera, calling attention to her control over how the camera and her audience view her. Alma also manipulates the light and the window curtain in the room and thus controls how dimly or clearly she's seen. With her pale skin, light hair, and sheer white nightdress, she moves freely—sipping wine, sitting, standing, pacing, turning her head, closing a curtain, lighting a cigarette—against the night-blackened bedroom walls, while her listener remains silent, never blinking.

To be sure, the ways in which women take "command," both in the O'Kaysons' hit and in Bergman's art-house classic, reflect men's fantasies. Often such fantasies serve to perpetuate self-flattering ignorance. In *Persuasion*, Jane Austen memorably summed up this long-standing obstacle to women's "command" of self-representation, with the heroine's reminder that "men have had every advantage of us in telling their own story ... the pen has been in their hands" and the conclusion that follows: "I will not allow books to prove anything." Despite her heroine Anne Elliott's protest, Austen's own books have at least demonstrated, if not "proven," the capacity of gaze objects to become effective actors and agents *sometimes*.

A century later Virginia Woolf metaphorically illustrated the impact of the misleading stories Anne Elliott denounced. She explained that that "women have served all these centuries as looking-glasses possessing the magic and delicious power of reflecting the figure of man at twice its natural size" and amplified this understanding by expressly identifying men's age-old entitlement "to rule over other people" as their "source of power," as a means of limiting women's aspirations to "command" and as one of "the pathetic devices of the human imagination." In Woolf's view, this looking-glass gaze and the command it authorizes guarantees "the enormous importance" of the "patriarch who has to conquer, who has to rule half the human race" and represent this female half as "inferior to himself."

If the looking glass Woolf describes does distort and exaggerate as much she claims, then some male gazers are likely to notice such grotesqueries. Reasoning aesthetically, if not morally, such attentive gazers may, in turn, recoil at the sheer the shabbiness of the "devices" Woolf describes and consequently find ourselves pressed to challenge and undermine the gaze-imposed and gaze-enforced domination Austen, Woolf, Mulvey, and others have exposed and justly protested. Men who thoroughly *objectify* women (see Chap. 4), who gaze intently enough, may begin actually to aspire beyond objectification, to a rigorous *objectivity*, when they've come to recognize the disparities and grotesqueries such writers have exposed. These male gazers my come to understand the narrative that Edna O'Brien once identified, explaining that "the body contains the life story just as much as the brain" (Roth, "Conversation"). Instead of gazing in pursuit of command and control, conceptually and aesthetically minded male gazers might come to gaze in pursuit of stories and even explanations.

The art historian Julian Bell recently encapsulated and amplified this distinction, arguing that even when "sex-driven" the male gaze often reflects an analytic impulse, a perspective inevitably tempered by a humbling appreciation of the limits of gazer's powers of perception:

> Objects, whether they be fruit or fruit trees or female bodies, are indefinitely various in appearance, since each has a separate history that causes it to pick up light in unique combinations of color and sheen ... There is to be no disguising, either, the conditions that separate the viewer from the object. The picture-maker can only observe things aspect by aspect, often obstructed ... He should acknowledge and analyze this partiality of vision. Equally, he should declare his interests, as a sex-driven voyeur: lay them on the table, submit them to intelligence. ("Great")

Consequently simply accepting the static views of male gazing as inevitably an instrument of domination, the view Mulvey has made so influential, begs the questions both Bergman and the O'Kaysons raised. In mass entertainment as in elite cultural marketplaces such performances address sexually mixed audiences and not only the male gazer, the masculine commander, Mulvey postulated. What she labeled "visual pleasure," along with the other pleasures movies, other images, and narratives provide also include pleasures that can threaten domination, sexual and otherwise. Even in Bergman's dark saturnine *Persona*, the gaze object Bibi Andersson plays includes "giggling" and "laughter" as part of her experience as a performing gaze object. The gaze object's giggle-worthy complicity in Bergman's male-gaze fantasy at least holds out the possibility that male gazing might, under some circumstances, work as a collaborative performance rather than invariably to reinforce gender hierarchy and sexual subjugation.

Male gazing can't always follow the same simplistic and inevitable script Mulvey described because gazers and their objects are invariably embedded in other kinds of social—economic, institutional, tribal, "racial"—relations. *Kingsblood Royal*, Sinclair Lewis's dark midcentury satire of race-thinking, for example, illustrates the extent of this embeddedness by exaggerating what Mulvey deems the male gazer's supposedly inevitable inclination to "command" the scene and "create the action." Lewis mocks the gazer's claims to command as simultaneously irresistible *and* clownishly marginal. His narrator introduces this gazer, Borus Bugdoll, as a "Negro" sporting "bright-blue trousers, a sports-jacket in wide checks, and a shrimp-colored bow tie … standing upright yet seeming to lounge." Striking this pose, the gazer "did not suggest cotton-fields but the musical comedy, the race track, the sweet shooting of craps." With the "hands and the poised shoulders of a middle-weight prizefighter," he conveyed "an animal beauty made devilish by his stare," the "bold and amused" gaze he aims at his hostess, a (white) suburban housewife named Vestal Kingsblood. Vestal, the novel's heroine, senses that Bugdoll is "laughing his head off at me," that "he had known every woman from Sappho to Queen Marie and had understood them all perfectly," and that "his eyes did not merely undress Vestal; they hinted that, in a flustered and hateful way, she was enjoying it." Despite this fascinated reaction, she ends up "saying to herself, "I've never in my life seen such a circus-clown get-up," while wishing that her husband "could wear clothes like that and still look romantic." Encountering the male gazer, paradoxically, as a charismatic laughing stock, drives Vestal from the room, from her own kitchen, "mumbling" and feeling intellectually discredited: "Vestal quaked, and with a mumbled something which did no especial credit to her intellectual superiority, she bolted from the kitchen." But Bugdoll's gaze also leaves her "grinning … not displeased." Becoming defiantly out of step with her milieu's racial and sexual decorum, Vestal ends up describing her gazer as a "gentleman." By accentuating Bugdoll's "race" and place, in the kitchen with "the help," Lewis prompts questions about the extent to which Bugdoll's male gaze serves to promote equality and challenge segregation and perhaps even to subvert all assumptions about external, readily performed social distinctions. Lewis leaves readers wondering whether Vestal's reference to him as a gentleman, despite his apparent boorishness, illustrates the conceptually and politically liberating potential of the male gaze—or, less sanguinely, whether Vestal's unease is simply another example of the unfairness of the male gazer's advantage or another symptom of feeling her relatively advantageous *racial* status threatened. By satirically raising these questions, Lewis confronts readers with more encompassing questions, the *cui bono* questions that male gazing (and racial gazing—"the white gaze") inevitably raise.

CLOWNING VS. GAZING

Lewis's view of the gazer as "a circus-clown" and of the experience of being gazed upon as an occasion for "grinning" suggests the extent to which for gaze-objects and gazers alike comedy and humor can level and disarm male gazing. Feminist scholars such as Cynthia Willet and Suzanne Lavin have documented the impact and reach of this equalizing challenge by women stand-up performers standing up to the male gaze over the course of the late twentieth century (Lavin 91).

Since the millennium, Sarah Silverman has perhaps done the most to sustain and enrich this legacy, which Lavin characterizes as "the shift of the woman performer as subject rather than object" (92). Caricaturing the object of male gazing, Silverman preempts the authority gazing has customarily afforded Mulvey's "command and control" male gazers. In 2007, on David Letterman's *Late* Show, Silverman equated herself with two of the millennial decade's most storied gaze objects, Britney Spears and Paris Hilton. Insisting that she'd prefer to discuss her perfume rather than her time in prison, Silverman claimed a superlatively feminine identity and objectified herself as a delicate source of aromatic sensory pleasure. Silverman then recalled telling her husband how fat and charisma-deprived she finds him. By thus transforming herself into an objectifier rather than an object, Silverman had forestalled the very prospect of objectification by both her spouse and by her audience, the very attitude she had encouraged in the first place with her references to Spears and Hilton.

A few months before Silverman performed this routine she appeared on the cover and as the subject of a photo spread in the October issue of the unabashedly sexist "lad" magazine *Maxim*.[11] In one photo Silverman poses "femininely." Clothed in a candy-cane striped bikini bottom and a white tank top and with her lips puckered, she gazes at the head of a gorilla whose skin wraps around her legs. This outré posturing extended Silverman's persona's sexual curiosity and the possibilities of sexual attraction beyond her own species. With this pose, she ratcheted up her eagerness to cast herself as a sexual agent rather than as sexual object. This self-objectifying gorilla-girl stance vividly illustrates Laura Kipnis' account of how Silverman's anti-cathartic "comic sensibility" produces performances that "leave nothing exactly the same" (*Men* 86). The seemingly clashing personae on the *Maxim* cover gel to reflect the motive for stand-up iconoclasm encapsulated in Sandra Bernhard's generalization about the male spectators who frequent her shows: "They'll look at you twice. Once to see your tits, the other to see what you're doing" (Lavin 91).

Such boundary-pushing became Silverman's trademark early on her career. One of her earlier routines, for example, opens with her disclosing that "I like having sex." Then she asks: "Any sex people in the room?" In identifying herself as one of the "sex people" and in soliciting kindred spirits, Silverman casts herself simultaneously as gazer and gaze object and grants her audience permission to do the same. The 2007 *Maxim* spread stresses Silverman's double identity as gazer and gaze object by offsetting poses signaling compliant femininity (like the candy-cane stripes-and-puckered-lips pose) with poses casting her as a masculine aggressor. The fear-mongering sloganeering on the cover, for example, designates Silverman a "SEXY BEAST" while a smaller subscript reemphasizes the larger-than-life threat she poses by heralding her as "The New Kong of Comedy" in a double allusion to the simian title character of America's most popular beauty-and the beast fable and to the fevered masculine aggressiveness and impotence Martin Scorsese searingly probed in *The King of Comedy*.

The overall effect of the images and captions in the *Maxim* feature is to wed girlish submissiveness with the rampaging, royal—"commanding"—hyper virility evoked by Ken Kalfus minimally fictional

---

[11] "Sexy Beast", *Maxim* cover. http://i.ebayimg.com/00/s/MTA1N1g4Nzc=/z/wncAAOxy3zNSh7G0/$_35.JPG.

effort to enter the mind of one of our era's most controversial embodi-
ments of imperiously rampaging virility, the French statesman–financier
and alleged rapist Dominique Strauss-Kahn. Kalfus's Strauss-Kahn boast-
fully analyzes male gazing by promoting himself as its "paragon":

> Not every man has my determination, but every man is just as concupiscent,
> whether he's married or single, getting it regularly or not. He may be the
> perspiring comb-over with a somber, heavy-lidded demeanor, or the goofy,
> buck-toothed busboy whose bedroom is postered with images of football-
> ers, or the wise, soft-spoken rabbi, or the hideously maimed war veteran.
> Every one of those men who is heterosexual is watching you and your sisters,
> Mariama, surreptitiously or candidly, judging the outline of a breast and then
> extrapolating, or assessing a tush, an ankle, or a pair of full, vermilion lips.
> The turn of a head and its momentary reveal of a long, slender neck give us
> a deep and abiding pleasure, regardless of what happens next. Count on it.[12]

By appropriating the traditionally "male" candor that Kalfus's Strauss-
Kahn voices, Silverman's comedy illustrates the extent to which, by century's end, the concept of male-gazing remained an instrument of critique.
The critique, however, had turned more dialectical and ironic than polemical in response to the widespread recognition that Mulvey's critique has
"become something of an orthodoxy" (Gamman and Marshment vii).

This ironic turn reflects a consensus among influential critics including
Michel Foucault, bell hooks (116, 125–126), and Stuart Hall (201) that
every orthodoxy contains its own tacit rebuttal and that rigorous critical
thinking obliges us to inhabit the space between beliefs that tempt us
and insights that frustrate such temptations. Consequently, our indebt-
edness to Mulvey for the timeliness and accuracy of her account of gazing as a traditional instrument of men's control of women needs to be
complemented with the recognition that however much such controllers,
the men in "command," exercised this power for purposes of subordina-
tion, women and men alike can readily adapt and transform traditional
male gazing into the oppositional gazing bell hooks has proposed as a
form of resistance.

---

[12] Compare: "Whistle, You Dumb Bastard!" cartoon George Booth, *The New Yorker*
(27 August 1973). http://www.art.com/products/p15063518123-sa-i6848715/george-
booth-whistle-you-dumb-bastard-new-yorker-cartoon.htm.

THE LIMITS OF RECIPROCITY

This resistance became a staple of American fiction during the twentieth century and a spanned the spectrum that Philip Rahv famously introduced in 1939, crudely but pithily dividing American literature's refined, cultivated, and implicitly effeminate "Paleface" writers and blunt, demotic, implicitly masculine "Redskin" writers. Among the twentieth century's most paradigmatically "Paleface" writers Edith Wharton and Willa Cather (Pinsker 484) were particularly attentive students of thwarted male gazing and of the accommodations and compromises that often results from such frustrations.

Wharton's 1919 novel *The Age of Innocence* prominently features two male gazers. The first of these, a well-born young New York lawyer, opens Wharton's narrative by admiring his fiancée. "'The darling!' thought Newland Archer, his glance flitting back to the young girl" who, he assumes, "doesn't even guess what it's all about" as "he contemplated her absorbed young face with a thrill of possessorship," a thrill Wharton attributes to Archer's "pride in his own masculine initiation" (see Chap. 4). Halfway through the novel, Archer spots another gazer, his nemesis and seeming romantic rival "Beaufort," who stands "tall and red-faced, scrutinizing the women with his arrogant stare." Neither gazer wins the affections of the same exotic beauty, Ellen Olenska, whom they pursue over the course of the narrative. While Archer's affection ultimately seems reciprocated (if unconsummated), Beaufort's "commanding" wealth and *chutzpah* overshadow this reciprocity for much of Wharton's story. Beaufort's advantages have little bearing on what sunders Archer from Ellen Olenska. Far more effective in keeping them apart is the "tribal" resistance, especially the gaze (the "countless silently observing eyes") of the matriarchy that governs this rarefied New York milieu. This resistance, Archer comes to realize, has relieved of him of the sense command he may have assumed as a privilege and obligation as a young man. What began as Archer's "masculine" prerogative, his entitlement to "possessorship," leaves him finally "shy, old-fashioned, inadequate: a mere grey speck of a man compared with the ruthless magnificent fellow he had dreamed of being."

Six years later in "Soldier's Home" the consummate "Redskin" Ernest Hemingway (Pinsker 485) showed readers another defeated gazer, one thwarted far earlier in his life and more traumatically than Newland Archer. Hemingway's hero, a combat-seasoned warrior named (far more prosaically than Newland Archer) Harold Krebs, at first cut a more conventionally masculine figure than Wharton's protagonist, at least until Krebs realizes the futility of his prerogative as a gazer. When Krebs returned home to Oklahoma from combat on the Western Front and occupation duty along the Rhine, he considered himself a seasoned gazer. Hemingway opens "Soldier's Home" by describing two photographs. The first photo shows Krebs in the exclusively male company of his fraternity brothers. The second shows him sporting his Marine Corps NCO stripes, a sign of having at least begun his apprenticeship as a "man-in-command." Krebs appears in this photo standing "on the Rhine with two German girls." Even though "they were not beautiful," he recalls feeling at ease in their company because:

> There was not all this talking. You couldn't talk much and you did not need to talk. It was simple and you were friends.

Gazing back home in Oklahoma, by contrast, Krebs *does* find beauty: "so many good-looking young girls ... he liked to look at." Sharpening this contrast, Hemingway registers what an attentive, analytic, and even fashion-conscious gazer Krebs has become among these "good looking girls":

> Most of them had their hair cut short. When he went away only little girls wore their hair like that or girls that were fast. They all wore sweaters and shirt waists with round Dutch collars. It was a pattern. He liked to look at them from the front porch as they walked on the other side of the street. He liked to watch them walking under the shade of the trees. He liked the round Dutch collars above their sweaters. He liked their silk stockings and flat shoes. He liked their bobbed hair and the way they walked.

The more detailed these observations become, though, the more removed Krebs feels from the objects of his sharp gaze. Close up, he feels defeated by what he takes to be *their* rules of engagement:

> ... their appeal to him was not very strong. He did not like them when he saw them in the Greek's ice cream parlor. He did not want them themselves really. They were too complicated ... Vaguely he wanted a girl but he did not want to have to work to get her. He would have liked to have a girl but he did not want to have to spend a long time getting her. He did not want to get into the intrigue and the politics. He did not want to have to do any courting. He did not want to tell any more lies. It wasn't worth it.

In "Soldier's Home," as in *The Age of Innocence*, male-gazing seems to have proven more demoralizing than empowering, a reason to surrender rather than a basis for command.

As The Gazer Ages

Now a familiar cultural staple, Mulvey's male gazer appears to have exercised far less of the authority to "command" and "create action" that Mulvey had ascribed to him. Likewise, Mulvey's catchphrase has lost much of its conceptual force and polemical edge. Regrettably, the very phrase "the male gaze" seems bound to serve more and more as a cue for cheap shots.

An exchange in Geoff Dyer's acclaimed 2009 novel *Jeff in Venice, Death in Varanese* illustrates the extent of this repurposing. Throughout its two-generation run, the phrase "the male gaze" has usually referred to someone else's gaze, often despairingly, polemically, or at least warily. Dyer's narrator, by contrast, speaking in the first person, concedes his complicity as a gazer. Like one of Henry James's floundering couriers, this narrator travels abroad in order to secure a rare picture, a drawing of aging beauty and renowned muse:

> He looked at her face in the drawing, but was unable to look at the face of the person who had handed it to him. There was the startling fact of the drawing showing her naked, but there was also an unsettling psychological quality to the picture ... She was letting this man, her lover, look at her and draw her. To gaze at their lover, naked: it was what men had always wanted to do. If the man was an artist—or just a teenager with a camcorder—then what he painted or filmed was not simply what he saw but the unchanging strength of that desire, that hunger to see ... Any love in his gaze was unreciprocated ... Look all you want, her expression said. You can see everything and you will see nothing except what I have in common with every other woman on earth. (Dyer 73)

As he shows the drawing a few hours later to a woman he's wooing, she warns him:

> 'You're not going to say something boring about "the male gaze" are you?'
> 'I was actually,' he said, looking at her. 'Did you only say that to make
> me look at you?' Which was all he wanted to do for the moment. (83)

"The male gaze," a phrase and a concept now both banal and ubiquitous, belongs in this exchange to everyone: to the admitted gazer, to the object of his gaze, and to critics and teachers who taught Dyer's narrator and his companion about the male gaze.

This understanding of gazing as collaborative rather than as invidiously uni-directional not only antedates Mulvey's coinage. It seems to have been central to modern and contemporary fiction for the past century. Perhaps the most famous or at least most extravagant example appears at the end of James Joyce's *Ulysses* in Molly Bloom's famous soliloquy. On her 1989 album *Sensual World* and on the accompanying video the British singer Kate Bush cast herself as Molly Bloom in the guise of a "Machiavellian girl wear[ing] a sunset." By identifying with Machiavelli, Europe's most influential and most misconstrued student of power, *and* with Joyce's heroine, an ardently desired, repeatedly objectified, scandalously venturesome wife and mistress, Bush seems to have adopted a persona at once subject to and yet complicit in what she calls the gazer's "powers o'er a woman's body."[13]

While recalling Joyce as a flagrant male gazer and disclosing the complicity between male gazers and the objects of their gazes, Bush seems to be arguing that women may have perennially acted as active partners in the male gazing that *Ulysses* and other classic "male" narratives famously depict. As Joyce presents her, Molly Bloom appears to insinuate and embed her own desired and desiring body, her "breasts all perfume" in particular, into its surroundings, both natural and human-made—"into an enveloping landscape consisting of both "mountain flowers" and a "Moorish wall." Bush's rereading of Ulysses echoes Richard Pearce's "male feminist" account of the novel as a series of dialogic parodies in which "the male gaze is continually broken," its "power" broken "most importantly, by Molly's monologue" (41, 45–46). According to Pearce's argument, Joyce ultimately reverses the gaze so that the ostensible gaze object, Molly Bloom, "turns the men around her "into objects" and exercises an "all-embracing" and "independent" gaze of her own (46–49).[14]

---

[13]"Her Greatest Lyric." http://www.youtube.com/watch?v=ASb7SyoWyeE 'date accessed' [9th May 2017].

[14]Compare "When She Catches Me Staring," Borus & Feinstein, *Girls & Sports* cartoon (21 February 2008) (no longer available online).

JOINT CUSTODY

The prevalence of the phrase "the male gaze" and its conceptual appeal seems to rest on a simple and compelling insight that has over years too often degenerated into facile oversimplification. For male-gazing, both the idea and the practice itself, to remain conceptually compelling as a conversation stimulant and as an opportunity for inquiry, writers, teachers, and male-gaze readers need to keep in mind the "reciprocal curiosity" that F. Scott Fitzgerald described as a prime goad to gazing almost a century ago in *The Great Gatsby* (see Chap. 4):

> I looked at Miss Baker, wondering ... Her gray, sun-stained eyes looked back at me with reciprocal curiosity.

Fitzgerald's early fiction presents a particularly apt illustration of how male gazing embeds itself in more ambitious moves toward cultural, historical, or philosophical reflection. In 1920 the monthly magazine *Smart Set* ran a Fitzgerald story titled "May Day" about a failed artist who "had loved to" sketch a woman whose "cherished ... pert arresting profile" he could draw "with his eyes shut" (*Stories*). During the five-year interval between the appearance of "Mayday" and the publication of *Gatsby* the young Fitzgerald seems to have grown from understanding gazing as form of solipsistic self-gratification to recognizing gazing as a reciprocal inquiry. Stewart O'Nan's *West of Sunset*, a fictional account of the end of Fitzgerald's career and his end-of-life stint in Hollywood as a screenwriter, details the extent to which Fitzgerald eventually came to regard rigorously curious gazing (including the kind of fashion-conscious attentiveness Hemingway described) as a professional necessity.

> The first thing he needed to figure out was how to use Joan Crawford. He studied her like a test subject ... in the flickering dark of Thalberg's old projection room ... watching her arch her eyebrows and smirk her way through *Possessed* and *Chained* and *Forsaking All Others*, trying to discern her strengths ... Bullock's Schwab's—the Troc—everywhere he went he pictured Joan Crawford, imagined her character parsing other women on the street. He began to pay attention to fabrics and headlines and to be dismayed at the epidemic of slacks. (O'Nan 157–58)

During the same year that "Mayday" appeared, *The Smart Set* also published Willa Cather's novella "Coming, Aphrodite!" In this story, far more extensively than Fitzgerald, Cather critically and sympathetically validated meticulous and reciprocal gazing. To the extent that the male gazer who serves as her viewpoint character comes to epitomize what, in Cather's view, modern artists, male painters, and perhaps women novelists alike ought to aspire to, Cather even comes close to idealizing male gazing. One obstacle Cather initially faced in getting the story published also suggests how discomfiting it may have been a century ago for a woman to write from the vantage point of a male gazer. Exerting pressure that verged on censorship, Cather's supposedly urbane editors at *The Smart Set* pressed her to replace the innocuous adjective "unclad" with the "girlish" circumlocutory euphemism "clad in a pink chiffon cloud of some sort" in characterizing a gazer's first impression of the arresting female body that comes to obsess him.

More provocatively, in "Coming, Aphrodite!" Cather stages a fraught conflict over the role of artists and the value of their work, working a much-mined vein among Victorian and early twentieth-century writers such as Dickens, George Gissing, Henry James, Jack London, Joyce, Woolf, Fitzgerald, Langston Hughes, Nathanael West. The antagonists in "Coming, Aphrodite!" are two heartland-born aspiring artists who find themselves next-door neighbors in a Washington Square walkup at the close of the nineteenth century. Over the course of the story Eden Bower (née Edna Bowers), a singer and actress who aspired as a girl to become "the czar's mistress" (a newly unlikely prospect when the story was published in 1920), rises to theatrical stardom. During her brief Village sojourn, Eden falls under the gaze and briefly under the spell of a contrarian painter in the adjoining flat. The painter, Dan Hedger, also becomes "successful," reputedly "one of the first men among the moderns," while eschewing Eden's more commonplace understanding of career success.

In a veiled autobiographical turn Cather depicts Hedger, paradoxically, as an anti-modern modernist who strove to "get away from all that photographic stuff." Recalling such cherished male gazers as Matisse and Renoir, Cather shows Hedger beset by what one commentator on these painters' work called "Arcadian obsessions, the longings of a modernist who didn't want to be modern" (Cotter). Recollecting his sojourn in France, for example, Hedger stresses that he had "never been in Paris," spending his entire French sojourn "in the south of France … studying with C—… biggest man among the moderns." This geographical reference and the chronological frame of "Coming, Aphrodite!" indicate that

"C" probably alludes to Paul Cézanne. Cather's description of Hedger's epiphanic discovery of Eden, moreover, recalls the full-frontal extended pose of Cézanne's 1899 portrait "Nude Woman Standing"[15] painted around the same time Hedger studied under "C's" tutelage. Though not evidently standing "in a pool of sunlight," Cézanne's model does face the viewer from the most brightly lighted area of the canvas. In "Nude Woman Standing" Cezanne's palette favors the lower end of the color spectrum—brown, yellow, orange—an effect Cather encompassed with a reference to a "golden shower" and "helianthine fire." The attributes that draw Hedger's gaze—Eden's appearance as "wholly unclad, doing exercises," swinging "her arms" fully in action—recall the way Cezanne shows his "Nude Woman's" arms bent over her head, with one arm higher than the other, and with her feet appearing to move, one foot in front of the other, toward the gazer. Cather's apparent move, like that of her male-gazing alter-ego Hedger, to align herself with the provocative candor that nudes by late nineteenth- and early twentieth-century French painters (Cézanne, Courbet, Matisse, Picasso, Renoir) brought to male gazing may be glimpsed in the *The Smart Set* editors' aversion to the adjective "unclad" (which Cather made of a point of restoring when "Coming, Aphrodite!" appeared in her second story collection, *Youth and the Bright Medusa*).

Despite this connection to modernity and modernism, Hedger sums up his apprenticeship in modernity with a nod to Golden Age nostalgia. Being in France, "Hedger concluded," "was being in Paradise." When asked whether French women are "very beautiful" and whether he had "awfully good things to eat and drink," Hedger calls to mind the extent to which male-gazing modernists and their successors tended to embed the gaze object in an encompassing context, in still life close-ups and in wide-angle landscapes.

In his *Diary of a Bad Year*, Nobel laureate J.M. Coetzee assiduously illustrates this embededness. After registering "my first glimpse of" a "startling young woman" wearing a "tomato red shift startling in its brevity," Coetzee's gazer becomes a pained philosopher and a speculatively mind-reading psychologist, recounting how "as I watched her, an ache, a metaphysical ache crept over me ... and in an intuitive way

---

[15] Paul Cezanne, *Nude Woman Standing*. http://uploads7.wikiart.org/images/paul-cezanne/nude-woman-standing-1899.jpg.

she knew about it [but] did not particularly like [it] ... though it was tribute to her beauty and freshness as well as to the shortness of her dress" (3, 7). Much later in his diary, Coetzee's narrator recounts a lesson in gazing from a dead friend. A consummate "womanizer ... keenly receptive to feminine beauty," the friend taught him that most powerful gazers confine their gazing to "the realm of imagination" (175). They learn to forgo material contact with the objects of their gaze and thus renounce any actual or imaginary claims to command them. Such consummate gazers opt instead to enjoy the pleasure of curatorial connoisseurship, "to capture a 'living image' of the beloved and make it their own." Some far-reaching benefits of this curatorial approach registers in the confession by one of our era's most renowned museum curators, the Metropolitan Museum's emeritus director Philippe de Montebello, that

> It was in displaced desire ... that his personal engagement with art began: by falling in love, in his early teens, with a black-and-white photograph of the thirteenth-century limestone head of Marchioness Uta in Naumburg Cathedral, with "her puffed eyelids, as though after a night of lovemaking ... I still think she's one of the most beautiful women in the world." (Bell, "There")

In Coetzee's account, this aestheticizing sublimation of gazing becomes a "technique" of inquiry and surveillance, an opportunity for "the erotic imagination" to "explore at leisure until the woman's every last secret was laid open" (175, 177).

Part of what makes Cather's "Coming, Aphrodite" such a crucial story in the male-gaze reader canon is that it shows a gazer integrating the gaze with his professional calling, treating gazing as a conceptually dense, emotionally fraught "exploration." Hedger thus serves as an exponent of inquisitive, socially alert, information-rich and ultimately life-changing gazing. In an exchange early in his and Eden Bower's courtship, Cather shows Hedger sounding like a careful professional observer of the life of the senses in which his artistic calling necessarily engages him. In answering Eden's trite question about the legendary charms of French women—"Are the women very beautiful?"—Hedger replies like a reporter or a traditionally meticulous "realist" novelist:

Hedger said some of the women were fine looking, especially one girl who went about selling fish and lobsters. About the food there was nothing remarkable,—except the ripe figs, he liked those. They drank sour wine, and used goat-butter, which was strong and full of hair, as it was churned in a goat skin.

Then he adds that "it's a beautiful country" and in answering the question "How, beautiful?" offers to "show" Eden "some sketches" he made of the Provencal landscape. For Hedger the beauty of the women around him is apparently inextricable from Provencal landscape, cuisine, and agricultural practices, as contexts and circumstances are for every accomplished male-gaze reader.

Conjectural evidence indicates that Hedger may be based on William Glackens, who hailed, like Hedger, from Pennsylvania, who was almost an exact contemporary of Cather; who studied in France, where he fell under the influence of Renoir (instead of "C") and developed a lifelong attachment to Provence; who became part of the emerging Greenwich Village "scene" at about the same time as Cather and her characters; who worked as a commercial illustrator like Hedger; and whose best-known portrait, *Nude with an Apple* (1910),[16] associates male gazing with Christendom's Ur-pursuit-of-knowledge narrative, the story of a couple that "ate apples ... and, after a while ... knew it all" (Foer).

Cather's representation of Hedger as a bohemian paragon as well as her authorial alter-ego helps establish his gazing as the plot pivot in "Coming, Aphrodite!" Cather's barely ambivalent preference for what Hedger represents at the expense of what Eden, his gaze object, represents privileges unapologetic gazing as integral to the view of artistic conviction and achievement Cather's narrative promotes. Hedger's gazing begins fortuitously when he discovers a previously hidden knothole "in the closet that was built against the partition separating his room from Miss Bower's":

When he took his overcoat from its place against the partition, a long ray of yellow light shot across the dark enclosure, a knothole, evidently, in the high wainscoting of the west room. He had never noticed it before, and without realizing what he was doing, he stooped

---

[16]William Glackens, *Nude with an Apple*. http://uploads4.wikiart.org/images/william-james-glackens/nude-with-apple-1910.jpg.

and squinted through it. Yonder, in a pool of sunlight, stood his new neighbor, wholly unclad, doing exercises... before a long gilt mirror. Hedger did not happen to think how unpardonable it was of him to watch her. Nudity was not improper to anyone who had worked so much from the figure, and he continued to look, simply because he had never seen a woman's body so beautiful as this one, positively glorious in action. As she swung her arms and changed from one pivot of motion to another, muscular energy seemed to flow through her from her toes to her finger-tips. The soft flush of exercise and the gold of afternoon sun played over her flesh together, enveloped her in a luminous mist which, as she turned and twisted, made now an arm, now a shoulder, now a thigh, dissolve in pure light and instantly recover its outline with the next gesture.

Cather shows Hedger occupying the position Bob Dylan, another Greenwich Village *wunderkind*, sang of in visualizing a condition to which male gazing often leads. Contrary to Mulvey's account of male gazers as in command, Hedger "winds up peeping through a keyhole down upon [his] knees," as in Dylan's ironically titled gazer's lament "She Belongs to Me" (see Chap. 4). According to Cather, this abjection has its compensations. "Stooping" and "groping in the dark for the eyehole" that "makes everything otherworldly," "enchanted" and "remote," Hedger completes but then transcends the transformation Mulvey and feminist successors ascribe to gazing. Aestheticizing Eden into an object of enchantment, he manages, in Mulvey's phrase, to "produce the woman as object." Eventually, as a suitor, though, he also manages to engage with her as an autonomous agent.

As Cather's narrative unfolds, this balance proves unsustainable. Cather elicits sympathy for Hedger by showing his artistic convictions undermining his affections as a lover and complicates what Hedger represents while leaving Eden Bower one-dimensional and self-objectifying. As a counterpoint to Eden's complacent stability, Cather's compounds Hedger's talent and status as a painter by highlighting over the course of his narrative his up-from-nowhere orphan-boy backstory, his commercial adroitness, his venturesomeness as a traveler, and his panache as a raconteur. As a painter, suitor, and storyteller, Hedger comes to incarnate what John Berger defines as "embodied" male power, which, Berger hastens to add, the embodier may claim without possessing, but can nevertheless exploit simply because he's male (45–46).

With an extreme close-up view of his hands, Cather shows Hedger signaling, and barely containing, the bodily assertiveness Berger identifies. Glued to his peephole while Eden "turned and twisted … now an arm, now a shoulder, now a thigh … with the next gesture," Hedger reaches the limit of Berger's truism about the "promise" of "men's power" over female sex objects—"men act and act and woman appear":

> Hedger's fingers curved as if he were holding a crayon; mentally he was doing the whole figure in a single running line, and the charcoal seemed to explode in his hand at the point where the energy of each gesture was discharged into the whirling disc of light, from a foot or shoulder, from the up-thrust chin or the lifted breasts.

This "discharge" or release seems to promise, paradoxically, liberation through obsession.

The liberating obsession available to scrupulous, assiduous male gazers, which Cather ascribes to Hedger, reverberates even more viscerally in an account by Andrew Wyeth of his discovery of his favored gaze object: Helga Testorf.[17] Like Eden in "Coming, Aphrodite," Helga was a close neighbor of the artist. Helga, however, "sat" for Wyeth over a fourteen-year period. She recalls feeling transformed and aroused, "filled up" and "in love," as a result of being subjected to Wyeth's gaze (Meryman 336, 338). Eden Bower seems to have felt similarly aroused by Hedger's gaze. Upon learning about Hedger's "peeping," however, Eden Bower comes to treat her arousal as a challenging epiphany. After "Hedger confessed his crime," he "was reproached and forgiven, and now Eden knew what it was in his look that she had found so disturbing."

This move from reproach to absolution may second the observation of a the narrator in "In the Cage," a 1898 novella by Henry James, the precursor Cather honored as "a mighty master of language and keen student of human actions and motives" (Curtin 248). James's nameless protagonist in "In the Cage," herself an aspiring student of human actions and motives, acknowledges both the imperative to express indignation at the gazer's leer ("the male glance") and the contingent disingenuousness of such outrage:

---

[17] "Andrew Wyeth's Stunning Secret." *Time Magazine* (18 August 1986). Cover. http://latimesblogs.latimes.com/culturemonster/images/2009/01/15/time_magazine.jpg.

When she watched, a minute later, through the cage, the swing of her visitor's departing petticoats, she saw the sight from the waist down; and when the counter-clerk, after a mere male glance, remarked, with an intention unmistakably low, 'Handsome woman!' she had for him the finest of her chills: 'She's the widow of a bishop.' She always felt, with the counter-clerk, that it was impossible sufficiently to put it on; for what she wished to express to him was the maximum of her contempt, and that element in her nature was confusedly stored. 'A bishop' was putting it on, but the counter-clerk's approaches were vile.

No such outrage follows from Hedger's surprisingly exculpatory confession of his own "vile" male glancing. Instead when the couple finally acts on their mutual attraction

faces were lost ... blurred in shadow, but the figures were a man and a woman, and that was their whole concern and their mysterious beauty,—it was the rhythm in which they moved, at last, along the roof and down into the dark hole; he first, drawing her gently after him. She came down very slowly. The excitement and bravado and uncertainty of that long day and night seemed all at once to tell upon her. When his feet were on the carpet and he reached up to lift her down, she twined her arms about his neck as after a long separation, and turned her face to him, and her lips, with their perfume of youth and passion.

Though Wyeth biographers report that, unlike Hedger and Eden, Wyeth and Helga never had sex, Helga did reciprocate Wyeth's gaze-inspired desire. According to Helga, simply sitting for "Andy" resulted in her falling in love with him. Another Wyeth subject recounts the frisson of being an artist's gaze object far more graphically than Helga recollected her "love" for "Andy" or than Cather's narrator describes Eden Bower's attachment to Dan Hedger:

...the second he started to sketch me ... I could feel him *really* looking—I felt the color going right to my face. That's the intensity. My nipples were erect three-quarters of the time (Meryman 338).

Like Hedger, Wyeth found this heady mixture of artistic inspiration and erotic excitement both freeing and consuming:

And now I meet this girl and I get right up to her crotch and really draw it. With no feeling of, oh, you can't do that. She was an image I couldn't get out of my mind (Meryman 338).

In the penultimate section of "Coming, Aphrodite!" in an exchange that ends up initiating Hedger's and Bower's mutual seduction Hedger fortifies the liberating force of his untoward gaze by becoming a vividly embodied narrator, a verbal as well as a visual artist, who wears a "savage and determined expression" while narrating a "brutal story." Reacting to his Mesoamerican folktale about a sexually voracious rain-goddess queen

> Eden Bower sat shivering a little as she listened. Hedger was not trying to please her, she thought, but to antagonize and frighten her by his ... Now she was looking at the man he really was. Nobody's eyes had ever defied her like this. They were searching her and seeing everything; all she had concealed ... He was testing her, trying her out, and she was more ill at ease than she wished to show. "That's quite a thrilling story," she said at last, rising and winding her scarf about her throat.

Adhering to widely accepted imperatives of modern art, Hedger has discomfited his audience. But he also fails over the course of "Coming, Aphrodite!" to command his gaze object or exercise any control over her actions, despite the sexual attachment that follows from the combination of his gazing and his adroitness as a storyteller.

Cather associates Hedger's art and his gaze with yet another dimension of modernism, with the modernist view of the artist's calling not simply as an antagonistic storyteller—a narrative provocateur—but as an experimental adventurer. Constantly "outliving a succession of convictions and revelations about his art" and "getting rid of ideas" he once embraced, Hedger embodies Cather's own understanding of artistic integrity, in opposition to Eden's male-gaze-sanctioned view of herself as a "marketable product" and of the commercial "success" that Eden embraces and then futilely presses on Hedger as a worthy aspiration. "Coming, Aphrodite!" ends a generation after Eden and Hedger's abrupt parting. Returning to Manhattan after a triumphant European stage career, Eden asks a carriage-trade 5th Avenue gallery owner whether Hedger "had great success."

> "Certainly. He is one of the first men among the moderns. That is to say, among the very moderns. He is always coming up with something different.

He often exhibits in Paris, you must have seen." ... M. Jules pulled at his short grey moustache. "But, Madame, there are many kinds of success," he began cautiously. Madame gave a dry laugh. "Yes, so he used to say. We once quarreled on that issue. And how would you define his particular kind?" M. Jules grew thoughtful. "He is a great name with all the young men, and he is decidedly an influence in art. But one can't definitely place a man who is original, erratic, and who is changing all the time."

Hedger's market-flouting commercial success as a painter and his authoritativeness as a storyteller, who leaves his audience "shivering a little as she listened," underscore the extent to which *he* rather than Eden Bower serves as Cather's viewpoint character and alter-ego.

It stands to reason, therefore, that the story implicitly but not very ambiguously makes a case *for* male-gazing, as not merely biologically determined or socially conditioned—as something that, in Mulvey's view, men do to women—but as an artistic resource and perspectival option. According to *New Yorker* theater critic Hilton Als, "few feminists have articulated the ways in which some women may find stereotypical male behavior necessary, if only because it enables them to act out its supposed counterpart, femininity." Als' reasoning echoes the understanding of gazing voiced by Cather. If we must, as the prevailing wisdom argues, treat "femininity" and masculinity as gender-producing performances rather than genetically coded identities, then male-gazing belongs to this larger repertory of gender-making and gender-bending performances and opportunities for exploring and staging the effects of desire both within and between the sexes.

Attention/At-Ease

Early in her 1948 novel *The Heat of the Day* Elizabeth Bowen demonstrates what happens when characters and narrators set out, at cross purposes, to stage male gazing. Bowen has her narrator fix the reader's attention on "an Englishman in civilian clothes" attending an *al fresco* concert in London's Regent's Park. "At every interval" he "would cast about his neighbors with a baited look" (*Heat* 5–6) making a point of not looking at any particular audience member. Next to him sat an orphaned teenage war widow and self-identifying "movie-goer" (168) androgynously named Louie. Louie, Bowen's narrator reports, appeared dressed and made-up in order to have an "effect." Habitually looking for company, Louie seeks to elicit her fellow concert-goer's withheld gaze by starting a conversation. Bowen, however, repeatedly thwarts this gaze-soliciting initiative. She not only sets this encounter in a formal performance space, an amphitheater; she also characterizes Louie as constrained to keep rehearsing, without ever actually getting to perform, for her new audience. This thwarted performance would consist of what to her mind she's already established as a successful routine for achieving "the effect she hoped to convey" (8). In setting up this failed performance, Bowen describes one of the Englishman's first reactions to having his gaze solicited: "he at once looked, distasteful, the other way" (6). "Discountenanced" by "the feeling of being looked at twice— being viewed then checked over again in the same moment" Bowen's gaze-seeking ingénue experiences a failure of "perseverance." Instead of a gaze, Louie's performance elicits only a "frown" and an "unkind tone" (9–10). She later remembers this "disheartening farewell" as "a smack in the face" (159). Despite the rebuff, Louie continues to "keep a lookout" for this stranger whom she describes to a neighbor as "funny," as if *he* had been performing for *her*.

Notwithstanding his aversion to Louie's come-on, Bowen does show the "Englishman" as knowing that he's supposed to gaze and as steeped in "the sense of being watched" (38). Despite his aversion to gazing, Bowen ends up identifying the Englishman as constitutionally inclined to perform, with "routine alertness," (9) his role as a male gazer. Apparently unavoidably, Louie's "caked" lips "struck him and could have moved him, only they didn't" (8). Through his refusal to play the role of the male gazer as it's customarily scripted, "the Englishman" seems so astute about playing this role that knows how to downplay it with devastating effect.

Much later in *The Heat of Day*, when the primary star-crossed lovers plot has usurped Louie and "the Englishman" as the narrative's focal point, Bowen shows this gaze resistance at work between intimates, in a private space, rather than between strangers in Regent's Park. The heroine's lover becomes momentarily dissociated, disavowing his status as gazer when "with an effect of deliberation, he fixed his eyes on her face—though somehow not, it appeared, on her. Nor did those eyes appear to her to be his" (228). In both passages Bowen positions men (known heterosexuals in each instance), who are socially scripted for gazing as their default stance, in circumstances where they disclaim the gazer's role. As Cather did a generation earlier, Bowen shows gazing as a performance, a solo or a duet, available to women as well as to men. Most broadly, what stands out in both Bowen's and Cather's narratives is the desire and capacity among women novelists to stand in as male gazers—to male-gaze on behalf of their readers.

Bowen also raises the stakes by stretching the possibilities of what both gazing and refusing to gaze might tell readers about a man's intimate and civic relationships. Both the male non-gazers in *The Heat of the Day* turn out to be morally compromised and less than persuasive in rationalizing their compromises. Robert, the heroine's lover and a wounded Dunkirk veteran, turns out be working for the Third Reich. Harrison, the rude concertgoer in the park, is the government agent pursuing Robert. In performing this patriotic duty, Harrison sets out to blackmail the novel's heroine, Robert's lover Stella. In exchange for sex, Harrison promises not to arrest Robert.

A movie reviewer as well as a novelist—"a fan, not a critic" ("Why" 207)—Bowen makes a gazer out of Stella by depicting her and Louie as moviegoers. Just as Mulvey shows her male gazers confirming their identities by looking at screens, Bowen shows Stella discovering the story of her life with Robert in "Technicolor" (*Heat* 125). Her unvoiced misgivings about Robert surface when her view of him calls to mind what happens "in the cinema when some breakdown in projection leaves one shot frozen, absurdly, on the screen" (106). From Stella's perspective, Robert becomes an on-screen "celluloid" gaze object. After describing her view of Robert as telescopically distant, Stella shifts metaphors, so that the light by which she sees Robert takes on the "glossy thinness of celluloid" (124–125). Once she's established this perspective, Stella takes "command" of the *mise-en-scène*—of what Mulvey calls the "stage"—and the "action." Changing both the shot and the lighting, Stella assumes the role of a director, not simply a moviegoer like Mulvey's male gazers, and thus an agent far more in command than any of the onscreen gaze objects Mulvey described. Instead, Stella "brought the scene back again into focus by staring at window reflections in the glaze of the teapot" (125). More decisively if more obliquely than Cather, Bowen has turned the male gaze and her women characters' appropriation of it into far more than a spectator's instrument of domination. Showing Stella at the movies—an exclusively male activity according Mulvey—and metaphorically making her own movies in whatever space she chooses, Bowen transforms gazing and the counter-gazing it elicits into cues for managing and manipulating one's social position and for negotiating questions of personal and civic loyalty.

When Louie last sees Harrison, dining with Stella, who is now primed to accept his extortion deal, she brings "her gaze to bear upon Harrison, re-assessing him, from the finger nails to the crown of his head, in a new and important light" and judges "that Stella should do better" (266). Bowen complements Louie's penetrating gaze with an ear for implication. Recalling Harrison's "remark" that he "seldom forgot a face," Louie extends her gaze beyond his hand and head and determines that "considering what a number of" faces "there are, it ought to be quite funny inside your head by this time." Stella's concurrence—"you're right … it is quite funny inside his head"—prompts Harrison to reassert his control of the scene with his male gaze by "fixing his eyes on her." This move fails because, as the narrator notes, Harrison's response proved ambiguous, abject and thus easily ignorable.

With a reaction Bowen characterizes as "an either equivocal or tormented expression," Harrison joins a millennia-old line of flustered, flouted gazers. His position, as a Crown security agent, a representative of established authority backed by the force of law during wartime, makes a cruel joke of his ineffectiveness. This comeuppance makes for an unmistakable caution against reflexively associating male gazing with domination.

CHAPTER 3

American Fiction: Gaze Canon

The Farmer's Daughter, the Seamstress and the Papist

Not surprisingly contemporary (post-Mulvey) male writers have been quick to identify gazing as a cognitive transaction; hence, novelist Gary Shteyngart's realization that all around him "men and women" were "exchanging small bits of sexual information with their eyes" (236). For poet Dan Chiasson, gazing promises a kind of knowledge more challenging and more rewarding than mere "information." Thus Chiasson compares the movement of a gazer's "eye across a lover's body" to the analytically rigorous cognition he pictures in "Bicentennial": "Moving as a mind moves across a math problem."

Informative, inquisitive gazing has always been part of American literature, and it hasn't been confined to men's writing either. In her 1917 novel *Summer* Edith Wharton describes the beginning of intimacy as the moment when the novel's heroine, a contested gaze object named Charity Royal, "became aware of a change in [her wooer's] face." When Charity discerns that the gazer, Lucius Harney, "was no longer listening to her, he was only looking at her, with the passionate absorbed expression she had seen in his eyes after they had kissed," he seems to be "scrutinizing her troubled face with [a] minute searching gaze … searching her face for more light on what she had revealed to him." Before beginning the love story that this kiss sets in motion, Wharton took pains to explain Charity's suitor's profession as an architect and an

© The Author(s) 2017
J.D. Bloom, *Reading the Male Gaze in Literature and Culture*, Global
Masculinities, DOI 10.1007/978-3-319-59945-8_3

architectural historian, in other words as a trained analytic observer and explainer of whatever his gaze encompasses.

In the US literary canon such "searching" metasexual gazing predates Wharton by nearly a century. It dates back to the Republic's earliest literary classics. In his much popularized, oft-adapted tale "The Legend of Sleepy Hollow" Washington Irving tells a story, like Wharton's *Summer*, of rival gazers—contending wooers—and the object of their desire. Both suitors, Irving's beset-upon hero Ichabod Crane and his physically commanding rival Brom Bones, gaze metasexually. Where Brom Bones, Irving's "rantipole hero," sees in their neighbor, Katrina Van Tassel, the "blooming ... object of" his "uncouth gallantries," the courtly schoolmaster Ichabod Crane sees much more. His perspective and that of Irving's narrator melds attention to ethnic heritage, fashion history, and agricultural economics with the male gazer's conventional condescension to the "fair" and "weaker sex."

> Katrina Van Tassel, the daughter and only child of a substantial Dutch farmer ... was a blooming lass of fresh eighteen; plump as a partridge; ripe and melting and rosy cheeked as one of her father's peaches, and universally famed, not merely for her beauty, but her vast expectations. She was withal a little of a coquette, as might be perceived even in her dress, which was a mixture of ancient and modern fashions, as most suited to set off her charms. She wore the ornaments of pure yellow gold, which her great-great-grandmother had brought over from Saardam, the tempting stomacher of the olden time; and withal a provokingly short petticoat, to display the prettiest foot and ankle in the country round ... the delicate little dimpled hand of Katrina Van Tassel ...

The topical diffusion surrounding what Katrina Van Tassel represents when first introduced illustrates the extent to which objectifying women isn't necessarily carnal and may not even reflect any interest in physically possessing a woman, controlling her body (Traister 118), or commanding the stage of her action (Mulvey, "Visual Pleasure"):

> Ichabod Crane had a soft and foolish heart towards the sex; and it is not to be wondered at that so tempting a morsel soon found favor in his eyes, more especially after he had visited her in her paternal mansion.

At the end of "The Legend of Sleepy Hollow" Irving followed his account of the triumph of Brom's "uncouth gallantries" in the contest over Katrina with rumors about Ichabod's material prosperity after fleeing Sleepy Hollow.

The uncertainty over who "won" this contest underscores the possibility that the motives for gazing might vary more than popular uses of the phrase allow. The effeteness Irving attributes to Ichabod suggests how much the desires that drive the objectification of women extend, in Irving's view, beyond sexual control to encompass an array of not necessarily gendered aspirations, including prosperity and material comfort (Traister 117).

Such representations of women as unsexed objects of desire, as legacy-bearers, and as real estate rather than as imagined sex partners reverberated throughout American writing during first half of the nineteenth century as the nation forged its cultural identity. Familiar examples include the lost loves who haunt Edgar Poe's tales and poems, such as Helen, Ligeia, Rowena, and "the beautiful Annabel Lee," as well as the fair-dark sister pairs, the "lurid poppy-blossoms" and "white lilies" (Lawrence, *Studies*) in need of rescue and marriage throughout James Fenimore Cooper's frontier novels. Throughout the American literary canon unsexed male gazing has tended to confound American writers' most memorable characters as well as challenge generations of readers.

Perhaps no American writer has done more to present male gazing as a source of "trouble" for gazers (to use Wharton's word) and as an occasion for conjecture and contextualizing than Nathaniel Hawthorne did in 1850 in *The Scarlet Letter*. This "trouble" deepens over the course of Hawthorne's "romance" as male-gazing narrators and male-gazing characters became less assured and authoritative about their perceptions and their inferences. Hawthorne began his tale of Hester Prynne, whom his narrative ultimately transfigures into a transgressing, self-contained, artistically powerful woman, by stressing his heroine's status as a gaze object:

> a pretty large number of the inhabitants of Boston; all with their eyes intently fastened on the iron-clamped oaken door ... The women, who were now standing about the prison-door, stood within less than half a century of the period when the man-like Elizabeth had been the not altogether unsuitable representative of the sex ... The bright morning sun, therefore, shone on broad shoulders and well-developed busts, and on round and ruddy cheeks, that had ripened in the far-off island, and had hardly yet grown paler or thinner in the atmosphere of New England ... The door of the jail being flung open from within, there appeared ... the offender ... the young woman ... stood fully revealed before the crowd ... with a burning blush, and yet a haughty smile, and a glance that would not be abashed, looked around at her townspeople and neighbors. On the breast of her gown, in fine red cloth, surrounded with an elaborate

embroidery and fantastic flourishes of gold thread, appeared the letter A. It was so artistically done, and with so much fertility and gorgeous luxuriance of fancy, that it had all the effect of a last and fitting decoration to the apparel which she wore; and which was of a splendor in accordance with the taste of the age, but greatly beyond what was allowed by the sumptuary regulations of the colony. The young woman was tall, with a figure of perfect elegance, on a large scale. She had dark and abundant hair, so glossy that it threw off the sunshine with a gleam, and a face which, besides being beautiful from regularity of feature and richness of complexion, had the impressiveness belonging to a marked brow and deep black eyes. She was lady-like, too, after the manner of the feminine gentility of those days; characterized by a certain state and dignity, rather than by the delicate, evanescent, and indescribable grace, which is now recognized as its indication ... Had there been a Papist among the crowd of Puritans, he might have seen in this beautiful woman, so picturesque in her attire and mien, and with the infant at her bosom, an object to remind him of the image of Divine Maternity, which so many illustrious painters have vied with one another to represent; something which should remind him, indeed, but only by contrast, of that sacred image of sinless motherhood, whose infant was to redeem the world.

With his painstaking description of his heroine's figure, face, hair, and garb, Hawthorne highlights the extent to which throughout the narrative Hester will become the object of a range of gazes, not all of them exclusively male. Hawthorne's insistence on this plurality of gazes becomes unequivocally explicit in the very title of the *Scarlet Letter*'s midpoint chapter (thirteen of twenty-four), bluntly titled "Another View of Hester."

In opening *The Scarlet Letter* with an account of Hester's release from prison Hawthorne introduces only the first of many gazers in his narrative. This most conspicuous male gazer "among the crowd" of seventeenth-century Bostonians Hawthorne coyly and only conjecturally identifies as "a Papist." Though presenting him as merely hypothetical and namelessly generic, Hawthorne does flesh out this "Papist's" frame of mind in identifying him as an aesthete attentive to what is "picturesque" and literally as an objectifier who looks at "objects" for transcendent meaning. By recalling how "many illustrious painters have vied with one another to represent" such a scene, Hawthorne adds the cautionary note that all the inferences gazing yields and any conclusion a gazer reaches need to be seen as precarious and subject to contestation.

Hawthorne's contemporary readers would have realized right away that in Puritan Boston (and in much of antebellum America) the perspective of this "Papist" gazer would have been subjected to far more than contestation; the gazer himself would have lived in fear of ostracism, abuse, or worse. By introducing this gazer as a Papist pariah, Hawthorne undermines the aesthetic and doctrinal impetuses governing his gaze. This gazer's precarious status may also account for his merely hypothetical and subjunctive presence in this scene and his subsequent disappearance from the rest of the narrative. His aesthetically dense and ideologically outlawed perspective subsequently yields to the more reductively objectifying, synecdochic views of Hester Prynne prevalent throughout the rest of the novel. In the service of others' ideological and emotional "interests and convenience," Hester is repeatedly "beheld" as well as "comprehended" and "discerned" as she becomes more and more of a cognitive challenge and less of an erotic gaze object:

> Those who had before known her, and had expected to behold her dimmed ... Children, too young to comprehend wherefore this woman should be shut out from the sphere of human charities, would creep nigh enough to behold her plying her needle at the cottage-window, or standing in the doorway, or laboring in her little garden, or coming forth along the pathway that led townward, and, discerning the scarlet letter on her breast, would scamper off with a strange contagious fear ... Behold, verily, there is the woman of the scarlet letter ... behold here the unhappy woman, Hester Prynne ...

In the eyes of her many beholders whose "gaze" she experienced as "peculiar torture," Hester comes to be seen as a cautionary lesson, a "general symbol at which the preacher and moralist might point," "a female problem" and "a *political* problem" (Berlant 72) about whom "there hath been much question," according to her colony's governor. An embodied question, Hester emerges perhaps paradoxically as both "a necessity to the state's semiotic apparatus" (Berlant 68) and a successfully self-promoting artistic prodigy:

> Children, too young to comprehend wherefore this woman should be shut out from the sphere of human charities, would creep nigh enough to behold her plying her needle at the cottage-window ... She possessed an art that sufficed ... to supply food for her thriving infant and herself. It was the art—then, as now, almost the only one within a woman's grasp—of

needle-work. She bore on her breast, in the curiously embroidered letter, a specimen of her delicate and imaginative skill, of which the dames of a court might gladly have availed themselves, to add the richer and more spiritual adornment of human ingenuity to their fabrics of silk and gold.

Hester's art and ingenuity cumulatively transform the very stigma imposed on her by the church's and state's gazing disciplinarians and usurps their authority (Berlant 136). Reinforced by "the gaze of the multitude," her scarlet letter becomes a protective shield and "a badge of sacredness." It becomes an instrument of resistance to state and church disciplinarians' power to command her. In frustrating their efforts to ferret out of Hester the identity of her daughter Pearl's father until it's too late to discipline or punish him, Hester has also turned herself from a frail woman in punitive and protective custody into a protector and creator in her own right. When the narrator observes midway through the narrative that "the scarlet letter had not done its office" because Hester has achieved "a freedom of speculation ... which our forefathers would have held to be a deadlier crime than that stigmatized by the scarlet letter," Hawthorne signals decisively that the male gaze has failed as an instrument of command and that, at least from the perspective of those who value intellectual freedom, the disciplinary male gaze deserves to fail.

FROM NOT PRETTY TO PRETTY

As Henry James points out, melodramatic clichés like adultery and scandals about out-of-wedlock motherhood were "to Hawthorne's imagination comparatively vulgar" (*Hawthorne*). Consequently, the question more in need of narrative resolution than questions about Pearl's paternity or her mother's extramarital partner in *The Scarlet Letter* turn on determining which "view of Hester" will come to predominate and who will make the determination: one of the male gazers who populate the narrative; the women gazers in "the marketplace" who view Hester en masse at the "prison-door"; "readers" whom Hawthorne frees in chapter twenty-three "to choose among theories" and among "views" of Hester; or Hester herself? Hawthorne seems to have resolved this question with a conclusion singling out Hester Prynne as a prospering, revered, beloved solitary survivor: "an object of love and interest ... looked upon with awe, yet with reverence."

In his 1879 biographical homage to Hawthorne, James reflected on the extent to which narrative tension in *The Scarlet Letter* depends in effect on gazing, on a sequence of competing views of Hester Prynne. Though acknowledging the novel's "genius," James questions the results of Hawthorne's "over-ingenuity." These results include "picturesquely arranged" "representatives" instead of full-blooded "characters," "a want of reality," and static narration "with little progression, though with a great deal … of … stable variation" that "contribute[s] little that helps" Hawthorne's narrative "to live and move."

Despite these cavils, James did follow Hawthorne's example by repeatedly assuming the pose of a male gazer throughout his own work. Both through first-person narrators (see the discussion in Chap. 1 of "The Beldonald Holbein") and often through third-person narrators, James seemed intent on avoiding the obliqueness and stasis he ascribes to *The Scarlet Letter* and on replacing "picturesque arrangement" and "stable variation" with more direct action and insight. Published a year before his study of Hawthorne, James's early novel *The Europeans* illustrates this turn. The heroine of *The Europeans*, the US-born Baroness Eugenia-Camilla-Dolores Munster, becomes part of what James regarded as the "artistic experiment" his novel conducts (*Letters* vol. 1 65). Forestalling perceptions of the baroness as static and merely "picturesque," James' narrator introduces her by accentuating how much she "represents a configuration" that those around her "cannot comprehend" and how much she functions in the narrative as a bearer of "complicated possibilities" (Poirier, *Comic* 101, 106).

James introduces these complications by echoing Shakespeare's gaze-skewing sonnet 130 ("My mistress' eyes are nothing like the sun") and by daring readers to begin judging the baroness according to the most superficial and hackneyed criterion for evaluating women's "looks." Characterizing the baroness' appearance with so uncharacteristically colloquial and so pointedly banal an adjective as "pretty," James may have also been questioning the accuracy or propriety of *prettiness* as a ubiquitous standard of judgment among male gazers:

> She was not pretty; but even when it expressed perplexed irritation her face was most interesting and agreeable. Neither was she in her first youth; yet, though slender, with a great deal of extremely well-fashioned roundness of contour—a suggestion both of maturity and flexibility—she carried her three and thirty years as a light-wristed Hebe might have carried

a brimming wine-cup. Her complexion was fatigued, as the French say; her mouth was large, her lips too full, her teeth uneven, her chin rather commonly modeled; she had a thick nose, and when she smiled—she was constantly smiling—the lines beside it rose too high, toward her eyes. But these eyes were charming: gray in color, brilliant, quickly glancing, gently resting, full of intelligence. Her forehead was very low—it was her only handsome feature; and she had a great abundance of crisp dark hair, finely frizzled, which was always braided in a manner that suggested some Southern or Eastern, some remotely foreign, woman. She had a large collection of ear-rings, and wore them in alternation; and they seemed to give a point to her Oriental or exotic aspect. A compliment had once been paid her, which, being repeated to her, gave her greater pleasure than anything she had ever heard. "A pretty woman?" someone had said. "Why, her features are very bad." "I don't know about her features," a very discerning observer had answered; "but she carries her head like a pretty woman." You may imagine whether, after this, she carried her head less becomingly.

In short order and on the basis of her "carriage" or bearing, James has transformed the baroness from "not pretty" to "like a pretty woman." In the process, he preempts and exhausts the variety of gazes that might be fixed on her. These gazes fix on her face, her age, her hair, her brow, her mouth, her eyes, her temperament and mood, her "foreign," "exotic," and "oriental" attributes. James' narrator also "translates" what he sees from what "the French say" and, resorting to mythological allusion, turns the countess into the Greek servant-goddess Hebe.

James closes this introductory description by disputing prior assertions about Eugenia. In raising these questions, James' narrator shifts the focus from description to inference, from Eugenia's appearance to what her appearance signifies. The introduction of "a very discerning observer," a connoisseur gazer (though not expressly male), and this observer's disingenuously humble confession that "I don't know about her features" agitates the uncertainty over what to make of the princess's "features." This uncertainty, which sustains James's narrative, may also reflect his efforts to save his novel from the stasis he ascribed to *The Scarlet Letter*. By affording his "discerning observer" one final opportunity to "imagine" and by allowing his gazer the last word in the initial description of Baroness Eugenia, James tilts the argument over Eugenia's appearance in favor of the observer and against the nameless, attribute-less (gender-less) "someone" who had disparaged her "features." Like the hypothetical male gazer standing "in the crowd" in

The Scarlet Letter, the Papist who regards Hester from the sectarian perspective of "sinless motherhood," James's "discerning observer" also moves to complicate male gazing. This "discerning observer" sees–or imposes–what the omniscient narrator had resisted recognizing: the heroine's prettiness.

Confounding gazers of both sexes becomes one of Baroness Eugenia's functions as a character, or "compositional resource" (James, "Preface"), throughout *The Europeans*. In chapter three, when the Baroness meets her American kinfolk, James singles out a "rigid" uncle, Mr. Wentworth (no given name). James's description of Uncle Wentworth's first view of the baroness exposes his thwarted plans and the assumptions about women that his reaction reflects. James' narrator also exposes Uncle Wentworth as a failed male gazer:

> He had arranged in his mind a little speech; but now it quite faded away. He felt almost frightened. He had never been looked at in just that way— with just that fixed, intense smile—by any woman; and it perplexed and weighed upon him, now, that the woman who was smiling so and who had instantly given him a vivid sense of her possessing other unprecedented attributes, was his own niece … He had a feeling that it was his duty, so long as the Baroness looked at him, smiling in that way, to meet her glance with his own scrupulously adjusted, consciously frigid organs of vision; but on this occasion he failed to perform his duty to the last.

More sanguine about this meeting but equally surprised, Eugenia's cousin Gertrude "had expected her, for mysterious reasons, to resemble a very pretty portrait of the Empress Josephine, of which there hung an engraving in one of the parlors … But the Baroness was not at all like that—not at all." Since the narrator has already answered the question of what the baroness *was* like—"like a pretty woman"—the answer to troubling questions about what the Baroness *was* like comes to matter less than the optical "adjustments" gazing demands of Mr. Wentworth and also to matter less than Gertrude's "mysterious reasons" for "expecting" a dead French empress instead of a young American baroness. James's implicit argument in this sequence of reactions to the baroness highlights how gazing can function as a goad to discovery, the kind of discovery that ideally leads to a change of mind or an expansion of awareness, the kind of learning Eugenia's American hosts experience in the face of her arguable "prettiness."

The Master, Colm Tóibín's 2004 biographical novel about Henry James, recalls how James became a meta-gazer, how he discovered male gazing as a boy, gazing not on his own account, but rather by spying his father in the act of gazing:

> There was a woman bathing, a young woman being watched by an older woman on the beach. The bather was large, perhaps even over-weight, and well protected from the elements by an elaborate costume ... Henry barely noticed her at first as his father stopped and made as though to examine something on the far horizon. Then his father walked forward for a while, silently, distracted, and turned back to study the horizon once more. This time Henry realized that he was watching the bather, examining her fiercely and hungrily and then turning away, observing the low dunes behind him, pretending that they also interested him to the same intense degree.
>
> As his father turned away once more and began walking towards home, he sounded out of breath and did not speak. Henry wanted to find an excuse to run ahead and get away from him, but then his father turned again, the expression on his face vivid, the skin blotched and the eyes sharp as though he were angry. His father was now standing on the shore, trembling, watching the swimmer who had her back to him, her costume clinging to her. His father made no further effort to seem casual. His stare was deliberate and pointed, but no one else noticed it. The woman did not look behind, and her companion had moved away. It was important, Henry knew, for him to pretend that this was nothing; there was no question that this could be mentioned or commented on. His father did not move, and seemed unaware of his presence, but he must have known he was there, Henry thought, and whatever this was, this keen-eyed drinking in of the woman bather, it was enough to make his father not care about Henry's presence. Finally, as he turned and set out on the journey home, his father stared back regularly with the look of someone who had been hunted down and defeated. The woman, once more, swam out to sea. (81)

The observation that this gaze object's "companion had moved away" (implying much more distance than, say, "moved on") focuses on one of those "commanding" figures Mulvey designated as paradigmatic male gazers. Oblivious to the presence of his son, James *père* extends his command beyond the object of his gaze itself by exercising his power to silence young Henry simply by dint of his commanding demeanor. Tóibín doesn't necessarily debunk the views of a gazer's power that he evokes. But he does show what happens when the gazer's reach exceeds his grasp, a condition James would attribute in his 1903 novel *The Ambassadors* to "being given over to uncontrolled perceptions" that "complicate" protagonist Lambert Strether's "vision" and "let his imagination roam." Tóibín magnifies this complication by taking into account the effect of gazing on the gazer and on the demeanor of the gazer when he becomes subjected to the someone else's gaze. According to both James and Tóibín, even the most commanding gaze can fail and in failing expose the gazer's impotence.

Despite Henry James Sr.'s calling as a transcendental philosopher and spiritual seeker (149), Tóibín's description of him as "trembling" like a "keen-eyed" drinker with his skin mottling and eyes sharpened by anger turns him into an entirely material earthbound container of thwarted lust. The younger James (as Tóibín renders him) "knew [to] pretend that" his father's gaze-prompted transformation "was nothing; there was no question that this could be mentioned or commented on" because as James wrote in his later years "there are decencies in the name of general self-respect we must take for granted, there's a rudimentary intellectual honor to which we must, in the interest of civilization at least pretend." When Lionel Trilling quoted this acknowledgment, in his 1940 essay "Reality in America," he was upholding James' "intellectual honor" and "the authoritative immediacy" of his writing (11) against what Trilling disparaged as a critical consensus favoring James's diametric opposite in the American literary canon: Theodore Dreiser (*Liberal Imagination*, 9–10). The (now long-lapsed) consensus Trilling was challenging favored Dreiser's work because of its crudity and roughness, exactly the traits exhibited by James's gazing father as Tóibín depicts him.

WOMEN KEPT AND UNKEPT

Trilling's much-cited phrase, "the dark and bloody crossroads where literature and politics meet" (8), often quoted context-free, first appeared in this James-versus-Dreiser essay. At this portentous junction Trilling pits Dreiser's "vulgar materialism," with its "lust for 'beauty' and 'sex,'" against James's "electrical mind" and "complex and rapid imagination" (16, 12). As a forthright male gazer, apparently alienated from the "decencies" Trilling attributed to James (11), Dreiser may be unsurpassed among major American novelists as a serial male gazer. The starkest evidence of his heedless passion for gazing is his late-career, two-volume collection entitled *A Gallery of Women* (1929). Arguably, the title encapsulates Dreiser's entire career since, taken as a whole, his oeuvre constitutes a "truly memorable gallery of women" (Eby 157). Confounding efforts to divide Dreiser's work between his fiction and his reportage, this series of single-chapter reminiscences of women Dreiser had known defies genre classification. Some forty years later, however, a Hollywood-sponsored director-playwright memorably adapted Dreiser's "gallery of women" approach to male-gazing for the big screen.

This updated "gallery of women" appears toward the end of Mike Nichols and Jules Feiffer's 1971 *succès de scandale Carnal Knowledge*, a dark satire on male gazing and its repercussions. This scene shows a burned-out corporate lawyer, played by Jack Nicholson, in his Manhattan penthouse presenting a slideshow that he's titled "Ballbusters on Parade." Ostensibly recounting a life of failed relationships, Nicholson's character, Jonathan Fuerst, can't escape cataloguing the physical traits of the women in and out of his life, praising one for her "great body" and another for her "build"; singling out others for more particular attributes such as their "asses" or "great tits"; noting another's resemblance to "Elizabeth Taylor in *National Velvet*." Nicholson ends his retrospect with Porky Pig's famously stammered sign-off "Th-th-th-that's all folks!" He then questions one of his guests, a young woman viewing the slideshow along with Jonathan and his Amherst roommate, about her crying, asking, "What are you crying for? It's not a Lassie movie." Jonathan's points of reference, a heroic lost dog and an inarticulate cartoon pig who always gets the last word, accentuate the disjunction between *his* take on his slideshow and its implications for its other audiences, the couple in his apartment and moviegoers around the world. Jonathan's focus on body parts and his habit of limiting his perspective to screen images and Hollywood animal stories—Porky Pig, Lassie, *National Velvet*—expose his maladroitness at reading the very images he has assembled to tell his life story. Jonathan's failure speaks more broadly to the gazer's challenge in articulating the relationship between women's visible, tangible attributes and the intangibles on which marriages, extramarital affairs, premarital liaisons, and even many supposedly casual hookups depend.

In *A Gallery of Women* Dreiser set out to sort out this mix of intangible attributes and the tangible marks of attractiveness that (we've been

incessantly reminded) preoccupy male gazers. Dreiser begins one chapter, about Ellen Adams Wrynn, an illustrator he hired while working as a
magazine editor, by recalling that "what interested me most ... was her
personality" (I, 133). His next sentence, though, gives short shrift to
this superlative "interest," stressing instead that "she was young, attractive" and only then proceeding to note her vigor and ambition. This
attention to "personality" remains cursory, as Dreiser next recalls her as
"more blonde than brunette, but certainly not so fair as dark—a chestnut blonde." Dreiser sums up his "first impression" by linking Wrynn's
appearance and interests, with the former taking precedence. Wrynn
apparently belongs to one of Dreiser's well-established classifications:
"another good-looking girl interested in art and the bohemian life" (I,
133). Even upon discovering her to be an accomplished painter and
praising her for it, Dreiser relates Wrynn's artistry to her various body
parts. Thus the figure in one of her paintings, "a boudoir scene" of "a
rounded, sensual girl," resembles Wrynn, whose "arms and torso and
thighs were warmly yet conservatively hinted at." The image, Dreiser
recalls, "had a sense of something exotic, and yet at the same time
repressed, in picture and in artist" (I, 134–35). "Interested in romance
and her particular type of beauty," Dreiser shifts his attention from
Wrynn's artistry and workplace professionalism to the "varietism" and
the "pagan, gay way of life of which Ellen ... was a part" (I, 137). After
recounting his unplanned encounters with Wrynn in the company of various men, Dreiser concludes that only in her absence, when he comes
upon her paintings, does he find their relationship "most thrilling":

> I was dumbfounded, really, for it so entirely different from anything I had
> seen signed by her or done of or presented in America or elsewhere ... and
> hence to me most refreshing and fascinating ... But gee! The light, the
> space, the daring, the raw reds, green blues, mauves, whites, yellows. No
> mere savory impaste here! No conservative and so traditional modulation
> ... no rich couch of underpainting. Instead, all glaring, direct, and reso
> nant ... it was also stirring and provoking. (145–46)

Dreiser's admission that "I studied her as much as I did her work, but
without the ability to connect the two" (163) illustrates how for Dreiser
in *A Gallery of Women* gaze objects provide the basis for those complex reflections of which, in Trilling's view, Dreiser was incapable (Eby
156–157).

An unpublished reminiscence about another of Dreiser's gazed-upon employees who fascinated him both sexually and professionally directly confronts both his urge and his inability to reconcile these not-quite converging interests:

> And an interesting fact was this that in spite of a clinging and rather décolleté dress which seemed intended to provoke sensual attention to her charms she had a certain clerky or brisk and upstanding office air such as somehow suggests one who comes with documents and notes, your charming, well-tailored stenographer, as it were. Yet with this other thing—intense sensuality. ("Gloom")

Throughout his career Dreiser seems to have been driven to find a conceptual place for "this other thing" without letting go of the relentless objectification of women, a large part of the vulgar materialism that provoked Trilling's reproach.

Thanks to his work as a magazine editor, which led to Dreiser's meeting Ellen Wrynn, Dreiser may be the only major American novelist with professional credentials as a male gazer. Though "Dreiser extensively wrote about women and wondered about them" (Eby 157), his most notable professional credential may be his 1907–1910 tenure as editor of the Butterick company's group of "women's" magazines: *The Designer*, *New Idea Women's Magazine*, and the largest, *The Delineator* (Swanberg 118–120), which had been established to sell its owner's sewing patterns. As it grew into a popular general-interest monthly, though, *The Delineator* claimed as its mission "human betterment." This mission entailed "appeal[ing] to the one great humanizing force of humanity— womanhood"—thereby helping "every woman in the land to live better." *Delineator* covers usually showed young fashionably dressed women and struck a balance between calling attention to their clothes and to their faces and figures.[1]

Dreiser's stint at *The Delineator* happened to fall between his first and second, arguably his most accomplished, novels, the eponymously titled *Sister Carrie* and *Jennie Gerhardt*. These novels illustrate the extent to which, as Claire Eby argues, "Dreiser does not have single way of depicting women; nor does he concentrate on a particular type as

---

[1] *Delineator* cover. https://s-media-cache-ak0.pinimg.com/736x/a1/4f/a6/a14fa632 ced090d5ca77c7b9f088e59f.jpg.

representative"; consequently, readers "can build a case for Dreiser as a progressive or reactionary in his views of women" (143).

Dreiser elaborates his understanding of male gazing as a prevalent modern social practice near the middle of *Sister Carrie*:

> The walk down Broadway ... was one of the remarkable features of the city. There gathered ... not only all the pretty women who love a showy parade, but the men who love to gaze upon and admire them ... Carrie stepped along easily enough after they got out of the car at Thirty-fourth Street, but soon fixed her eyes upon the lovely company which swarmed by and with them as they proceeded. She noticed suddenly that Mrs. Vance's manner had rather stiffened under the gaze of handsome men and elegantly dressed ladies, whose glances were not modified by any rules of propriety. To stare seemed the proper and natural thing. Carrie found herself stared at and ogled. Men in flawless top-coats, high hats, and silver-headed walking ticks elbowed near and looked too often into conscious eyes.

This view of modernity as a "showy parade," a spectacle bathed in "kaleidoscopic glitter" (Dreiser, *Jennie*), reverberates throughout Dreiser's fiction (see Chap. 4). Such spectacles belong to what Irene Gammell identifies as a "panoptic universe" (65–66) that encompasses those "bundles of passions and vague desires" introduced early in *Sister Carrie*, the very desires that foster male gazing. Within this universe Dreiser individualizes Carrie's and Jennie's gazed-upon female bodies. As Stephen Brennan argues, Dreiser semiotically opens these bodies to a range of readings and introduces them as instruments of individual men's projections (147).

In *Sister Carrie*, for example, Dreiser dwells as much on what the gazer brings to gazing as he dwells on the gazer's "text": Carrie's appearance. Dreiser pays as much attention to *how* gazers "read" women's bodies as to the bodies themselves. This apportioning of the narrator's attention, between *what* questions and *how* questions, surfaces when Dreiser introduces Drouet, Carrie's first sex partner, the salesman who picks her up onboard a Chicago-bound rail coach. After tersely noting that Carrie "felt him observing her mass of hair," no texture or color noted, Dreiser characterizes Drouet, by contrast, with an account of his emotional and (minimally) intellectual attributes, by ascribing to him "a strong physical nature, actuated by a keen desire for the feminine ... a mind free of any consideration of the problems or forces of the world" and by a "love of variable pleasure." After establishing Carrie and Drouet as a settled couple with a domestic routine, Dreiser fleshes out Drouet's gazing style and its effect:

> They had been dawdling over the dishes, and their eyes had frequently met. Carrie could not help but feel the vibration of force which followed, which, indeed, was his gaze. He had a way of touching her hand in explanation, as if to impress a fact upon her. He touched it now as he spoke of going.

Hurstwood, the second and more significant of Carrie's domestic partners, a saloon manager and "a successful and well-known man about town," brings more savvy and nuance—and, finally, it turns out, more neediness—to his male gazing.

In contrast to Dreiser's account of Drouet as a gazer, his characterization of Hurstwood as a gazer abounds with modifiers indicating tentativeness, hesitation, and intangibles:

> ... slowly, after a slight pause. He had raised his eyes solemnly and was looking into her own. He assumed that he had struck a deep chord. Now was a slight chance to say a word in his own behalf. He leaned over quietly and continued his steady gaze. He felt the critical character of the period.

The impact of this gaze extends beyond Hurstwood's individual physical stimulus-response reaction to encompass one of Dreiser's and his era's favorite abstractions: "nature." Carrie, Dreiser's narrator observes, "endeavored to stir, but it was useless" because "the whole strength of a man's nature was working." Likewise, the impact of Carrie on Hurstwood shifts from a one-dimensionally demeaning expectation on Hurstwood's part: that Carrie would provide "new baggage of fine clothes and pretty features" and an opportunity to "indulge in an evening of lightsome frolic, and then lose track of ... forever." Instead, Dreiser turns from Hurstwood's reductive objectifying to pondering the semantic limits and the failures that confront the sophisticated gazer:

> A woman whose youth and beauty attracted him. In the mild
> light of Carrie's eye was nothing of the calculation of the
> mistress. In the diffident manner was nothing of the art of the
> courtesan.

An even more sophisticated gazer usurps Hurstwood's place in Carrie's affections late in the novel. As Carrie's acting career flourishes, she meets the entrepreneurial inventor Robert Ames. In elaborating slowly, over several pages, Carrie's reaction to Ames, Dreiser links the apparent lack of sexual chemistry between them—her impression that he had "nothing of the dashing lady's man about him" (256)—to the appeal of Ames' intellect.

> This strong young man beside her, with his clear, natural look, seemed to get a hold of things which she did not quite understand, but approved of. It was fine to be so, as a man, she thought … He seemed wiser than Hurstwood, saner and brighter than Drouet. He seemed innocent and clean … exceedingly pleasant. She noticed, also, that his interest in her was a far-off one. She was not in his life, nor any of the things that touched his life, and yet now, as he spoke of these things, they appealed to her.

The seeming chasteness of their connection notwithstanding, the distance between Carrie and Ames closes and their "far-off interest" in each other becomes emotionally and even physically charged, with Dreiser's narrator's announcement that "Carrie thrilled to be taken so seriously." Carrie's frisson follows from Ames' explanation of Carrie's artistic promise, an explanation focusing on her attractiveness. "As one pleased with a puzzle," Ames explains, analytically rather than concupiscently, the effect of "something about [Carrie's] eyes and mouth." Ames amplifies this visual appreciation by noting how Carrie's voice complements this "something." In the course of presenting Ames' explanatory lecture, Dreiser also characterizes Ames' and Carrie's visual responses to each other, highlighting the reciprocity of their gazes:

> 'the expression in your face is one that comes out in different things. You get the same thing in a pathetic song, or any picture which moves you deeply. It's a thing the world likes to see, because it's a natural expression of its longing.' Carrie gazed without exactly getting the import of what he meant. 'The world is always struggling to express itself,' he went on. 'Most people are not capable of voicing their feelings. They depend upon others. That is what genius is for. One man expresses their desires for them in music; another one in poetry; another one in a play. Sometimes nature does it in a face-it makes the face representative of all desire. That's what has happened in your case.' He looked at her with so much of the import of the thing in his eyes that she caught it. At least, she got the idea that her look was something which represented the world's longing.

The extent to which Carrie had felt, during her early liaisons, the "dependence" Ames cites underscores the repetitive continuity of Carrie's relationships with the series of suitors and gazers she's encountered. Even in realizing herself "easily the center of interest" during her first stage appearance, when her "intensity" "aroused feeling" from a recalcitrant theater audience, Carrie continues to depend of the responses of both Hurstwood and Drouet" who "viewed her pretty figure with rising feelings."

> The fact that such ability should reveal itself in her, that they should see it set forth under such effective circumstances, framed almost in massy gold and shone upon by the appropriate lights of sentiment and personality, heightened her charm for them.

Throughout *Sister Carrie* Dreiser marks the milestones in Carrie's emergence from this dependence on the thwarted command-driven gazes of her early suitors.

Carrie's realization that her appeal as a gaze object extends beyond Drouet and Hurstwood and might appeal to a larger public coincides with her pursuit of economic autonomy. Deciding that "she did not want Drouet or his money when she thought of it, nor anything more to do with Hurstwood," Carrie acknowledges her debt to the gazers, to the seducers who set in motion her transformation into an independent, self-consciously commanding gaze object:

> … there was one change for the better. She knew that she had improved in appearance. Her manner had vastly changed. Her clothes were becoming, and men—well-dressed men, some of
>
> the kind who before had gazed at her indifferently from
>
> behind their polished railings and imposing office partitions—now gazed into her face with a soft light in their eyes. In way, she felt the power and satisfaction of the thing.

As Carrie persists in pursuing a theatrical career she takes these lessons to heart and transforms herself, as Dreiser's culinary metaphor emphasizes, into an irresistible consumable mass-market product:

3 AMERICAN FICTION: GAZE CANON   81

In the second act, the crowd, wearied by a dull conversation, roved with its eyes about the stage and sighted her ... sweet-faced, demure, but scowling. At first the general idea was that she was temporarily irritated, that the look was genuine and not fun at all.

As she went on frowning, looking now at one principal and now at

the other, the audience began to smile. The portly gentlemen

in the front rows began to feel that she was a delicious

little morsel. It was the kind of frown they would have loved ...

The audience, the more it studied her, the more it indicated its delight.

Under Ames' tutelage, in response to his efforts to instruct and inspire her to master and profit from gazers' reactions to her appearance, Carrie becomes more than a "morsel."

This transformation from an imitative "maiden," from an ingénue keen on acting "pretty, yes, indeed" and content to play the part of a kept woman and to serve as Drouet's or Hurstwood's "delicious morsel," into a "life-size" public figure who keeps herself rather than being kept culminates when the gazer who once dominated Carrie casts his gaze on her and finds himself compelled to look *up* to her:

> At Broadway and Thirty-ninth Street was blazing, in incandescent
> fire, Carrie's name ... was so bright that it attracted
> Hurstwood's gaze. He looked up, and then at a large, gilt-framed
> posterboard, on which was a fine lithograph of Carrie,
> life-size.

This glimpse of Carrie's outsize image stirs a desire to gaze on her again in the flesh, prompting him to enter the theater and repeatedly voice his need to gaze on Carrie once more.

> 'I want to see Miss Madenda,' he said.
> 'You do, eh?' the [attendant] said, almost tickled at the spectacle.
> 'Get out of here,' and he shoved him again. Hurstwood had no
> strength to resist.

'I want to see Miss Madenda,' he tried to explain, even as he was being
hustled away
The man gave him a last push and closed the door ... He began
to cry and swear foolishly ... begging, crying, losing track of his
thoughts, one after another, as a mind decayed and disjointed is
wont to do.

This abasement of the gazer serves, according to the narrative logic of
Sister Carrie, to authenticate Carrie's "success story." This far-from-heartening "success story" represents in turn a distinctly modern "concept of female power" (Gammel 76). By participating in a "dissemination of sexuality" and assuming the lifelike form that Hurstwood believes he discovered, Carrie became an "incarnation of commodified sex-at-distance" (97).

A decade later, in *Jennie Gerhardt*, Dreiser showed this second novel's eponymous gaze object as at once more dependent on the male gazers who "kept" her as a mistress *and* freer of their projections than Carrie managed to become. The complications that Ames introduces, belatedly and briefly, to *Sister Carrie* reverberate throughout *Jennie Gerhardt*. The elaboration of such questions in *Jennie Gerhardt* may account for Trilling's grudging concession in singling out this novel as "the only exception" to Dreiser's moral nihilism, his lack of intellect, and the corrosiveness and solipsism of "Dreiser's pity" (15–16). Dreiser's treatment of gazing in *Jennie Gerhardt* helps account for what Trilling saw as the novel's unique place in Dreiser's oeuvre: instead of sharply delineating the styles and consequences of differing gazes (as he did in *Sister Carrie*), in *Jennie Gerhardt* Dreiser ascribes a conceptually ambitious curiosity about Jennie to the anonymous gazers Jennie encounters and to the men with whom she lives.

The novel's opening paragraph features an anonymous gaze, by a hotel desk clerk. His very anonymity, along with the gendering adverb "manlike" with which Dreiser identifies him, aligns his gaze with that of everyman in his reaction to "the evidence of beauty in distress," which he associates with Jennie's apparently "innocent helplessness." Dreiser's everyman has apparently softened his perspective in the interval between *Sister Carrie* (where man-on-the street gazes "were not modified by any rules of propriety") and *Jennie Gerhardt* (where gazers view the heroine more as part of an "abstract 'system'") (Fiedler 252–253) than as a "morsel." Thus the novel's first nameless gazer, Dreiser's stand-in for everyman, seems inclined to infer a narrative from the gaze object he beholds and to leaven his gazing with sympathy, even if it's the stock sympathy that resonates in a melodramatic phrase like "beauty in distress."

Three chapters later, Dreiser's narrator fleshes out this everyman response with an aesthete's eye, a couturier's confidence, a cosmetician's enthusiasm, a psychologist's assured conjectures, and a sophisticated moralist's disillusionment:

> There was developing in her that perfection of womanhood, the full mold of form, which could not help but attract any man. Already she was well-built, and tall for a girl. Had she been dressed in the trailing skirts of a woman of fashion she would have made a fitting companion for a man the height of the Senator. Her eyes were wondrously clear and bright, her skin fair, and her teeth white and even. She was clever, too, in a sensible way, and by no means deficient in observation. All that she lacked was training and the assurance of which the knowledge of utter dependency despoils one. But the carrying of washing and the compulsion to acknowledge almost anything as a favor put her at a disadvantage.

The combination of the appeal and vulnerability described here arouse curiosity and desire in not just "any man"; it piques the desire of the hotel's most prominent resident, Brander, a fiftyish US senator who becomes Jennie's first lover. Less impulsive than the younger gazers and mass gazers in *Sister Carrie*, Brander brings to his gazing an aesthetic and narrative perspective—a knowing gaze. A "restored" (de-bowdlerized) 1992 edition of Jennie Gerhardt accentuates how fully Brander's gaze encompasses his attention to texture, form, and the effects of time passing.

> a sidewise glance told him, even more keenly than his first view, of her uncommon features ... the high, white forehead, with its smoothly parted and plaited hair. The eyes he knew were blue, the complexion fair. He had even time to admire the mouth and the full cheeks, but most of all, the well-rounded, graceful form, full of youth, health, and all that futurity of hope, which to the middle-aged and waning, is so suggestive of all that is worth begging of Providence. Without another look he went dignifiedly upon his way, but the impression of her charming personality went with him. (8)

This question Dreiser raises about whether collecting impressions, as Brander does, fortifies the gazer's mastery or curbs it has a distinguished pedigree.

Over a century earlier, in "The Solitary Reaper," William Wordsworth described his alter-ego beholding "yon Highland lass" and insisting that her "music in my heart I bore long after it was heard no more." Dreiser ascribes a similar impulse to Brander, the curatorial impulse of the Romantic aesthete, who carries "with him" a durable "impression of" Jennie's "charming personality." Dreiser's emphasis on time passing and on advancing age (on the "waning [of] futurity") reflects moreover an appreciation of the imperatives to treat gazing as a disciplined inquiry and an investment in continuously refining one's gaze:

> Brander studied her face … and he thought he saw something exceedingly pathetic there. The girl's poor clothes and her wondering admiration for his exalted station in life affected him.

Brander's studious gazing and his conjectural "thought" underscore Dreiser's implicit argument that male-gazing encompasses more than a stimulus-response reaction. Though it encompasses the will-to-dominate, according to this argument, gazing ideally prompts the gazer to construe articulated meaning out of his male gazing.

After Brander's death early on in the story, the primary gazer (and eventually the father of Jennie's daughter Vesta) becomes the wealthy dilettante Lester Kane. In the "restored" text Kane's gazing not only seeks significance; it also conveys it:

> Once she caught him looking at her with a steady, incisive stare. She quailed inwardly, and took the first opportunity to get out of his presence. Another time he tried to address a few remarks to her, but she pretended duty somewhere else. He watched her at other times … when she was not looking, and she could feel his gaze … Now he was more insistent in his observation of her … He looked into her big, soft-blue eyes with his dark, vigorous brown ones. A flash that was hypnotic, significant, insistent passed between them. (121–23)

However much these observations seem to aggrandize Kane, this attention to his gaze and to its impact on Jennie concludes by intimating—at least aspirationally—an insistence on treating gazing as reciprocal.

So intent is Dreiser's narrator on complicating male gazing that he interrupts the story of Lester and Jennie's relationship in order to stifle the possibility that readers will respond to Kane's hyperbole as merely self-serving lechery. To ensure that readers won't "judge quickly" or form any "hasty and ill-conceived opinion" on the basis of "a single action," Dreiser sets out "to present" at length "a competent analysis of this man here and now."

> Although on the face of things he appeared to be a hunter and destroyer of undefended virtue, he was yet a man of such a complicated and interesting turn of mind that those who are inclined to be radically intolerant of his personality had best suspend judgment until some further light can be thrown upon it. Not every mind is to be calculated by the weight of a single folly, not every personality judged by the drag of a single passion. (125)

To stress how little Kane resembles the predatory male gazer of cautionary melodrama, Dreiser goes so far as to echo Wordsworth's description of the consummate Romantic visionary (Wordsworth himself) who can "see into the life of things" ("Tintern Abbey"). Thus he characterizes Kane as "endowed with the power to see into things." What vitiates this perspicacity, however, is the "kaleidoscopic glitter" Dreiser associates with modernity, "which is much more apt to weary and undo than to enlighten and strengthen the observing mind." Suffering from "a sort of intellectual fatigue," according to Dreiser's diagnosis,

> Kane was ... an example of the influence of this condition which we have described. His was a naturally observing mind, Rabelaisian in its strength and tendencies, but confused by the multiplicity of evidences of things, the vastness of the panorama of life, the glitter of its details, the unsubstantial nature of its forms, the uncertainty of their justification. Raised a Catholic, he was no longer a believer in the Divine inspiration of Catholicism; raised a member of the social elect, he was not altogether a believer in that innate superiority which is too often supposed to exist in those socially elect; brought up as the heir to a comfortable fortune and with the *opportunity of taking unto himself a money-endowed maiden of* his own plane, he was not believer in the necessity or wisdom of such a choice. Marriage itself was not an institution which he by any means was ready to justify. It was established. Yes, certainly. But what of it? The whole nation believed in it. True, but other nations believed in polygamy. There were other questions that bothered him—such questions as the belief in a single deity or ruler of

the universe, and whether a republican, monarchial or aristocratic form of government was best. In short, the whole gamut of things material, social, spiritual had come under the knife of his mental surgery and been left but half dissected. Life was not proved to him. Not a single idea of his, unless it were the need of being honest, was finally settled. In all other things he wavered, questioned, procrastinated, leaving to time and the powers back of the universe that which he could not solve.

In evoking Kane's intellectual turbulence, Dreiser modernizes Wordsworth's idealization of male gazers as Romantic visionaries. While the transcendence-minded Wordsworth complained that "we murder to dissect" ("The Tables Turned"), Dreiser presents the conceptually ambi- tious gazer as a dissector and displaces Wordsworth's self-aggrandizing, spiritually reassuring Romantic gazing with a more unsettling view of the male gazer as a proponent of the Romantic skepticism John Keats (a trained surgeon) called for in advocating "negative capability" (Keats, *Letters*). While Dreiser shows Kane approaching but not achieving this ideal ability to live "in uncertainities, mysteries, doubts, without any irritable reaching after fact and reason," the sequence of the narrator's "competent analysis" identifies Kane's intellectual aspirations and their partial realization with his male gazing.

LET GERTRUDE STEIN CALL YOU SWEETHEART

In sonnet 65, Shakespeare asks how beauty can contend with or accom- modate itself to rage.

> How with this rage shall beauty hold a plea,
> Whose action is no stronger than a flower?

In 1990 Tim O'Brien revisited this 400-year-old question in *The Things They Carried*. Since its publication this assemblage of linked war stories has, arguably, become the most widely taught, anthologized, and dis- cussed book about the Vietnam war and about the war's implications for American manhood. O'Brien introduced male gazing to the war- ravaged Vietnamese highlands in a section of *The Things They* Carried titled "The Sweetheart of the Song Tra Bong." This first-person as- told-to frame narrative recalls "a young medic" stationed at a remote mountain outpost and recounts how he finagled to "bring in a girl" and, in the words of one of the tale's incredulous listeners, "import [his] own personal poontang" (86). "Girl," "poontang," and the title noun, "sweetheart"—all these literally inaccurate or egregiously sexist ways of referring to a grown woman—had, by 1990, become provocative fighting words among educated and especially progressive-minded readers of "literary" fiction. Each noun connotes a different way of looking at and thinking about adult women, so that their inclusion in the same conversation insinuates some of the conflicting male-gaze perspectives that O'Brien shows his narrators weighing throughout the story.

Mark Fossie, the determined and love-besotted soldier whom O'Brien aligns with the "sweetheart" perspective, needed to declare a separate peace in order to accomplish his private mission. Citing his unit's non-combatant work, its "ideal duty" (87), Fossie insists that there's "no war *here*" (89), adopting the position Gertrude Stein voiced in her reflections on World War Two, *Wars I Have Seen*:

near a war is not always very near. Even when it is here. It is very funny that but it is true. Perhaps if one were a boy it would be different but I do not think so. I think even when men are in a war it is not very near, it is here but it is not very near. That is the way it seems to me from all I can hear and from all I can see. (5)

Stein's demurral about her own "natural" gender perspective, the perspective of neither "men" nor her hypothetical "boy," reflects Karin Cope's conclusion that "much of Stein's life and work" constitutes "an argument against natural gender" and lends credence to Cope's depiction of Stein as a provocateur who "embodied a gender unknown" (201, 200). My pairing of Stein and O'Brien draws not only on Cope's view of Stein as a consummate gender bender. This pairing also looks to Chris Vanderwees' compelling case for "The Sweetheart of the Song Tra Bong" as a critique "of normative masculinity": a critical account of "gender instability" and of the "elusiveness of gender categories" in which O'Brien "inverts gender power relations" (192–193, 200).

O'Brien also sets "Sweetheart" in an ambiguous war space, in a location where war is both "not very near" and "here," like the wartime France that Stein describes. Song Tra Bong rests on a riverside bluff with "virtually no security at all" that provides "a curious sense of safety" (87, 88), which one single-minded corporal transforms from a theater of operations into a theater for male gazers.

Like generations of male gazers throughout American fiction, the main narrator of "The Sweetheart of Song Tra Bong" records but doesn't dwell on his gaze object's physical attributes. Though registering his first impression of "Mary Anne" as a "tall big-boned blonde" with "long white legs and blue eyes and a complexion like strawberry ice cream" (89), he seems more interested in detailing her sociological backstory. Not only does he distinguish Mary Anne with a name and an affect: "very friendly, too" and later, "a kind of come and get me energy, coy and flirtatious" (91). He goes on to recount her stateside life story, including individuating information about her age (17), her hometown schooling (Cleveland Heights Senior High), and her girlhood aspirations:

> Mary Anne Bell and Mark Fossie had been sweethearts since grammar school. From the sixth grade on they had known for a fact that someday they would be married, and live in a fine gingerbread house near
> Lake Erie, and have three healthy yellow-haired children, and grow old together,
> and no doubt die in each other's arms and be buried in the same walnut casket.
> That was the plan. They were very much in love, full of dreams, and in the
> ordinary flow of their lives the whole scenario might well have come true. (90)

Like Fossie himself (and like many of O'Brien's readers), his narrator has been schooled to appreciate this utopian "sweetheart" narrative from the inside, as his detailed account emphasizes. Unlike Fossie, though, the narrator is also attuned to its implausibility and the entertainment value of Fossie's aspiration to import this narrative to and keep it intact in war-ravaged Vietnam.

Though picturing Song Tra Bong as "surrounded by tangled rolls of concertina wire … and reinforced firing positions," O'Brien adopts Stein's "funny but true" war-story aesthetic. O'Brien's narrator becomes so enrapt with reconstructing and embellishing his initial gaze, his first sighting of Mary Anne, that his condescension to this "cute kid" starts to sound like the enthusiasm of a child accessorizing a Barbie doll, and not simply confining her to a suburban Ohio "gingerbread house." Barbie's "biographer," M.G. Lord, argues that, thanks largely to her

accoutrements, like the ones O'Brien's narrator singles out, even Barbie
"the prom queen ... baton-twirler" could also be a "social mountaineer"
who "has never stayed home against her will" (182, 129).

> This cute blonde—just a kid, just barely out high school—she shows up
> with a suitcase and one of those plastic cosmetics kits. Comes right out to
> the boonies. I swear to God, man, she's got on culottes. White culottes
> and this sexy pink sweater. There she is. (O'Brien 86)

Despite this wardrobe, Mary Anne's qualifications for mountaineering,
social and otherwise, become immediately apparent to O'Brien's narrator. In noting Mary Anne's "sexiness" and "attractiveness," O'Brien's
narrator singles out her "too ... wide shoulders" (90), which Hollywood
turned into a code for "assertive, confident, masculinity" and independence earlier in the twentieth century (Banner 280–282). Then he dwells
on her "terrific ... legs and... eyes" (O'Brien 89); on her wardrobe,
"cutoff jeans" and "black swimsuit top" (91); and her cheerleader affect
(92). O'Brien's narrator refrains, however, from turning his gaze and his
phrasing where the conventions of manly storytelling and visual representations of women typically lead, to breasts and buttocks (Lord 209,
211–212, 267–268). O'Brien both highlights and discredits this staple
of male gazing by recalling how one squad member's ridicule of Mary
Anne as combining "D-cup guts" with "trainer-bra brains" (92) met
with unanimous dissent from his fellow warriors. What O'Brien emphasizes and what he downplays in these descriptions presage the disarming,
even neutering impact of Mary Anne's emerging combat-zone confidence and authority (93–94).

This disarming impact extends beyond the narrating gazer to her
sponsor, her fiancé Mark Fossie, and to their entire squad. Mary Anne,
the narrator realizes, has joined them in order to educate squad members
about what they "just don't *know*" about Vietnam (O'Brien 106) as well
as, more predictably, to entertain and beguile them. Mary Anne's sur-
name, Bell, which the narrator keeps mentioning, spotlights his appreciation of this pedagogic impact: that of a school bell summoning boys to
their lessons or the bell that ends Keats's "Nightingale Ode" and "tolls
[the poet] back to his sole self" and to a realization of his own limitations. The recognition of Mary Anne's martial savvy seconds Stein's
impression of "boys" and women at war as emotionally interchangeable.

O'Brien's narrator echoes Stein's anti-sexist demurral—"perhaps if one were a boy it would be different but I do not think so."

In an earthy, impatient homage, O'Brien's story-within-the-story narrator, Rat Kiley, rejects the condescending "sweetheart" narrative and the reductive misogynist "poontang" metonymy:

> 'She wasn't dumb, 'he'd snap … 'A *girl*, that's the only difference, and I'll tell you something: it didn't amount to jack. I mean, when we first got here—all of us—we were real young and innocent, full of romantic bullshit, but we learned pretty damn quick. And so did Mary Anne.' (93)

No longer a "cute" Barbie, Mary Anne Bell becomes instead a paragon of candor and intellect. "No timid child" (91) and not "afraid to get her hands bloody" (93), Mary Anne proves herself curious and a quick study. "She liked to roam around the compound asking questions" and learning about weapons, bivouac cookery, her Vietnamese neighbors, the landscape while "picking up little phrases of Vietnamese" and explaining, "I'm here. I might as well learn something" (91). What Mary Anne learns changes more than her outlook. Physical changes follow as Mary Anne adapts, easily and eagerly, to war and realizes that "everything I want is here," in the boonies, where, she claims, she's "never been happier" (94–95). As her "body begins to "seem foreign" to her fiancé, "too stiff … too firm where the softness used to be," so too does her affect, her "bubbliness" and giggling, along with her voice: "It seemed to reorganize itself at a lower pitch" (94–95). As in much American storytelling by male-gazers, this sequence turns the gazer's and readers' attention away from its point of departure: the gaze object's body.

In a departure from this convention, Mary Anne changes so much that she escapes male gazing entirely. She's simply "gone" to where Mark Fossie and the primary narrator, Rat Kiley, "can't find her" (95). O'Brien shows these squad members initially reacting conventionally, by assuming that Mary Anne has started sleeping with another soldier. It turns out, however, that the reason for her disappearance "wasn't sex or anything" (97), apparently referring to a default male explanation of women's unavailability. To the extent that "The Sweetheart of the Song Tra Bong" sustains a rhetorical agenda, it seems to entail sabotaging such customary narratives and removing the "blinders … about women" that Rat Kiley ascribes to his incredulous listeners: "You got to get rid of your sexist attitude," he harangues them (102). What made Rat's audience incredulous was the actual reason for Mary Anne's disappearance: her decision to join the elusive night warriors, the Green Berets, encamped nearby, who come and go mysteriously, "out on fuckin' *ambush*" (97).

In order to complete her escape from Fossie, from his combat-averse medic comrades, and from their convention-bound gazing, Mary Anne was obliged to stage one final performance as a gaze object. During her final stay with the squad, she and Fossie present "a model of togetherness" as Mary Anne caricatures the silenced, demure retro suburban matron she once felt fated to become.

> Mary Anne's hair was freshly shampooed. She wore a white
>
> blouse, a navy blue skirt, a pair of plain black flats. Over
>
> dinner she kept her eyes down, poking at her food, subdued
>
> to the point of silence ... others tried to nudge her into
>
> talking about the ambush ... but the questions seemed to give her trouble. Nervously, she'd look across the table at Fossie. She'd wait a moment, as if to receive some sort of clearance, then she'd bow her head and mumble out a vague word or two. There were no real answers. (98)

Gazing, O'Brien's narrator stresses, became a conspicuous feature of the couple's relationship during its closing act:

> If Mary Anne happened to move
> a few steps away from him, even briefly, he'd tighten up
> and force himself not to watch her. But then a moment
> later he'd be watching. (99)

Mark Fossie's effort to maintain his gaze, to keep an eye on Mary Anne, soon yields, though, to his realization that "she's already gone" (107).

When Mary Anne and her fellow warriors return from the "wilderness" (104) a few weeks after this first disappearance the narrator "didn't recognize her" and finds it difficult to distinguish her from the other members of her (all male) patrol (101). In the narrator's account, Mary Anne's metamorphosis was so complete that she not only completely ignored Fossie; her conventionally pretty blue eyes had turned "a bright glowing jungle green."

92

92

J.D. BLOOM

O'Brien pointedly closes the story with an improbable image that links Mary Anne's discovery of her vocation as a nocturnal stalker "ready for the kill" with the gaze object she was scripted to become. The narrator ends his homage to Mary Anne by picturing her "wearing her culottes and her pink sweater," and by presenting her as powerful gazer in her own right, rather than a gaze object. As "she gazed down at Fossie ... her eyes: utterly flat and indifferent ... no emotion in her stare," Mary Anne sports a new piece of "jewelry": "a necklace of tongues" (105). This "full change" transformation into a powerful gazer crystallizes when Rat Kiley at first fails to recognize Mary Anne among her Green Beret comrades. Reacting to the perplexing change in her eye color, Kiley suggests that she had altered her gaze to match and help her master her surroundings. O'Brien emphasizes her active pursuit of this metamorphosis by immediately following this description of Mary Anne's eyes with an image of her "cradling her weapon" and "swiftly" disappearing into the company of her fellow killers (101). In Rat Kiley and Mark Fossie's final sighting of Mary Anne she appears dressed to be gazed at while gazing and speaking powerfully enough to silence Fossie so forcefully that he "seemed to shrink away," "busted to PFC" and physically diminished (107, 110).

Mary Anne's last look "down at Fossie" exhibits "the composure of someone perfectly at peace with herself." It also acidly counterpoints Fossie's and Mary Anne's relative gazing positions upon her arrival. Then, the narrator recalls, Fossie "gazed down at his pretty girlfriend" soon after boasting to his comrades of the "pair of solid brass balls" that emboldened him to transport Mary Anne from Cleveland Heights to the Song Tra Bong (89).

Mary Anne's gaze unequivocally in command, she completes the power inversion that O'Brien sets in motion and that leaves the self-professedly ballsy Fossie far more diminished than Washington Irving left the bookish Ichabod Crane. First, Mary Anne silences Fossie, indicts his innocence, and belittles his "brass balls," insisting that "there's no sense talking" because "you just don't *know* ... You hide in this little fortress, behind wire and sandbags, and you don't know what it's all about" (106). Mary Anne literally flouts one of the most venerable attitudes toward women and their supposed "place." She warns Mark Fossie, "you're in a place ... where you don't belong." Mary Anne's dismissal decisively reverses a narrative pattern as deeply scored into English-language and European fiction as any.

The novel that has perhaps most famously kept a woman in her place and thus buttressed the tradition that O'Brien shows Mary Anne Bell flouting was singled out a generation before Laura Mulvey made male-gazing such a byword, before the concept of male-gazing attained its discursive ubiquity. In 1951, R.P. Blackmur singled out Gustave Flaubert's *Madame Bovary* as the consummate aesthetic distillation of the male gaze. More recently, *New Yorker* movie reviewer Anthony Lane, identified the dilemma confronting screen interpreters of *Madame* Bovary by differentiating filmmakers who "fortify the male gaze" from directors inclined to "unpick [sic]...the male gaze." These filmmakers, Lane argues, cue the audience to "reflect on the eyes of [Emma Bovary's] beholders" and on the gazers' own "moral vision" ("Wouldn't" 81). Half a century ahead of Lane, Blackmur also treated such confrontations with gazers as central to Flaubert's rhetorical agenda in *Madame Bovary*.

Writing about Emma Bovary in the first-person plural (48, 52–53, 55, 58), Blackmur envisioned readers of the novel, along with Flaubert himself and the men who bedded Emma Bovary, as beguiled male gazers held by "all the extraordinarily visualized detail which stands for we do not know what unformulable identifications of Emma's body, in all its parts and movements, with the story .... it is thus that we undress" her (61, 67). In reading *Madame Bovary*, such readers will find "the shape of a woman," "the shape of desire" and "a structure of imagination" in which "we can count on sexual force to fill up ... the hollow spaces" and turn this force into "sentiment" (48). In turn, Blackmur concludes, "this sentiment will be turned into a force." This reader response that Blackmur traced bears a remarkable resemblance to the attitude that both inspired and defeated Mark Fossie in "Sweetheart," the attitude that Mary Anne Bell taught Rat Kiley to overcome, the lesson Kiley and O'Brien himself imparted by sharing her story.

Kiley thus comes to represent a new kind of male gazer. By the end of "Sweetheart," he has displaced Fossie as Mary Anne's "lover." Fossie is a conventional male gazer to whom, like Emma Bovary's husband Charles, "all the platitudes of marriage" and courtship were "perpetually fresh" (Blackmur 71). Fossie views Mary Anne as a standard-issue "sweetheart" whom he can move around at will (across America, across the Pacific) and whom he can contain in this single shopworn narrative: "one of those women to whom things happen," as Blackmur describes Flaubert's heroine (64). By contrast, Kiley learns how to value Mary Anne by letting her go without ever seeing her again or without ever having bedded or controlled her. As he finally confesses,

> Suddenly, Rat pushed up to his feet, moved a few steps away from us, then stopped and stood with his back turned. He was an emotional guy.
> 'Got hooked, I guess,' he said. 'I loved her'. (108)

Unlike conventional male gazers, Kiley loves Mary Anne for her power, what academics might call her "agency," her effectiveness in transcending the narratives, connoted by nouns like "sweetheart" and "poontang," designed to contain her.

What follows from the conflicts between such narratives and a gaze object's aspiration to flout them furnishes the title phrase for Blackmur's Flaubert essay. The phrase "beauty out of place" seems readily applicable to Mary Anne Bell, more so than it did to Emma Bovary. Each "prodigal daughter" (Blackmur 57) embodies "the drive in each of us to overreach" to such an extent that "the passion for the act of ... reaching" becomes self-defining (49). As a result, for transmuted gazers like Rat Kiley, women's gaze-worthiness comes to rest not on what they look like but on what they aspire to and on how they dramatize themselves and "unit[e] their bodies with their surroundings" (Blackmur 54). Such heroines become appealing not because of where the gazer's appetite leads him but because of where the gaze objects' aspirations lead *them*. In making this argument, Blackmur locates the point in *Madame Bovary* where Flaubert shifts the focus from what Emma Bovary looks like to the power of her craving:

> she went to fetch a bottle of curacao from the cupboard, reached down two small glasses, filled one to the brim, poured scarcely anything into the other, and, after having clinked glasses, carried hers to her mouth. As it was almost empty she bent back to drink, her head thrown back, her lips pouting, her neck on the strain. She laughed at getting none of it, while with the tip of her tongue passing between her small teeth she licked drop by drop the bottom of her glass. (55)

Where Flaubert assigned his omniscient narrator the task of evoking Emma's cravings and her suitor's appreciation, O'Brien's let Mary Anne speak for herself, at length, on behalf of "the passion of her reach":

'I want to swallow the whole country—the dirt,
the death—I just want to eat it and have it there inside me.
That's how I feel. It's like ... this appetite ...
I feel close to myself. When I'm out there at night, I feel
close to my own body, I can feel my blood moving, my skin
and my fingernails, everything, it's like I'm full of electricity and
I'm glowing in the dark—I'm on fire almost-I'm burning away into
nothing—but it doesn't matter because I know exactly who I am.'
(106)

With Rat Kiley's sympathetic gloss on this vivid articulation by Mary
Anne of her eccentric appetites and of her "romantic conception of herself" (Blackmur 57), O'Brien affirms that both her eloquence and grit
merit our sympathy, and even our love:

For Mary Anne Bell, it seemed, Vietnam had the effect of a powerful
drug: that mix of unnamed terror and unnamed pleasure that comes as
the needle slips in and you know you're risking something. The endor-
phins start to flow, and the adrenaline, and you hold your breath and creep
quietly through the moonlit nightscapes; you become intimate with dan-
ger; you're in touch with the far side of yourself, as though it's another
hemisphere, and you want to string it out and go wherever the trip takes
you and be host to all the possibilities inside yourself. Not *bad*, she'd said.
Vietnam made her glow in the dark. She wanted more, she wanted to
penetrate deeper into the mystery of herself, and after a time the wanting
became needing, which turned then to craving. (109)

With these ideologically and aesthetically conflicting moves, both Mary
Anne Bell and Emma Bovary come to represent, in Blackmur's essay's
title phrase, "beauty out of place" (48, 58, 63, 66, 73).

Emma Bovary's aspiration, which Flaubert set out (as Blackmur put
it) "to anathematize, to exorcise," gruesomely "destroyed her" (63,
50). Mary Anne Bell, by contrast, lives on, "somewhere out there in
the dark ... sliding through the shadows ... part of the land" (O'Brien
110). In "Sweetheart of the Song Tra Bong" O'Brien makes a place for
the beauty that Flaubert sentenced to death on behalf of a cultural tradition that has long ruled such "beauty out of place." In giving Mary
Anne Bell's beauty a voice and a place, O'Brien has begun to reorder
what Mulvey characterizes as "a world ordered by sexual imbalance"
so that "pleasure in looking has been split between active/male and

passive/female." What Mulvey indicts as the power of the "determining male gaze" to project its fantasy" remains all too prevalent. Nevertheless, these fantasies, in O'Brien's account and gradually over the course of American literary history, seem increasingly to damn rather than to foster the "imbalance" that Mulvey decried and that today's prevailing consensus continues to decry.

BEAUTY OUT OF PLACE—GAZING ACROSS THE COLOR LINE

Few narratives have rendered the damnation of the gazer more forcefully than Chester Himes' 1945 novel *If He Hollers, Let Him Go*. Its narrator, Bob Jones, becomes such a consummate male gazer that during a single evening he shifts from recognizing his will to gaze as operating under his own direction to conceding that the direction of his gaze lies beyond his control. This narrator recalls first that "I let my gaze rest on her ... taking in the delicate lines of her chin and throat, the sensitive lines about her mouth, and the clean curved sweep of her neck" (59). A few hours later the narrator concedes that "my gaze followed her on its own" (66). In the first instance, the narrator was gazing across a restaurant at "a very blond girl in a gorgeous print dress." In the second he was gazing across a San Pedro living room at "a short dumpy brown-skinned girl" who "wasn't even half pretty" despite her "animal sensuousness" and "animal grace" (65–66). The sharp contrast between the conventional beauty of the first gaze object and the narrator's discovery of "beauty out of place," the unexpected pleasure the second gaze prompts, complements, and complicates the equally sharp contrast in this sequence between interracial gazing and intraracial gazing.

Over the course of *If He Hollers*, these swings between interracial gazing and intraracial gazing bedevil efforts by the narrator, a young factory worker in World War Two-era Los Angeles, to overcome one treacherous impediment—racial, sexual, economic, and discursive—after another. This "goddamned world" in which Jones feels himself cast among "the lowest people on God's earth" (76, 79) wearies, oppresses, and eventually defeats him. Boasting repeatedly about "know[ing] any number of chicks....plenty of chicks I could go to bed with" (72, 91), Jones finds his daily rounds rife with a range of gazing opportunities: "a peroxide blonde" with large, bright-painted, fleshy mouth" and "big, baby bluish eyes ... mascaraed like a burlesque queen ... well-sexed, rife but not quite rotten"; "an Arkansas slick chick, rife loose teenage fluff, with a broad face and small eyes, and a hard mouth, and straggly uncombed hair"; "a big sloppy dame"; "bright yellow" and "long, angular, dark" women at whom he can't help but "sneak a look" (19, 74, 76, 79). Along with all these opportunities for gazing and for sex, the narrator's daily rounds also expose him to numerous fellow male gazers and their varying approaches to gazing, as their response to the "Arkansas slick chick" in a Little Tokyo bar illustrates: "Some studiedly ignored her; a couple of black boys at the bar kept turning around to look at her; two Filipinos sitting directly in front of her stared at her with hot burning eyes and forgot to eat" (75). Himes' narrator's own gazing repertory includes what he calls the "gaper's bit" (134), a move he gets to make when a co-worker bends to over to pick up some trash enabling Bob to glimpse her "breasts hanging loose inside her [shirt]waist."

One of the novel's early sequences, an account of the narrator's drive home from work and the stops he makes en route, illustrates at once the ordinariness of interracial gazing and the conceptual, conversational impasses it leads to. During first stop, at a bar near his factory, Jones finds himself subjected to female gazing before falling into his customary male-gazer pose.

> The white woman next to me stopped talking and looked around. I could feel her gaze on me ... I turned to look at the white woman by my side. Our eyes met. She had brown eyes, frankly curious, and blonde hair, dark at the roots, piled on top of her head. In the dim orange light her lipstick didn't show and her mouth looked too thin for the size of her other features. She had taken off her brassiere on account of the heat and the outline of her breasts showed distinctly through her white rayon blouse. (39)

After leaving the bar the narrator picks up a group of hitchhikers, white GIs stationed in Los Angeles. He has "a lot fun" joking with them, "playing a guessing game about" the lives of the women they pass along the way until

> we came to a dark brown woman in a dark red dress ... They didn't say anything at all. I wanted to say something to keep it going ... If we had all been colored we'd have laughed. like hell because she was really a comical sister. But with the white boys present, I couldn't say anything. I looked straight ahead and we all became embarrassed and remained silent for a time ... We didn't talk about women any more. (39, 42)

In these passages showing him gazing across the color line, Jones' gazing appears motivated by "frank curiosity," an eagerness to take interest in other people, even to the point of (offensively) peering through a stranger's "white rayon blouse." Himes also highlights the extent to which gazing *should* but ultimately can't provide an impetus to sharing thoughts and to conversing, across the color line.

Like *If He Hollers*, much of the most influential and provocative work by twentieth-century African American novelists has confronted taboos and examined the discursive impasses that result from these taboos. Among the classics of African American fiction, Zora Neale Hurston's *Their Eyes Were Watching God* stands out for its forthright treatment of gazing as a give-and-take transaction and not simply an oppressive imposition. Hurston opens *Their Eyes* by highlighting the cognitive economy of gazing elicited by protagonist Janie Crawford's return to her hometown:

> The men noticed her firm buttocks like
> she had grape fruits in her hip pockets;
> the great rope of black hair swinging
> to her waist and unraveling in the wind
> like a plume; then her pugnacious breasts
> trying to bore holes in her shirt.
> They, the men, were saving with
> the mind what they lost with the eye. (2)

The similes and metaphors ("grape fruits ... rope ... plume ... bore holes") establish the narrator's position as a gazer who, after transforming her gaze object into an elusive (grapefruit-bearing) nurturer and into a "pugnacious" threat, presents herself as a judge of the surrounding male gazers, of their losses and their "savings." Throughout the novel, Hurston extends this understanding of transactional gazing beyond Janie herself so that it encompasses her neighbors, the women

> down the street making out they are pretty by the way they walk. They
> have got that fresh, new taste about them like young mustard greens in the
> spring, and the young men on the porch are just bound to tell them about
> it and buy them some treats. (67)

The contrast that Hurston's narrative turns on, between Janie's unsatisfying marriage to Joe Starks and her fulfilling romance with Tea Cake

Woods, is shaped in part by the difference between the role that gazing plays in each relationship. While Joe "ordered Janie to tie up her hair around the store" he owns, because "she was there in store for *him* to look at, not those others" (55), Tea Cake encourages Janie to take as much pleasure in—"git [as much] enjoyment from"—her own hair and eyes as he and "other folks" do (103–104). Inasmuch as the academy now typically reads Hurston's work as a critique of racial and sexual oppression, this passage may presage the hope poet Rosmarie Waldrop recently voiced that the "representation of pleasure," such as the pleasure Tea Cake promotes, might "through desire, motivate change" (70).

Like Hurston, Himes turns male gazing into an instrument for both ferreting out and pleading on behalf of the kind of beauty out of place that Himes' narrator encountered in San Pedro. Unlike Hurston, though, Himes confronts the inevitability of such beauty remaining out of place, even doomed to destruction. While Himes skewers the taboos that legitimate these dispiriting impulses, his narrator only narrowly escapes a climate in which gazers ignore at their peril the prospect of being "lynched for looking" (Himes, *Hollers*, 125).

Spanning the half century between the depths of Jim Crow, marked by the Supreme Court's 1896 Plessy ruling, and its landmark reversal of legally sanctioned "separate but equal" segregation in the 1954 Brown decision, novels by Charles Chesnutt and James Baldwin feature male-gazer protagonists whose gazing begins with seemingly conventional heterosexual affirmations of privilege and status only to deepen and darken in ways that expose the limits and tragic consequences of the desires male gazing supposedly serves.

Chesnutt's 1900 novel *The House Behind the Cedars* draws subversively on the "tragic mulatta" clichés that dated back to antebellum fiction, while pioneering "the passing narrative" that James Weldon Johnson and Nella Larsen would soon establish as an American literary staple. Chesnutt's subversion entailed a critique of the prevailing racial epistemology that obliged Americans to look at one another's infinitely variable skin colors and reductively designate what they saw as *race*, the nearly unanimous superstition (Barzun) that allowed white American men to maintain the economic and sexual prerogatives slavery afforded them before the Civil War and long after slavery's legal abolition. Though Chesnutt's critique of this epistemology or superstition pervades *The House Behind the Cedars*, he needed to spell it out explicitly, in a magazine article, five years after the novel's publication:

> I take no stock in this doctrine [of race] … It seems to me a modern invention of the white people to perpetuate the color line … I can scarcely restrain a smile when I hear mulatto talking of race integrity or a quadroon dwelling upon race pride … Race prejudice will not perhaps entirely disappear until the difference of color shall disappear. (Chesnutt, *Speeches* 232)

Much of the dialogue and even more of Chesnutt's omniscient narrator's commentary in *The House Behind the Cedars* articulate this critique by dramatizing the implications and repercussions of male gazing across the color line.

The opening passage of *The House Behind the Cedars* lays the groundwork for Chesnutt's critique by introducing a male gazer, a prosperous-looking mysterious visitor to the North Carolina city where most of the narrative action occurs. Immediately upon arriving in the center of town, the visitor, who calls himself John Warwick, finds his path "converging" with that of "a young woman." This convergence triggers his gaze:

> Warwick's first glance had revealed the fact that the young woman was strikingly handsome, with a stately beauty seldom encountered. As he walked along behind her at a measured distance, he could not help noting the details that made up this pleasing impression, for his mind was singularly alive to beauty, in whatever embodiment. The girl's figure, he perceived, was admirably proportioned; she was evidently at the period when the angles of childhood were rounding into the promising curves of adolescence. Her abundant hair, of a dark and glossy brown, was neatly plaited and coiled above an ivory column that rose straight from a pair of gently sloping shoulders, clearly outlined beneath the light muslin frock that covered them. He could see that she was tastefully, though not richly, dressed, and that she walked with an elastic step that revealed a light heart and the vigor of perfect health. Her face, of course, he could not analyze, since he had caught only the one brief but convincing glimpse of it.

Warwick's urge to analyze sets in motion a second convergence. Since curiosity customarily serves as a stimulus for analysis, Chesnutt cues his reader to wonder not simply about the effect of "the girl's" appearance but also about the implications of Warwick's attraction, an attraction powerful enough to reduce him from an apparently prominent southern

"gentleman" in the narrator's view, or a "South Ca'lina bigbug" according to the locals, to a besotted stalker overwhelmed by a "decided thrill
of pleasure."

> The young woman kept on down Front Street, Warwick maintaining his
> distance a few roads behind her ... The sound of her voice gave Warwick a
> thrill. It was soft and sweet and clear—quite in harmony with her appear-
> ance ... Once she threw a backward glance at Warwick, thus enabling him
> to catch a second glimpse of a singularly pretty face ... 'A woman with
> such a figure,' thought Warwick, 'ought to be able to face the world with
> the confidence of Phryne confronting her judges.'[2]

Chesnutt's reference to Phryne, a fourth-century BCE Athenian courte-
san, reveals both Warwick's libertine tendencies and his erudition (that
of an autodidact bibliophile we learn later). The reference to Phryne's
"judges," moreover, reminds readers that Warwick (who trained as
lawyer, as we also learn later) has been presenting himself as a judge as
well as an "analyst" of his gaze object's beauty. According to accounts
by Phryne's contemporaries, an Athenian court acquitted her of impiety
simply because during her trial she disrobed and exposed her breasts to
her judges' male gaze.

Though the Phryne reference carries the implication that, as with
Phryne's judges, Warwick's infatuation has overwhelmed his judgment and reason, Chesnutt shows him striving to dignify his stalker's
impulse and to sublimate his lecherous fascination into curiosity about
his surroundings and about his gaze object's social location. Thus
Warwick becomes

> conscious that something more than mere grace or beauty had attracted
> him with increasing force toward this young woman. A suggestion, at first
> faint and elusive, of something familiar, had grown stronger when he heard
> her voice, and became more and more pronounced with each rod of their
> advance; and when she stopped finally before a gate, and, opening it, went
> into a yard shut off from the street by a row of dwarf cedars, Warwick had
> already discounted in some measure the surprise he would have felt at see-
> ing her enter there had he not walked down Front Street behind her.

---

[2] Jean–Léon Gérôme, *Phryne In Front of the Judges.* http://www.shafe.uk/wp-content/
uploads/gerome_phryne_in_front_of_the_judges_1861.jpg.

Warwick's cognitive exertions appear, at this point at least, to have paid off with the realization that the object of his fascination or "thoughtful regard" is no stranger.

> 'It must be Rena,' he murmured. 'Who could have dreamed that she would blossom out like that? It must surely be Rena!' ... As she came forward, Warwick rose, put his arm around her waist, drew her toward him, and kissed her affectionately, to her evident embarrassment ... He kissed her again, and then drew her down beside him on the sofa.... 'You're a very pretty girl,' said Warwick, regarding his sister thoughtfully.

Apparently convinced that sublimation has won out and that fraternal benevolence is the basis for his "regard" and for what makes it "thoughtful," Warwick confesses to having stalked his sister and justifies himself by citing his appreciation of her beauty. He confesses that "I followed you down Front Street this morning, and scarcely took my eyes off you all the way; and yet I did 't know you, and scarcely saw your face. You improve on acquaintance; to-night, I find you handsomer still."

In unfolding the plot of *The House Behind the Cedars*, Chesnutt explains that Rena's beauty and grace persuaded Warwick to invite Rena to join him on the other side of the color line, on his South Carolina plantation, where he's been passing, assuming the role of a planter patrician, since leaving home as a teenager.

> Her graceful movements, the quiet elegance with which she wore even the simplest gown, the easy authoritativeness with which she directed the servants, were to him proofs of superior quality, and he felt correspondingly proud of her. His feeling for her was something more than brotherly love,—he was quite conscious that there were degrees in brotherly love, and that if she had been homely or stupid, he would never have disturbed her in the stagnant life of the house behind the cedars. There had come to him from some source, down the stream of time, a rill of the Greek sense of proportion, of fitness, of beauty, which is indeed but proportion embodied, the perfect adaptation of means to ends.

Two taboos converge in Warwick's gaze, as described by Chesnutt, and determine the decision Warwick's gazing occasions: taboos against incest and against racial imposture or "passing." In describing Rena's neck as "an ivory column," a characterization later echoed in a suitor's beguilement by her "ivory complexion," Chesnutt insinuates that her racial ambiguity, her ability to pass, contributes to her allure. This allure qualifies Rena—born legally black, but, like Warwick, visibly white—to join Warwick's conspiracy to "pass."

Toni Morrison once wrote that her literary "project," which *mutatis mutandis* recalls John Warwick's life project for himself and Rena, entailed shifting readers' gazes "from racial objects to racial subjects" and relocating attention "from the described and imagined to the describers and imaginers" (90). This distinctly literary, reader-centered application of the "double-consciousness" that W.E.B. DuBois introduced to the American cultural lexicon in 1903 informs both the narrative and the spectacle in which Warwick contrives to enmesh Rena. In a scheme she envisions as a Cinderella-like transformation, Warwick casts Rena as a replacement for his dead ("white") wife and hence as the mistress of his plantation. As envisioned, this scenario literally completes the last item on Morrison's agenda: the metamorphosis of the "servers [into] the served." By showing Warwick so intently sexualizing Rena from the outset of *The House Behind the Cedars*, however, Chesnutt tweaks—and arguably warps—Morrison's formulation by redirecting his reader's gaze. During her brief stint as a white chatelaine, Chesnutt sustains Rena's status and desirability as a *sexual* object. But for the time being Rena no longer needs to endure living as a "racial object" and is freed to enjoy life as a would-be racial *subject*, becoming, like her brother, a master rather than a victim of her own hereditary racial classification.

Chesnutt ended the novel by elaborating the failure of Warwick's project and of Rena's Cinderella aspirations and by dramatizing the repercussions of these failures to reconcile "the warring ideals" with which "double-consciousness" had to reckon. These repercussions begin with rejection by the cavalier suitor who had been so beguiled by Rena's patrician grace and her "ivory complexion" only to abandon her upon discovering her origins. After re-crossing the color line, Rena endures sexual harassment at the hands of the "mulatto" politician who hired her as a schoolmarm. During her flight back to her North Carolina home, Rena dies of brain fever. (According to a prevailing melodramatic literary convention) the combination of a broken heart and a fever contracted in a gloomy forest during a storm of Shakespearean proportions maddened and then killed Rena. Even in death, Rena remains a racial question and a sexual object, which men, white *and* black, are meant to be "doin'

[something] with." Bearing Rena homeward to die, the neighbor trans-
porting her encounters a suspicious traveler, "a young white man, who
peered inquisitively into the canopied cart":

> 'Hello!' exclaimed the stranger, 'who've you got there?'
> 'A sick woman, suh.'
> 'Why, she's white, as I'm a sinner!' he cried, after a closer inspection.
> 'Look a-here, nigger, what are you doin' with this white woman?'
> 'She's not w'ite, boss,—she's a bright mulatter.'

When her remorseful suitor reaches Rena's home to find her mother
and neighbors in mourning, he asks one of her neighbors who died.
Introducing the last sentence in the story, the neighbor replies, "a young
cullud'oman, sah." This reply stresses that all that remains of Rena are
her inescapable racial identity and her status as a woman. As a body subjected, even in death, to men's observation, Rena endures solely as a
conversation topic among men.

The concluding description of Rena undercuts repeated remind-
ers throughout *The House Behind the Cedars* that, according to narrator's omniscient and complicating gaze, Rena is not, despite her legal
status, a "cullud'oman." Nevertheless, when a decision needs to be
made about what she is and what her body represents, Chesnutt (a
lawyer by training) falls back on Rena's rigidly constrained legal status
as "cullud," or colored. Since her brother's attraction to her and his
incestuous male-gazing occasioned her fatal attempt to pass, Rena's
"reversion" attests to the power of the twin taboos Chesnutt set
out—quixotically—to challenge and probe: taboos against passing and
against incest.

For all their punishing power, though, these taboos were often subservient to a third. Reviled almost as much as it was flouted among
white southerners, the taboo against miscegenation may explain why
Chesnutt's narrator treats Warwick's incestuous lechery so lightly and
why this southern gentleman can so easily deny the implications of his
"more than brotherly" gaze at his Phryne-like sister Rena. Warwick's
gaze recalls and reenacts the first step in the gazing, by southern slave
owners and overseers, which led to ubiquitous miscegenation and within
a generation or two after the introduction of slavery to the Americas,
produced circumstances in which nobody was unambiguously black or
white (assuming anyone ever had been). In the slave South, where few

belonged exclusively to the racial, supposedly genetically determinant group to which law and custom assigned them, where paternity typically remained unacknowledged by white fathers of enslaved children, incest became as ubiquitous as it was unmentionable. Chesnutt described the consequences of this conceptually dissonant norm in a magazine article published during the same year that *The House Behind the Cedars* appeared:

> To start with, the Negroes are already considerably mixed—many of them in large proportion, and most of them in some degree—and the white people, as I shall endeavor to show later on, are many of them slightly mixed with the Negro. But we will assume, for the sake of the argument, that the two races are absolutely pure. We will assume, too, that the laws of the whole country were as favorable to this amalgamation as the laws of most Southern States are at present against it; i.e., that it were made a misdemeanor for two white or two colored persons to marry, so long as it was possible to obtain a mate of the other race-this would be even more favorable than the Southern rule which makes no such exception. ("Speeches" 124)

The "assumptions" Chesnutt proposes here "for the sake of argument" about the freedom to mate across the color line have now, after a long and often brutal struggle, been resolved, with a result "favorable to [the] amalgamation" Chesnutt envisioned. In our century, struggles for such intimate freedoms still rage, though on a different front, as courts, legislatures, and churches remain embroiled in disputes over whether sexuality should govern any consenting adults' freedom to couple.

Struggles Continue

Coinciding with the beginning of the end of race-based legal restrictions on these personal freedoms, one of the twentieth century's most durably controversial American novels fired one of the earliest salvos on behalf of these still-contested sexual freedoms. James Baldwin's 1956 novel *Giovanni's Room* highlighted the promise of male gazing as an instrument for asserting this freedom and for challenging the *invisibility* Ralph Ellison had placed at the core of African American manhood only four years earlier in *Invisible Man*. As his narrative unfolds, however, Baldwin exposes the futility of the novel's narrator's investment in gazing as an instrument of liberation from his era's implacable bigotry. In Baldwin's *exposé* the "command" effect Mulvey would come to ascribe to male gazing a generation later in "Visual Pleasure and Narrative Cinema" proves no match for the sexual oppression many male gazers faced or for the invisibility they endured. Baldwin discredits sweeping indictments of men in general as privileged and exploitative male gazers endowed with an exclusively male freedom "to command the stage" and "create the action" by the sheer force of their desire.

Though ultimately discrediting it, Baldwin begins *Giovanni's Room* by acknowledging and articulating this understanding of male gazing as empowering, as authorizing "command," and as a means of "controlling" others. The opening paragraphs introduce the novel's first-person narrator construing a self-aggrandizing account of how others see him: as a representative of American manhood, superlatively equipped by virtue of his heritage to triumph in what Camille Paglia characterizes as "the agon of male will" (*Personae*, 7). Imperious, self-regarding, and alone, he gazes on his own mirror image and sees a face Baldwin would later describe as belonging to someone "invested with the power of the world" (*Nobody* 170). Along with this "face" of both "generic whiteness" (Abur-Rahman 481) and of American manly authority comes a voice asserting its ancestry-sanctioned prerogative to command (Holland 275). Bearing the scripturally resonant regal name David, Baldwin's narrator describes his mirror image as "tall … like an arrow" and notes how his "blond hair gleams" (3). Positioning himself historically—and hierarchically—as part of a *Herrenvolk*, David identifies himself as a birthright master, as the heir of "ancestors" who "conquered a continent" by "pushing across death-laden plains."

In ascribing to his narrator such a decidedly *Herrenvolk* stance, Baldwin turned passing from a plot device for exploring a ubiquitous but tabooed social practice into an ironically dominant rhetorical position. In this instance passing also turned out to be a career-threatening provocation because by publishing *Giovanni's Room* Baldwin stepped away from his growing stature as a chronicler of African American families, suspended the role he had begun to play as a mordant antagonist of America's deeply inscribed color line, and jeopardized the reputation he had begun to earn with his *Harper's* and *Partisan Review* essays and had recently secured with his first essay collection in 1955, *Notes of a Native Son*. Once these essays cemented Baldwin's position as a public intellectual, his first novel, a Harlem *Bildungsroman* titled *Go Tell It on the Mountain*, appeared in 1953. Its favorable critical and popular reception turned Baldwin into a literary celebrity, "the next 'Negro novelist,'" according to Baldwin's publisher, Alfred A. Knopf (Campbell 86). Despite its contract with Baldwin for a second novel, Knopf refused to publish *Giovanni's Room* because it was neither "a Negro novel" nor was it "set in Harlem" (96, 105). Characteristically flouting "the imperative of racial authenticity" (Abur-Rahman 479), Baldwin spurned the role Knopf had scripted for him. Hence in the autobiographical introduction to *Notes of a Native Son*, Baldwin voices his anticipation of and "hope" for the day when "I could … write about" more than "being a Negro" (8). With his racial imposture in *Giovanni's Room*, Baldwin positions his uber-white alter-ego as one of the apparently unimpeachably "commanding" men distinctly entitled according to Mulvey to the prerogatives of male gazing.

Early in the novel, Baldwin establishes what should be obvious to any understanding of male gazing, a point Mulvey would heteronormatively (if understandably) overlook: male gazing can be directed at men as well as at women. In a brief paragraph opening with two short sentences, which grammatically needn't be separate sentences, David announces:

> Giovanni looked at me. And this look made me feel that no one in my life had ever looked at me directly before. (36)

Both the brevity of the paragraph and the grammatically questionable move to begin the second sentence with "and" serve to bracket David's realization as epiphanic and Giovanni's look or gaze as transformative. "*Made* me feel," moreover, calls attention to the authority and even the coercive force male gazing can exert.

About halfway through the novel Baldwin fleshes out this dimension of the narrative by confronting David with another mirror image. In contrast to the novel's initial mirror scenes, this mirroring refracts more than it reflects. Spotting an American sailor in Paris (91–92), the setting for most of *Giovanni's Room*, and intently "staring at him," David finds himself "wishing I were he… younger than I had ever been, blonder and more beautiful." David wishes to wear "his masculinity as unequivocally as [the sailor] wore his skin." Perhaps imagining and projecting more than he perceives, David finds the sailor's gaze "lewd and knowing" and compares it to the "look he might" recently have aimed at a "desperately dressed nymphomaniac or a trollop who was trying to make him believe she was a lady." This gaze, were it to "erupt into speech," would exclaim "some brutal variation of *Look baby, I know you.*" Equating gazing at women, "trollops" and "nymphomaniacs," and gazing at a man, at the "knowing" sailor, has a leveling effect on the very act of gazing and thus begins to call into question the sense of command Mulvey attributed to male gazers. So too does the physical sensation that leaves David feeling diminished rather than in command. With his face flaming, his heart hardening and shaking, his step accelerating, David turns inward. Blighted by gazing, David realizes that "affection, for the boys I was doomed to look at, was vastly more frightening than lust."

One of David's first intuitions during this encounter results in his admitting that "women baffled him." Although *Giovanni's Room* focuses on a tempestuous, blighted love affair between two men—David and the title character, an Italian café waiter—Baldwin repeatedly recounts both David's and Giovanni's heterosexual backstory attachments. Anxiety about masculinity reverberates throughout Baldwin's work. Thus in *Giovanni's Room* as David "seeks a refuge in the conventional, outward trappings of manhood" (Baldwin, *Essays* 815; Gordon 83; Adams 37), he recounts as many heterosexual as same-sex intimacies over the course of his narrative. This apparent symmetry notwithstanding, the novel's "only explicit sex scenes take place between David and a woman" (Garber 128). Nevertheless, the novel's lasting reputation doesn't reflect this "queering" symmetry. While escaping ghettoization as a "black novel," *Giovanni's Room* now often finds itself confined to the "gay novel" shelf. Writing from the standpoint of a frankly commercial novelist and from the perspective of an heir to Baldwin's legacy, Edmund White praises *Giovanni's Room* as a category-killing classic of resistance. In recanting his eagerness as a novice writer for sequestering "gay literature," White reminisced about an era "before the category of 'gay writing' was invented when books with gay content" like *Giovanni's Room* "were widely reviewed and often became bestsellers" (184). Despite promoting antagonism to fixed identity classifications, *Giovanni's Room* has fallen to the forces of the cultural marketplace that White decries: it now lends its name to a Philadelphia bookshop that bills itself as "America's world-class lesbian, gay, bisexual & transgender bookstore for queers & our friends." Not surprisingly, on prime-time TV, in 2001, Baldwin's novel was glibly tagged as "too homosexual" on the popular NBC series *The West Wing* ("Two Cathedrals").

Even when writing autobiographically and polemically, Baldwin has forthrightly cast himself as heterosexual. In his 1963 civil rights manifesto *The Fire Next Time*, for example, Baldwin recalls realizing what "had not occurred to me before" and recollects the onset of puberty among his teenage neighbors, especially "girls, only slightly older ... who sang in the choir or taught Sunday school" and who:

> underwent, before my eyes, their incredible metamorphosis, of which the most bewildering aspect was not their budding breasts or the rounding of their behinds but something deeper and more subtle ... they became, in the twinkling of an eye, unutterably and fantastically *present*... one watched them turning into matrons before they became women... they understood they must act as decoy's for God. (18)

By characterizing these youngsters' transformation as occurring in "the twinkling of an eye," Baldwin broadcasts that, despite his same-sex affinities, his interest in these young women was that of conventional a male-gazer. "Girls," "matrons," "women" "decoys": the very sequence of Baldwin's nouns reflects an understanding of the impossibility of settling once and for all the social, sexual identities of the girls and women among whom he came of age; however, "decoys," the final noun in this sequence, does objectify these Harlem neighbors, begging the question of whether Baldwin the gazer objectified them or they objectified themselves. Such questions about who's objectifying whom unsettle questions such as those Mulvey and her successors purported to have answered about who's empowered by and who's diminished by male gazing.

In contrast to Baldwin's polemical autobiographical persona in *The Fire Next Time*, Baldwin's alter-ego in *Giovanni's Room* appears unequivocally as an objectifying gazer who subjects both of his heterosexual partners in the story to reductive sociological, demographic pigeonholing. In the case of the first of these partners and David's secondary heterosexual attachment in the novel, his efforts to represent her appear markedly sketchy. Sue, David recounts, "came from Philadelphia" where "her family was very rich" (95). In introducing Hella, with whom he has more sustained relationship, David proves at once sociologically more thorough and more trite. In a letter to his father announcing their engagement, David reports "her name is Hella Lincoln, she comes from Minneapolis, her father and mother still live there, he's a corporation lawyer and her mother's just the little woman" (*Giovanni* 124). "Just the little woman": David's cliché accentuates the extent of his reductive, hackneyed ways of talking about women and of his haste to objectify. With this eagerness to pigeonhole the women who pique his interest, David traps himself within the boundaries Baldwin set out to erase or at least blur.

David's limitations as a generic, hopelessly self-parodying heterosexual gazer surface most egregiously in his first description of Sue's appearance. His phrasing accentuates his impulse to distance himself from her when he calls her "a girl named Sue" (95). David burnishes his own status a stereotypical male-gazer by recalling that "the moment she appeared I began mentally to take off all her clothes." Like Mulvey's moviegoer, subject to "the magic of Hollywood," David introduces Sue by insisting on her conformity to mass media typecasting. "Blonde and rather puffy," Sue exhibited "the quality, in spite of the fact she was not pretty, of the girls who are selected each year to be Miss Rheingold" (95).

In 1956, readers—especially New York-area readers—would have recognized Baldwin's Miss Rheingold reference and associated it with one of America's most successful mass rituals for male gazers, for up to twenty-million gazers by 1959.[3] From 1940 to 1964, Miss Rheingold was the title awarded the winner of an annual poll that encouraged patrons of bars and stores selling Rheingold beer to vote in response to posters mounted in participating establishments.[4] Sue, David continues, "wore her curly blond hair cut very short," had "small breasts and a big behind. In order no doubt, to indicate … how little she cared for appearance and sensuality…[she]wore tight blue jeans." With this description David sets

---

[3] "Now! Elect Miss Rheingold 1953" poster. https://ephemeralnewyork.files.wordpress.com/2009/10/missrheingold1953.jpg.

[4] The Miss Rheingold contest ended in the mid-1960s because of what we now call "identity politics," when Liebmann Breweries, owners of the Rheingold brand, designated an African American Miss Rheingold instead of allowing the public to choose the winner as they had done in past years. Liebmann, which had been the first brewer to sponsor TV shows featuring black entertainers such as Nat King Cole, realized that integrating or diversifying the Miss Rheingold pool was a lose-lose proposition because it would diminish market share among alienated white ethnics, their traditional customers, while failing to become more inclusive would limit sales to the New York area's growing African-American and Latino populations:

> Rheingold was after the Harlem market … By the mid-60s, six lily-white girls no longer reflected the ethnic mix of the city. Rheingold found itself in a no-win situation: Keeping the status quo would anger the black and Hispanic communities, but adding nonwhite candidates might lose the blue-collar white males who bought the beer. (Diehl 2000)

out to articulate Mulvey's view of the gazer as intent on "command" because, both syntactically and lexically, he commandeers the entire discourse of women's attractiveness. The phrase "in spite of the fact she was not pretty" awkwardly disrupts, literally intervenes in, David's move to pinpoint and provide a context for the defining "quality" of Sue's appearance. Baldwin amplifies David's attention to what Sue is *not* by noting the sex-aversion her clothes signal. In the course of their pre-coital conversation, even this signaling fails, with David's attention to her affectations of "discontentment" diverted by glimpses of "the way her thighs moved against her jeans." To the extent that breasts stand preeminent among the female secondary sexual characteristics supposed to engross conventional male gazers, "her small breasts" direct even more attention to Sue's apparent "defects" as a gaze object. David's attention to Sue's "big behind" finally suggests, however, that for all its defects, her apparent bulk engages David. Even if she doesn't actually attract him, seeing Sue "both dismay[s] and relieve[s]" him. His unsettling interest in Sue rests in part on her social location, the milieu on which, in David's view, her identity rests. After establishing Sue's Miss Rheingold qualifications, David introduces her, as he introduced himself in the opening passage, as the product of a distinctive American caste: her "very rich" Philadelphia family whom she either "reviled" or when "drunk in another way, extolled for their virtues of thrift and fidelity" (95).

Neither sexual nor "sensual," Sue's appeal appears to rest on a mix of her Miss Rheingold attributes and her Main Line pedigree just as status and pedigree preoccupied David when he introduced himself at the beginning of the novel. Hence David's male gaze proves more conceptual than carnal. It encompasses what women represent more than it concerns itself with how they look. By ascribing to David the "manly" perspective of a Miss Rheingold barroom voter, Baldwin demonstrates the distinctly penetrating and authoritative understanding of "American masculinity" he would later claim as his forte (*Nobody* 172). Like celebrity models, movie stars, and (once upon a time) debutantes and socialites, Miss Rheingold represents what heterosexual conventional male gazers—are *supposed* to—and were once virtually required to desire (Sedgwick 136, 193–194, 196, 210). Sex with Miss Rheingold can confirm a man's sexual "normality" or masculinity and satisfy his obligation to "want" and "get the Girl" (Baldwin, *Collected Essays* 597–598). Such couplings affirm the dominion of what Eve Kosofsky Sedgwick has described as "heterosexual compulsion" (196, 210). David's encounter with Sue *should* confirm his power as a gazer since Miss Rheingold begins as a two-dimensional image widely available to millions of men but *may* become incarnate, immediately available for only a select few. In contrast to models' and screen stars' promoters, Miss Rheingold's packagers downplayed her carnality, further damping male gazers' hope of ever "having sex" with her. According to customary views of where male gazing ought to lead, David has succeeded resoundingly, by bedding "Miss Rheingold."

David's triumphant gazing, though, brings no pleasure. In a notably anhedonic sex scene, a "grisly act of love," David finds Sue constricted by "grave distrust," then "giving herself" as "a gesture of great despair" (99–100). Anticipating an aftermath, the point at which "we would hate each other," David girds himself to do "something awful to her ... a job of work" necessarily done "in an unforgettable manner." During this grim performance, David gazes narrowly, at Sue's thighs and legs, feeling her "tom-tom fists on my back." Listening to "her sobs" becoming "higher and harsher," he wonders about "how soon I could be free" and thinks to himself, in a phrase reminiscent of prize fights and bar brawls, "Well, let her have it for Christ's sake get it over with." Affirming his masculine prowess, he decides that "my performance with Sue was succeeding even too well." So well that he fears having to stick around and dine with her. This fear lingers and leaves David feeling deprived of the sense of the command and control male gazing is supposed to afford. "Ashamed" and "afraid to go out into that night which had seemed to be calling" him (101), David casts his final gaze narrowly, on a single body part:

> the strangest smile I had ever seen... pained, vindictive, humiliated... she inexpertly smeared across this grimace a bright girlish gaiety—as rigid as the skeleton beneath her flabby body. (102)

Instead of seeing Sue as diminished by his conquest, as his belittling physical description augured, David departs haunted by fears that Sue's demeanor, her smile in particular, might "kill" him.

David's gazing, as Baldwin tracks it, begins with the objectification that Mulvey postulated and described. David "takes" Sue as an "object" and "subjects [her] to a controlling and curious gaze." David's gazing departs, however, from the gazer's progress as hypothesized by

Mulvey: Baldwin opts not to show David's gaze following the trajectory Mulvey traced, a trajectory showing David identifying with "the patriarchal order." His gazing doesn't inspire vicarious "participation in" the "power" that Hollywood and other prevailing phallocentric narratives inspire in male spectators. Such inspirations include the "conquerors," the forbears, with whom David associates himself in the opening paragraph of the novel and the Miss Rheingold "voters" with whose eyes he initially judges Sue. Instead David departs Sue's flat humbled, if not humiliated. Newly attuned to the repercussions of male gazing, he finds himself identifying with the object of his gaze instead of with the commanding gazers Mulvey envisions.

BODY SHOPPING

After David's grim tryst with Sue, Baldwin's story focuses on his primary heterosexual connection in *Giovanni's Room*: with his fiancée— "my girl, Hella"—who occupies David's thoughts but remains absent from Paris, "gone" from David's life (4), during the first hundred or so pages of the novel. In contrast to the way he brings Sue into the narrative, Baldwin introduces Hella without showing David dwelling on her physical attributes, let alone her thighs and breasts. David's first description of Hella appears in a reminiscence about how "elegant, tense [and] glittering" she appeared in "the light" surrounding "the salon of an ocean-liner, drinking … laughing, watching the men" (4). David also reminisces fondly about their "nights in bed" and what had made them "so delightful." These memories couldn't contrast more sharply with David's jaundiced recollection of his one-night stand with Sue. David's seemingly fond memories of Hella lack the vividness and thus the credibility of his accounts of sex with Sue. They consist entirely of affirmative disembodied abstractions: "innocence and confidence… freedom" (5). Among these abstractions "innocence" in particular preoccupied and infuriated Baldwin. In Baldwin's view, "the truly awesome attempt of the American … to preserve his innocence" shelters an "innocent country" and its "innocent people," who run from the "storm of life," in order to deny in good conscience the violence we perpetrate (*Essays* 597; *Fire* 6–8; *Nobody*, 172).

The second passage in *Giovanni's Room* spotlighting Hella is epistolary. David's unsettling reaction to the sailor he passes, an encounter that depletes David's "confidence" and mocks all claims to "innocence," punctuates his reaction to a letter from Hella. The disconcerting sailor appears between David's visit to American Express to fetch his mail and his delayed decision to open and read Hella's long-awaited letter (90). It begins with an assemblage of apercus from a callow, precociously sophisticated tourist. It includes observations about Paris's "crazy statuary and absurd parks" in contrast to "beautiful, sunny, stony, and lonely" Spain— its "olive oil, fish castanets and tambourines" and a must-see bullfight. Hella followed this brochure boilerplate with complaints about fellow tourists, notably "old hags" who "make eyes at anything in pants" (93). In these hags Hella sees her own future and looks to "loving" David to save her from this generic fate as a discarded gaze object.

As envisioned by Hella, David seems as disembodied to her as she seems to him. Just as David first imagines Hella in a public commercial space, "the salon of an ocean liner," she deems him her "dear knight in Gimble's [sic] armor" (93). Many sophisticated readers in 1956 would have heard Hella's reference to "armor" as an allusion to Wilhelm Reich's post Freudian theory—or notion—of "body armor." Reich's ideas became popular among literati in the 1950s. During the years Baldwin spent working on Giovanni's Room, Norman Mailer, American letters' most celebrated proponent of Reich's ideas, became Baldwin's "very dear ... loving" friend as well as a very public antagonist (Nobody 172, 174). For Reichians, this armor metaphor explained America's supposedly endemic emotional repression and sexual frustration, which Reich set out to cure by releasing his patients' "orgone energy" (Mailer 209, 342, 389; P. Robinson 23–26). By working this allusion into Hella's correspondence, Baldwin casts a cold eye on Hella's view of David as a liberator or rescuer. Baldwin explicitly registered his own disdain for "mad" Reichian "panaceas" in Esquire five years after the publication of Giovanni's Room (Essays 662) and again in Playboy in 1985 (826).

Hella also strains to sound worldly by playing on the childishly archaic cliché "knight in shining armor." Hella replaces "shining," the customary modifier, with the name of a once famous New York department store. With her misspelling of "Gimbels," though, Baldwin pierces Hella's veneer of sophistication and thus discredits her "knightly" masculine image of David. Hella's move to brand David as Gimbels merchandise becomes as forced as David's move to brand Sue as Miss Rheingold. In contrast to David's depiction of Sue, Hella's disembodying displacement of David, however, succeeds: Hella believes her own simplification. Hella's phrasing prefaces this simplification by describing David's "future" as "this *business* of loving me" (93, emphasis added). During Baldwin's lifetime Gimbels had, with its "select, don't settle" advertising slogan, positioned itself among its competitors by promising more than any "business" or product could consistently deliver. The promise implicit in Gimbels' "select, don't settle" message was modest, though, in comparison to the hope for miraculous transformation aroused in the late 1940s when the retailer's flagship Herald Square store took a star turn (along with its more durable upscale neighbor and rival, Macy's) as the setting for Hollywood's feel-good Christmas classic *Miracle on 34th Street*.

LETTING GO

Baldwin's description of David and Hella's reunion emphasizes "hope" and promises reconciliation and even "glory" (121, 123), but departs from the earlier passages in the novel that focused on Hella's physical absence. During this reunion Hella's "marvelously living body" occupies the foreground, though the lovers each see a different body. Greeting her at the *Gare d'Austerlitz*, David finds Hella "stock still ... with her wide-legged boyish stance" (119) and once they're alone he sees her as a powerful horsewoman "holding the reins of her strong desire strongly in her hands" (122). Hella also singles out particular bodily functions. She represents herself to David, however, with a stark departure from his gender bending focus on her strong, loose, "boyish" extremities. Hella confides:

> I'm not really the emancipated girl I try to be… I guess I just want a man to come home to me every night… Hell, I want to be knocked up. I want to start having babies…it's all I'm good for. (123)

Agreeing "Yes ... I've always wanted that," David assents to Hella's renunciation of the "boyish" equestrienne image that his gaze had construed and reveled in. Hella's boyish allure thus banished, David begins precipitously to relinquish any interest in looking at, let alone engaging with her. Hella's observations about estrangement between women and men and about misogyny, commitment, and attachment (125–126) further David's disenchantment. Baldwin telegraphs David's recoil from Hella by registering his bodily responses and his body language.

"Tongue-tied" at first, David mostly listens while Hella muses aloud. But when Hella promises complete submission, David feels only "cold" (122, 126). This coldness, though, animates him enough so that he shakes "his head in mock confusion." David adds to this mockery by "laughing" repeatedly at Hella's reflections on their attachment to and future with each other. He disingenuously voices his "mock confusion" by claiming "I don't know what you're talking about... I don't understand you" (126). Patronizing Hella with a banal endearment, "You're adorable," David prompts Hella to close the conversation with a cliché, reassuring David that "we're both taking to" our life together "like ducks to water" and with a definitive pronouncement that they're both "fine," a conclusion the rest of the narrative starkly contravenes (126–127).

Baldwin marks this decisive retreat from commitment and engagement by having Hella change the subject entirely. Passing a bookshop, she decides to enter and buy "a trivial book" (127). Instead of pursuing their discussion about marriage and motherhood, Hella opts to shop for something "trivial." As she shops, David gazes at her. David follows Hella's earlier cue to view their relationship as a movie (122), a medium designed according to Baldwin for watching (white) women from a "distance" (*Essays* 493), and watches Hella from afar "with amusement." "Amused" but apparently not engaged, David recalls that he "wandered idly" away from Hella to the "farthest book shelf" where his gaze shifts to Jacques, a mutual friend of David's and Giovanni's. When Hella joins the pair, David turns his gaze to an imagined future, watching "as though I were watching an imminent disaster from miles away" (128). As his gaze shifts, David's demeanor presages his defeat. His body language becomes that of a supplicant with a "smile ... begging" Jacques "to be kind to me."

"Unaesthetic"

At this point, Baldwin stages the triangulation–the rendezvous with chagrin–that has been looming throughout the narrative. Giovanni enters the bookshop "staring" at Hella "with black, steady eyes as though he had never seen a woman before" (129). This stare assaults Hella's "composure" and stuns "her entire body" into "a kind of wild shrinking." By introducing Giovanni's stunning stare after describing David's helplessly supplicant "watching," Baldwin confirms Giovanni's position as an alpha gazer and recalls Giovanni's claim to this status early on in the novel, in

3 AMERICAN FICTION: GAZE CANON   117

David's recollection of Giovanni's uniquely compelling gaze during their first encounter (36–37). David's late observation that Giovanni "swaggers" while his nemesis Guillaume, a rich old Latin Quarter regular—"a silly old queen" according to Giovanni's bar friends—"prances" (153–156) underscores Giovanni's effectiveness in performing masculinity. Like David's, Giovanni's power to compel both men and women doesn't result in the "command" and "control" Mulvey attributes to male gazing. Instead Giovanni finds himself on death row waiting to be guillotined for killing Guillaume. Guillaume had raped Giovanni when he balked at fulfilling their money-for-sex bargain. After highlighting Giovanni's power as a gazer, Baldwin turns him into an abject self-consuming gaze object who destroys himself and loses David. Envisioning Giovanni in prison, David casts him as a tarnished gaze object, "like a falling movie star" who "has lost his drawing power," whose "secrecy has been discovered" and about whom "everything is known" (156). This dark but romantic picture of Giovanni is prompted by the hysterical, homophobic press coverage that Guillaume's murder provoked (157; Abur-Rahman 484).

David's view of Hella, with whom he lives throughout Giovanni's ordeal, moves in the opposite direction. David remains attentive to the workings of her body and continues to act like a conventional male gazer by "watching her naked body" closely and critically (158). His gaze and sense of Hella "moving" when she returned from Spain stirred a desire to "put my head on her breast ... to lie there" (123). Reacting to Giovanni's ordeal, David replaces this *gemutlich* tenderness toward Hella with a feeling that made his "flesh recoil," a feeling of being "fantastically intimidated" by her nakedness, especially by her breasts. Eventually he comes to disdain Hella's "body [as] uninteresting ... unaesthetic... grotesque" (158). This sequence of adjectives compounds and darkens David's previous responses to Hella as an aesthetic object, as do his view of her in the bookshop and his architectural image of her as a gated "walled city" (123).

Since the very concept of male-gazing originated in a critique of an art form (cinema), "unaesthetic" seems especially notable in connection with David's position as a male-gazer. Aestheticizing, including male gazing, extends beyond seeing as sensory perception. Harvey Teres has recently argued for such a broad view of what it means to aestheticize. Aestheticizing, in his view, fosters human connections and thus provokes ethical questions (108, 113). As such, aestheticizing obliges gazers to articulate their perceptions and often to furnish a narrative, even an argument, about what makes one's perceptions compelling. David's failure as a gazer, as an aestheticizer, decisively marks his rupture with Hella, a dissolution that culminates with a realization of the unfulfillably aesthetic basis of their relationship: a recognition that "we no longer seemed to see things to point out to each other" (159).

Nevertheless, David's will to gaze persists. And this persisting will to gaze and to aestheticize surfaces where Mulvey positions it: at the movies. All that's left for the couple to share by the time they part, David laments, is pub-crawling and going "to a lot of movies" (159). All this movie watching notwithstanding, David's loss of Giovanni and then of Hella severs his will to gaze from any imperative to aestheticize.

At the close of *Giovanni's Room* narcissistic self-contemplation has displaced David's "aesthetic" recoil from Hella's body. Baldwin once again shows David in solitude gazing at his own reflection. Pondering his own culpability for Giovanni's imminent execution, David reckons with the repercussions of his own gazing. Regardless of their sex, their gender, their sexuality, or the degree and purity of their attractiveness, David's gaze objects are all gone by the end of his story despite the *Herrenvolk* legacy, the gazer's *droit du seigneur* patrimony, that he claimed at the beginning of the novel. With David's abjection, Baldwin joins two centuries of American novelists in demonstrating that for all the plausibility and rhetorical appeal of Mulvey's argument, male gazing and the desires it reflects, whether thwarted or seemingly fulfilled, are as likely to lead to defeat as to facilitate domination, as likely to result in solitary confinement as well as to authorize men to "command the stage."

CHAPTER 4

Scopes on Trial

MEN AND THEIR EQUIPMENT

Robert Frost's 1928 poem "The Bear" characterizes its eponymous carnivore as hunting with a "scientific tread." Relying prosthetically on "the telescope at one end of his beat and at the other end the microscope" to track his prey, Frost's predator's reliance on optical technology is one of many such accounts throughout modern and contemporary writing, and especially American literature. Such work typically shows stymied gazers, like Frost's bear, falling back on familiar instruments of visual enhancement to compensate for their limited natural endowments. A narrator in one recent account, Phil Klay's prizewinning 2014 collection *Redeployment*, recalls, "I spent so much time looking at women through scopes ... But I never scratched the surface" (121–122), despite the rich array of lenses available to twenty-first-century gazers like Klay's soldier storytellers.

Such a sequence, trying and failing to scratch the visual surface and seeking technological backup, animates what's probably the second most quoted passage among classic American novels (after "Call me Ishmael" at the beginning of *Moby Dick*). The passage appears in the closing paragraphs of *The Great Gatsby*. Most quoters seem to favor the novel's fatalistic last sentence, which reminds us that we're all ships borne back ceaselessly into the past. Male gazers, however, are likely to find the antepenultimate paragraph far more quoteworthy. This closing meditation begins with Fitzgerald's narrator, Nick Carraway, speaking in

© The Author(s) 2017
J.D. Bloom, *Reading the Male Gaze in Literature and Culture*, Global
Masculinities, DOI 10.1007/978-3-319-59945-8_4

the first-person singular. In closing, with his image of "ships against the current," though, he speaks in a first-person plural voice. Beginning to speak *as* a male gazer, Nick Carraway claims, as the novel ends, to speak *for* male gazers. Thus he begins his memorable peroration gripped as much by the very act of seeing as by the story he's been telling:

> I became aware of the old island here that flowered once for Dutch sailors' eyes-a fresh, green breast of the new world. Its vanished trees, the trees that had made way for Gatsby's house, had once pandered in whispers to the last and greatest of all human dreams; for a transitory enchanted moment man must have held his breath in the presence of this continent, compelled into an aesthetic contemplation he neither understood nor desired, face to face for the last time in history with something commensurate to his capacity for wonder.

Male gazers are likely to find it all but impossible to avoid dwelling on the breast trope in this passage. Historically minded gazers may find themselves identifying with the gazers in the passage, the Dutch sailors Fitzgerald imagines approaching the North Shore of Long Island three centuries earlier. To the extent that we identify with these explorers, we're likely to feel flattered by the description of such vicarious breast-gazing as "aesthetic contemplation." The pleasure this flattery brings may even extend beyond the satisfactions of seeing our gazing idealized as aesthetic contemplation, at once artistic and philosophical. In associating modern male gazers with a "historical first" and with the European explorers who (as many living gazers once were taught) "discovered" America, Fitzgerald has flatteringly enlisted ordinary everyday male gazers in one of Western Civilization's most self-satisfying adventures. As vicarious contributors to the European Renaissance and the Age of Discovery it spawned, subsequent generations of male gazers also become agents of the Enlightenment and the industrial and political revolutions that followed from the Age of Discovery that Fitzgerald idealizes at the end of *Gatsby*.

As a trope, connections between breast-centered male-gazing and the discovery of "the New World" date back to the so-called Age of Discovery itself, a connection John Donne famously celebrated circa 1600 as he cast his European gaze on a "far fairer world":

> Unpin that spangled breast-plate, which you wear,
> That th' eyes of busy fools may be stopp'd there.
> Unlace yourself, for that harmonious chime

Tells me from you that now it is bed-time …
Your gown going off such beauteous state reveals,
As when from flowery meads th' hill's shadow steals …
Licence my roving hands, and let them go
Before, behind, between, above, below.
O, my America, my Newfoundland …
How am I blest in thus discovering thee! (Elegy)

Where Donne cast an intimate, close-up, and essentially unmediated gaze, Fitzgerald left it up to readers' imaginations to decide whether the Dutch sailors' gazed breastward with their naked eyes or with the assistance of one of the visual-enhancement tools that facilitated various Renaissance-spawned revolutions. Fitzgerald's readers were likely to have pictured these sailors using one of the spyglasses often included in illustrations of explorers first gazing on New Worlds. These explorers were likely to have been early adopters, adapters, and beneficiaries of the paradigm-shifting, "new, improved spyglass" technology that in Italy, in Galileo's hands, came to be known as the telescope (Lipking 202–203).

Since the so-called Enlightenment, vision-enhancing technologies, particularly microscopes and telescopes, have become instrumental in determining what we see, how we see, and how we think about the very act of seeing. Richard Holmes has documented how such technologies have encouraged us to treat seeing as a way of actively intervening in, rather than as passively contemplating and observing, the surrounding material world (xviii). Lawrence Lipking has explained how Galileo's telescope became more than an instrument of inquiry and how it became an essential rhetorical tool: a resource in the many disputes and debates that Galileo sparked and relished. Lipking argues that what Galileo discovered with his "marvelous spyglass" piqued his "polemical style" (31), dealing a deathblow to geocentric Ptolemaic superstition.[1]

By the twentieth century, movie cameras also became part of this Renaissance legacy. And, at least according to Laura Mulvey's analysis of the male gaze, movie technology joined microscopes and telescopes among widely available instruments of active visual intervention. As a contrivance that "collapses distance," "narrative cinema," in Mulvey's view, became instrumental in fostering an "ideology of representation"

---

[1] *Galileo Offering His Telescope to Three Women*. Anon. 1665. http://lcweb2.loc.gov/service/pnp/cph/3c10000/3c10000/3c10400/3c10447r.jpg.

("Visual"). Perpetuating what Mulvey characterizes as "Renaissance space," these ideologically skewed technologies can obscure and obfuscate as well as disclose and illuminate. Close examination of the evolution of all this interventionist visual technology, from Galileo to Edison and beyond, may call into question the extent to which such interventions have proven as conducive to male domination as Mulvey has alleged. Much of the fiction and poetry of the past two centuries has, in fact, kept open questions about whether or not modern visual technologies have sustained what Mulvey regards as men's power to "command the stage of action." To what extent, much of this writing asks, have these technologies continued to empower and aggrandize the men who use and enjoy them? To what extent have they blunted and diffused the power Mulvey imputed to male gazers?

Two late twentieth novelists, Italo Calvino and Jeffery Eugenides, have probed the promise of technologically enhanced male gazing, explored the lives of men and boys susceptible to this promise, and dramatized the disappointment that follows from counting on such promises. The very title of *Mr. Palomar*, Calvino's reflective and episodic 1983 novella, calls to mind modernity's faith in the power of our vision-enhancing instruments to extend our collective knowledge and enhance human mastery of the universe. Calvino's epynomic title alludes to one of the world's foremost astronomical observatories: the California Institute of Technology's Palomar Observatory near San Diego. The telescope this facility houses became part of this triumphalist narrative of human mastery when upon its completion it was hailed as "the perfect machine" (Florence).

"The Naked Bosom," an early section of Calvino's novel, shows Palomar strolling along a beach where he encounters a sunbather. Noticing that she has "her bosom bared," Palomar entertains the hope that his "gaze" will effectively "express" his pleasure (9–11). In keeping with his "discreet nature," however, Palomar initially frets about this seemingly serendipitous encounter. He fears it could lead to "insecurity and incoherence" rather than foster the "freedom and frankness" popularly associated with nude sunbathing by a "generation" for whom the "nudity of the female bosom was associated with amorous intimacy," at least by those whom the narrator associates with his era's "more broad-minded society." With this reaction Palomar joins the ranks of the millions of male gazers, such as those readers of *Hustler* magazine whom Laura Kipnis pityingly identifies as "saturated with frustrated desire" and (contra Mulvey) as inclined to view "sex [as] an arena of failure, not domination" (*Men* 15). Palomar plans to endorse this supposedly liberating—or at least libertine—"change in customs" and to "express" this endorsement "with his gaze." But instead of savoring his opportunity, Palomar turns away from the sunbather and shifts his gaze telescopically toward "the horizon," only to find there "in the distance the outline of a bronze-pink cloud of a naked female torso." Once again, Palomar averts this gaze, away from the horizon, so that "the trajectory of his gaze remains suspended in the void" and thus "guarantees his civil respect for the invisible frontier that surrounds people." Palomar's restored composure proves precarious. He immediately becomes unsettled by the possibility that his civility may prove "indiscreet and reactionary." He worries about "relegating the bosom ... to the semidarkness" to which "centuries of sexomaniacal Puritanism" have confined it, about upholding "the dead weight of an intolerant tradition," and about "reinforcing the convention that declares illicit any sight of the breast." This deference to tradition, he fears, will "create a kind a kind of mental brassiere suspended between my eyes and that bosom."

Palomar finally escapes his quandary by drawing on our Enlightenment legacy as he submits his gaze to scientific discipline:

> [He] keeps his eyes fixed straight ahead, so that his gaze
> touches with impartial uniformity the foam of the retreating
> waves, the boats pulled up on shore, the great bath
> towel spread out on the sand, the swelling moon of lighter
> with the dark halo of the nipple, the outline of the coast
> in the haze, gray against the sky. (10)

This commitment to scientific "impartiality ... neutral objectivity" and the increasingly telescopic trajectory of his gaze, toward "the sky," becomes confounded, though, by Palomar's metaphoric transformation of his gaze object's nipple into "the swelling moon." This moon, which Palomar's scientific bent and his very name oblige him to view telescopically, morphs into an evanescent abstraction, owing to Mr. Palomar's determination to see ever more abstractly an "outline ... in the haze." As the gazer's perspective turns microscopic rather than telescopic, the moon becomes a nipple halo, not even an entire breast, let alone pair of breasts. With Palomar's moon trope, Calvino has sabotaged his hero's effort to reconcile his impulse to enjoy and his impulse to sublimate male gazing.

Mixing sympathy and ridicule, Calvino allows Palomar (for the space of brief single-sentence paragraph) to congratulate himself for having achieved both the pleasure and sublimation that actually eluded him:

> There he reflects—pleased with himself … I have
> succeeded in having the bosom completely absorbed by the landscape,
> so that my gaze counted no more than the gaze of a seagull or a hake (10).

Palomar seems to have achieved the peace-of-mind Walt Whitman claimed in *Song of Myself* by declaring that "I think I could live with the animals, they are so placid and self-contained" (sec. 32). But this Whitmanesque turn to self-contained placidity proves no match for the passions that inspire and roil male-gazers. These passions, Palomar discovers, preclude peaceful cohabitation between deferential gazers and their gaze objects. Palomar has achieved only a precarious Whitmanesque peace of mind by living, only briefly, among "the animals," as a fowl or fish so distant from his gaze object that he flies or swims in an entirely different medium than she inhabits. No longer a terrestrial creature, Palomar feels like he no longer even treads the same earth as the sunbather on the beach.

Palomar's various failures—to achieve peace of mind, to feel part of his era's so-called "sexual revolution," to articulate his appreciation of his gaze object's anatomy—confront him with an ethical dilemma and exacerbate the ideological anxiety that every "enlightened," progressive-minded gazer confronts. His increasingly labored syntax over the course of this stroll highlights these stresses:

> … is this really the right way to act?—he reflects further …
> does it not mean flattening the human person to the level
> of things, considering it an object and, worse yet, considering as
> object that which in the person is the specific attribute of the
> female sex?
> Am I not perhaps perpetuating the old habit of male superiority,
> hardened over the years into habitual insolence? (10)

Confessing his inclination to objectify, Palomar seems to have taken a feminist turn with this self-interrogation. But instead of catharsis or enlightenment, his seeming disavowal of male gazing only aggravates his ideological agitation, prompting him to fret that any "underestimation of what a breast is and means" constitutes a devaluation of the woman attached to it.

Palomar's punctiliousness in weighing the allure of the aesthetic pleasure Fitzgerald ascribed to New World "discoverers," the demands of impartial scientific curiosity, the ethical imperatives and the evolving "customs" of his era all fail him. Palomar finds himself thrown back on an ancient language and a decidedly unscientific, amoral, retrograde conceptual framework—Greek mythology—in recognizing the sunbather's view of him as a "tiresome[ly] insisten[t] satyr" and her indifference to his "most enlightened intentions" (12). Midway through the novel Calvino's troubled hero has become so consummate a gazer and so invested in this retrograde myth-based conceptual framework that even panoramic views of inanimate objects become occasions for the defeat of male gazing. Beaches and sunbathers behind him, Palomar surveys Rome's skyline. As only the most bemused male gazer could, he finds there only "domes that make outlines against the sky, in every direction and every distance, as if to confirm the female, Junoesque essence of the city" (55). Palomar's erudite aestheticizing and his complacent reliance on ancient mythology ultimately only "confirm" how far from observable reality his gazing has led him.

In Jeffrey Eugenides' 1993 novel *The Virgin Suicides* a group of teenage first-person narrators becomes as intent on refining acts of gazing into a conceptual activity as they are on viewing the actual objects of their gazes. Contravening stereotypes of testosterone-addled adolescent boys, Eugenides' protagonists turn gazing from a carnal reflex into an occasion for the beguiling "aesthetic contemplation" that Fitzgerald's narrator prized. These apprentice gazers come of age together and by gazing together they cultivate both solidarity among themselves and sympathy for their shared gaze objects: five elusive, alluring, unanimously suicidal teenage sisters. Also presented *en suite*, these sisters belong to an aloof, engimatic neighborhood family, the Lisbons. Thus rather than focusing on a single female body, Eugenides' neighborhood gazers treat their preoccupation with the Lisbon girls as a sustained interpretive social inquiry. Collectively, the boys hope that what appears at one point as "all dots and dashes" might crystallize as "the interpretation" of these sister's behavior, which might definitively "tell [us] with authority … what the girls felt" (163–164). Consuming their entire adolescence, these inquisitive gazers' repeated attempts to encompass and understand

their objects, with the assistance of traditional spyglass technology—
binoculars and a telescope (141, 142, 184, 195)—yield only unassem-
bled "pieces of the puzzle ... oddly shaped emptiness ... countries we
couldn't name" (241).

The most beguiling of the sisters, the one who made herself most
visible to these boys' gaze (136, 140–145), Eugenides named Lux
(for *light*), underscoring the gap between what these apprentice gazers
sought and what they never found. Ultimately, their collective gazing
produces the condition Mulvey described as the "eroticized phantas-
magoria" that "make[s] a mockery of empirical objectivity." Thus the
narrative arc of *The Virgin Suicides* constitutes yet another challenge to
Mulvey's claim for the empowering and pleasuring effect of male gazing. Eugenides illustrates how, despite all our miraculous technologies of
visual enhancement, "the power of" men's "erotic look" to "investigate"
and "demystify" seems fated to falter.

GENTLEMEN

'Faith' is a fine invention
When gentlemen can see
But microscopes are prudent
In an emergency. Emily Dickinson (#185)

If any social group in the English-speaking world, especially throughout the British Empire and the American South, has been positioned
to command as Mulvey envisioned, it's likely to consist of the gentlemen that Emily Dickinson singles out in "Faith Is a Fine Invention."
Dickinson contrasts conditions that allow men "to see," or at least to
believe that they can see, with the blinding "emergencies" that impede
seeing, like the suicides and other mishaps that repeatedly draw emergency medical personnel to the Lisbon home in *The Virgin Suicides*. In
a poem beginning with the noun "faith" bracketed by quotation marks,
Dickinson pushed up against the limits of male gazing and the impetus
to "command" that (in Mulvey's view) motivates gazers. In the space of
four lines Dickinson telescopes three centuries of paradigm shifts from
Luther through Copernicus and Newton to the discoveries of her older
English contemporary Charles Darwin. These discoveries called "faith"
into question to such an extent that Dickinson apparently needed to
quarantine the whole concept of faith inside quotation marks.

Dickinson scholars date the composition of this poem to the early 1860s. Not only was Dickinson composing in the faith-shattering aftermath of the 1859 publication of Darwin's *Origin of Species* (Guthrie, Willis). During these years, her nation also endured its most seismic "emergency," the Civil War, which, a scholarly consensus holds, had a profound impact on Dickinson's writing (Wolosky; Pollak). Understood crudely but candidly, the Civil War can be plausibly (if offensively, even unutterably) understood as a crusade to save the absolute privilege or "command" that law and custom had long granted to a large class of male gazers, a caste that tradition allowed to confer upon themselves the title of *gentlemen*. Popular and some supposedly scholarly histories tend to treat the Civil War as a contest over slavery in general or, among a diminishing number of apologists and "whitewashers" (Ball), over a red herring called "states rights." Recently, though, Civil War histories have begun to consider slavery as an institution that guaranteed and helped sustain itself by guaranteeing "southern gentleman" and many of their less "genteel" (white) subordinates unchallengeable sexual access to women held in bondage. Paul Oliver has characterized such custom-sanctioned rape as a virtual rite of passage: "casual and often brutal unions enforced by the younger southern white men who often marked their adolescence with the rape of a slave girl" (70). "The extreme brutality" of these rapes Oliver judged especially "staggering" in a culture "that prided itself on the courtly manners and aristocratic bearing of the Southern Gentlemen." With this "ritual" in mind it may not be much of a stretch to add sociopathic adolescent sexual entitlement, neuronally and hormonally fueled and buttressed by three centuries of tradition, to our history teachers' more G-rated lists of "the causes of the Civil War." In the face of increasing antipathy to slavery and growing resistance to the apologist "reasoning" sustaining it among their fellow Americans, "Southern Gentlemen" were facing as Dickinson wrote a dire "emergency": an existential threat to their freedom to rape with impunity and to their absolute privilege of seizing the enslaved objects of their gaze and doing with them whatever they wanted.

Writing during the Civil War, John Stuart Mill descried how the caste-wide visceral shock of this threat provoked these (armed) "gentlemen" to view themselves as victims (Gallagher and Nolan 197–198). In his apocalyptic celebration of the demise of this privilege, Mill prophesied that "the day when slavery can no longer extend itself, is the day of its doom. The slave-owners know this, and it is the cause of their fury" (190).

Threatened by the kind of all-encompassing "emergency" to which Dickinson referred, "southern gentlemen" and their dependent followers took up arms to maintain their "right" to seize at will whatever enslaved woman or girl they gazed upon. In order to sustain an entitlement infinitely more consequential and unimaginably more brutal than the vicarious power that Mulvey would ascribe to twentieth-century male moviegoers, the Americas' slave-owning gentlemen precipitated the most dire emergency in American history.

IN AN EMERGENCY

Nearly every emergency so-named is a metaphor, since few actually experience "emergencies" as *emerging*. As flashing lights and blaring sirens too often remind us, emergencies tend to overwhelm and even ambush victims and witnesses alike; in emergencies sufferers and observers face what Wordsworth once experienced as "untoward thoughts." Such an emergency can become (as Dickinson implicitly argues in "Faith") an opportunity for the reflection and meditation Wordsworth promoted in poems such as "Resolution Independence."

> ... it sometimes chanceth, from the might
> Of joy in minds that can no further go,
> As high as we have mounted in delight
> In our dejection do we sink as low;
> To me that morning did it happen so;
> And fears and fancies thick upon me came.

In my lifetime, one poet in particular built a career on exploiting and exploring this understanding of poetry as a response to emergencies. *Meditations in an Emergency* by Frank O'Hara may be the most durably canonic volume of poems published in the USA during the Cold War. In 2009, some fifty years after its publication, a reminder of this durability surfaced in an episode of the most acclaimed TV drama to premiere during the millennial decade: *Mad Men*, a series cited for the way it "explore[s] the male gaze and the damage it can wreak" (Lyons). Early in the second season of this perennial Emmy favorite, series protagonist (and relentless male gazer) Don Draper buys O'Hara's collection after being told at a Greenwich Village bar "I don't think you'd like it ("For Those Who Think Young"). After reading *Meditations in an Emergency*, Draper finds himself struck by a line in the book from a poem celebrating another notorious male gazer, the revolutionary-era Soviet poet Vladimir Mayakovsky. Titled simply "Mayakovsky," this poem evokes the sense of emergency heralded in the book's title, a reference to the "catastrophe of … personality" (202)—a likely allusion to Oscar Wilde's realization that "catastrophes in life bring about catastrophes in Art" (Ellmann 532). Writing in the (London) *Times*, Stephen Amidon argues that in these lines from *Meditations in an Emergency*, by "the most 'interesting, and modern' poet at work during the … time frame of *Mad Men*," O'Hara echoes Draper's thoughts and adds "another layer to this most complicated of television heroes" ("O'Hara").

The title poem of *Meditations in an Emergency* opens as a lament over lost love followed by a plea for "boundless love" (197). The poet's meditation then turns to the vicissitudes of gazing, an unsurprising turn since in an earlier poem O'Hara confessed his proclivity for gazing by describing himself as "wear[ing] a hook in my look to be sexy" (121). In "Meditations in an Emergency," the poet's "eyes" come to stand for his entire self, the body parts that might enable him to "do something." Acknowledging this pressure to "do something," O'Hara's "meditator" succumbs grudgingly to the "duty to be attentive" and thus to the "anxiety"-ridden objects that surround him. Thus he finds himself subservient to "things"—the condition that vexed Emerson when he lamented in his 1836 "Concord Hymn" that "things are in the saddle and ride mankind." Accordingly, O'Hara's thing-ridden speaker objectifies himself, and, surrendering, grants agency to things. With this surrender, he relinquishes the male position of being in "command" with which Mulvey endows male gazers. Thus subjugated, O'Hara's speaker faces his "emergency" or the "catastrophe" cited in "Mayakovsky."

In "Meditations in an Emergency" this catastrophe takes the form of "Heterosexuality!…inexorably approaching." Thus O'Hara casts the "orientation"—or the "sexuality"—customarily aligned with the norm that male gazing assumes and supposedly sustains as a threat rather than as a secure position of command and control. After identifying this threat, the speaker parenthetically wonders, "how discourage her?" The pronoun "her" implicitly answers the poet's question—by turning "heterosexuality" itself into a woman, subject to the speaker's command. Facing this threat of normative sexuality, O'Hara's "meditator" proclaims himself an irrepressible life force driven by "the ecstasy of always bursting forth" to "will my will," in order to escape an exhausted "plot" or "trap" envisioned as a narrative ambush: "a final chapter no one reads because the plot is over." The poem's rhetorical confidence and metaphorical density assure the speaker's escape by transforming him into a "famous ... mysterious ... legend" who needs only to "spit in the lock and the lock turns." The ensuing exit springs him from the "trap" set by his jilting lover, by unrequited affection and attraction, and by normative sexuality.

Throughout *Meditations in an Emergency*, O'Hara treats male desire itself as a chronic emergency and depicts defeated gazers as mock-victims of such "emergencies." In "The Hunter," for example, the speaker describes a generic, seemingly prehistoric rite of passage. The title character, "the hunter," has completed this rite of passage and appears triumphant, even in "command": "manna fell ... he was now approved, and his strength increased ... He thought, why did I come? And then, I have come to rule" (167). In a sudden reversal, though, "the hunter" ends up "humiliated" and exposed, "alone in the clouds," at the very point of asserting his dominion. O'Hara's sequencing suggests that this reversal sets in as the hunter becomes a male gazer, when he looks to "rifts in the clouds, where the face of a woman appeared, frowning."

Elsewhere in *Meditations*, in "Jane Awake," O'Hara impersonates a (heterosexual) male gazer well known to readers of English poetry and particularly to students of the Romantic sublime. After opening with blazons celebrating "the opals hiding in [Jane's] lids" and how her "curls tumble languorously," O'Hara's speaker transforms his gaze object from a source of pleasure into a threat. In place of a beautiful experience, which reassures the gazer with a sense of control, male-gazing becomes a sublime experience, which (working as "the sublime" is supposed to) overwhelms the gazer (Burke). As Jane turns "unsmiling" and "savage," her "volcanic flesh" reveals its power to defeat the men who might search her out. She can "strangle policemen" and "hide everything from the watchman." The police and the watchman arguably represent male authorities empowered to observe and apprehend Jane. Closing the poem by speaking in a first-person plural voice, O'Hara has established an alliance with his gaze object against these authorized male gazers and thus pays deferential homage to the "savage" resistant object of male gazing.

"WHAT MAIDENS LOTH?"

Like countless poets before him, O'Hara's explorations of male gazing often looked to the canon and in particular to classical mythology as O'Hara does in one of his early poems, "An Image of Leda," which also shows gazers overwhelmed. O'Hara presents them as "spread-eagled" and cowed by the "cruelty" of cinema, rather than in command. Instead of accepting defeat, though, the speaker in "An Image of Leda" celebrates the compensatory rewards of movie-going, particularly the deceptive "pleasure in loving a shadow and caressing a disguise" (36). In arguing for this view of gazers as cheerfully subjugated, O'Hara seems to have been responding to a predecessor's image of Leda and answering the question that closes perhaps the most unsettling male-gaze sonnet in the Anglophone canon. The question, which William Butler Yeats's posed in 1924, in "Leda and the Swan," focuses on the impact of gazing on the gaze object. "Did she put on his knowledge with his power?," Yeats's speaker demands to know at the end of the sonnet. Among British and American poets, Yeats stands out as a notably versatile male gazer. His gaze stances range from resigned understatement in "A Drinking Song," which concludes "I look at you and I sigh," to the steadfastness of the wandering Aengus whose gaze transformed a "silver trout" into "a glimmering girl" whom he pursued till the end of time. "When You Are Old" features a subtler though equally persistent male gazer, a superannuated writer paying retrospective homage to a lost lover's perennially irresistible "changing face."

The vantage point in Yeats's Leda sonnet is that of a witness, an inquisitive voyeur in fact. He watches a rape by Greek mythology's most notoriously predatory male gazer, Zeus (disguised in the Leda legend as a swan). Yeats casts Leda in what Mulvey deems women's "traditional exhibitionist role." In this role, women become part of an "erotic spectacle ... simultaneously looked at and displayed, with their appearance coded for strong visual and erotic impact" and "displayed as sexual objects." This "erotic spectacle," Mulvey argues, serves "to freeze the flow of action in moments of erotic contemplation." In a narration that recounts "the action of the protagonist" rather than that of Leda Yeats's speaker plays the male gazer almost exactly as Mulvey describes him: "by means of identification" and "through participation in" Zeus's power. Yeats completes the scenario Mulvey spelled out when he "allows the spectator"—the speaker of the sonnet and its readers—to "indirectly possess" Leda along with the omnipotent, all-commanding Zeus.

After serving as the object of Zeus's gaze and bearing the brunt of his impregnating assault, Leda became, in Greek mythology, the mother of Helen of Troy. Thus allusively acknowledging the political (dynastic) repercussions of Zeus' gaze, Yeats's speaker's account of what he witnessed proceeds to raise a series of speculative questions. In the last of these Yeats's speaker wonders whether Zeus's victim "put on" Zeus's divine "knowledge" as a result of being subjected to his heedless "power."

By provoking readers to imagine rape as a source of "knowledge" in "Leda and the Swan," Yeats anticipated O'Hara's less objectionable account in "An Image of Leda," of movie-going as a transformative, educational assault. In raising similar questions about the relationships between knowledge and power in "An Image of Leda," O'Hara also plays the interrogator. Like Yeats, he inquires into the effects of gazing on gazers and on gaze objects and into feelings of diminishment and empowerment that gazing can occasion. But instead of setting the gaze exchange in the timeless open space in which Yeats positions his witness, O'Hara situates gazing in a twentieth-century movie theater. In contrast to Yeats, O'Hara eschews the distant observer's stance in favor of that of a genderless participant in a communal ritual (watching movies), a spectator who at once gazes and feels gazed upon. Like Leda and like Yeats's speaker in "Leda," who needs an entire quatrain to find his subject (and even to reach the grammatical subject of his opening sentence), O'Hara and his fellow movie-watchers appear at a loss. "The cinema," variously "cruel" and "like a miracle," takes O'Hara's community of gazers by surprise. These movie-goers find themselves, as Yeats depicted Leda, "caught up" and "mastered." When "the empty white space," the movie screen as O'Hara pictures it, "suddenly despite us... blackens," the audience's experience transforms them into vulnerable gaze objects. This vulnerability subjects them, like Leda, to a vanquishing power:

> ... naked
> on the river bank
> spread-eagled while
> the machine wings
> nearer.

By insisting that "there is no message," O'Hara prompts an interrogatory response akin to the questioning with which Yeats concluded his "Leda" sonnet. Instead of delivering a message, a lesson, or a conclusion, O'Hara's speaker also asks questions:

... Is
it our prayer or
wish that this
occur? Oh what is
this light that
holds us fast?

Even though in asking about the relationship between knowledge and power Yeats closed with an apparently open-ended question, this closural device allows readers to treat this closing question as a rhetorical question with "no" as its answer: nothing learned, nothing gained, from the rape of Leda. Yeats's sonnet's third quatrain, split by the following sentence fragment, nods allusively to the sonnet's Homeric source and thus stresses the lack of "knowledge"—of foresight and wisdom—that brought bloody catastrophe to the heirs of this union, to their kin and to their countrymen.

The broken wall, the burning roof and tower
And Agamemnon dead.

Though not decisively answered, O'Hara's questions in "An Image of Leda" (35) also prove less than entirely open-ended. Without expressly answering the poet's questions about prayers, wishes, and light, "An Image of Leda" does end with an affirmation. As the movie-goers collectively embrace the deception and manipulation to which "the cinema" subjects them, they transform their subjugation to the movies and their apparent "disgrace" in being so subjugated into a gender-neutral carnal pleasure.

A half-century after "Leda and the Swan" and a generation after "An Image of Leda," Mulvey would come to present movie-watching as an agent and expression of men's Zeus-like power over women. When he wrote "An Image of Leda" in 1950 O'Hara was, *avant-la-lettre*, articulating Mulvey's point that "cinema satisfies a primordial wish for pleasurable looking." But he was also solving the problem that agitated Mulvey. He was dispelling her claim that "pleasurable looking" among movie-goers is one-sided, resting as it does on an "active and passive heterosexual division of labor." O'Hara's move to sever the supposed satisfactions of "command" from the pleasures of gazing in general and male gazing in particular antedates twentieth-century movie-going and the controversies Mulvey's intervention has prompted over the past several decades—including the argument I've just staged between O'Hara's and Mulvey's understanding of the movie-watching experience.

Among the landmarks of English poetry, this disjunction between the powerlessness of the gazer and the pleasures of gazing itself appears perhaps most memorably in the poetry of John Keats. Probably his most recognized poem (thanks to its endlessly debated ending), "Ode on a Grecian Urn," traces the working of a repeatedly thwarted inquirer for whom gazing (apparently at "maidens") becomes an ambitious pursuit to determine what humans can know and what humans should know. All-encompassing wisdom instructing readers about "all ye know on earth and all ye need to know" is the lesson the ode's speaker claims to have learned from the inanimate object, the titular Grecian urn, that cues his reflections. Keats begins the poem by immediately displacing its title. Instead of considering the titular object, "a Greecian urn," or any inanimate object, Keats's ode's speaker begins these reflections as a would-be male-gazer. Looking, as male gazers typically do, at images of women, he opens his mediation by asking, "what maidens loth?" Nothing in the poem, however, indicates why the speaker believes that the women pictured on the urn's surface are maidens rather than, say, courtesans or mothers. And even though "maidens" in effect instructs the reader to think of these figures as virgins, the speaker's very interest in virginity, his very first concern, also reminds us that these women are potentially—perhaps inevitably—sexual actors. Keats's disclosure of his speaker's sexual preoccupation anticipates similar explorations in one of American fiction's most influential texts, a work that appeared a century after Keats's odes: Sherwood Anderson's 1919 volume *Winesburg, Ohio*. Like Keats' "Grecian Urn" speaker, Anderson's *Winesburg* narrator also concentrated the male gaze on "maidens" as objects of the male gazer's desire. In contrast to Keats's voiceless maidens, though, Anderson exposed the maidens in *Winesburg* to harassment that prompted them to "protest shrilly" ("Hands") and to attentions that allowed them to enjoy quiet "half expressed intimacy" ("The Thinker"). Anderson's focus on maidens raises questions similar to those raised by Keats, Yeats, and O'Hara about the disconnect between the alleged omnipotence of male gazing and the apparent impotence of many gazers. Anderson graphically illustrates this dissonance in his account of the courtship of one of Winesburg's most sought-after maidens. Interchangeable gazers at first, her "suitors ... talked to her of passion and there was a strained eager quality in their voices and in their eyes when they looked at her" ("Twisted Apples"). Eventually, two rival "suitors" with diametrically opposing courtship styles emerge from this pack:

> The two who were different were much unlike each other. One of them, a slender young man with white hands, the son of a jeweler in Winesburg, talked continually of virginity. When he was with her he was never off the subject ... For hours she sat in silence listening as he talked to her and then she began to be afraid of something. Beneath his talk of virginity she began to think there was a lust greater than in all the others. At times it seemed to her that as he talked he was holding her body in his hands. She imagined him turning it slowly about in the white hands and staring at it.

Persuading his gaze object that his "staring" is as forceful as an embrace, this suitor possesses the object of his gaze as much as the speaker in Keats's Grecian urn ode had held and beheld the mystifying urn in his hands. Though this suitor consequently seems commanding enough to make *staring* and *holding* interchangeable, his courtship fails: he loses to a rival, "a black-haired boy with large ears" who "said nothing at all but always managed to" maneuver the maiden "into the darkness" (where gazing becomes impossible) "where he began to kiss her" until "she became in the family way."

Opposing Selves

The rivalries between gazers that Anderson depicted, the tensions between emerging and lingering zeitgeists that plagued Mr. Palomar, the cognitive elusiveness of the gaze objects themselves as they appeared on Keats' Grecian urn are only a few of the frustrations confronting male gazers who read and write about the objects of their gazes and the experience of gazing itself. What I hope has become apparent by now is the extent to which such obstacles may shape and complicate male-gazing in ways that the male-gaze conversation Mulvey set in motion some forty years ago hasn't taken into account. What I hope has become even more apparent is the extent to which Mulvey's intervention didn't simply inaugurate a contemporary conversation but also contributed to the much older, more or less timeless male-gaze discourse, that has kept these complications and obstacles alive.

In his Pulitzer-winning 1964 volume of poems *77 Dream Songs* John Berryman painfully and comically confronted these complications, most memorably in the fourth of these dream songs. Composed in 1963, the year in which, according to Philip Larkin, "sexual intercourse began," Dream Song # 4 features Berryman's alter-ego as an over-eager would-be participant in the genesis Larkin heralded (see Chaps. 1 & 5). This persona (named Henry throughout *The Dream* Songs) begins his song by recalling a vexing instance of male gazing. Sitting in a restaurant with "dazed eyes," hungering and "fainting with interest," at the sight of a fellow patron's "delicious body ... the hottest one for years of night ... black hair, complexion Latin, jeweled eyes," Henry first assumes the thwarted gazer's stance, which he intermittently strikes throughout *77 Dream Songs* and in Berryman's second book of *Dream Songs* in 1969. In the later volume, in Dream Song 350, Henry elaborated this stance, by confessing his preoccupation with "all the girls ... their tops and bottoms and even ... their middles." Even a photograph "from Heaven" of a Miss Birnbaum, whose "knees, harmful and fair," fill the world, "tortures" and "trances" Henry in Dream Song 227 so much that he finds himself longing for

> a medium where 'Fuck you' comes as no curse
> but come as a sigh or a prayer.

The two forms of expression with which this dream song ends, with "a sigh or a prayer"—both often expressions of need and privation—mock the promise of "command" that, Mulvey insists, gazing fulfills. The gazer's disempowerment, lamented throughout the dream songs, cumulatively comes to stand for the limits that repeatedly stymie Henry over the course of both Dream Songs collections. "Burdened with feeling," Robert Pinsky argues, Henry experiences "feeling [as] beyond or apart from action" with the result that "the "pressure against such limits" distinguishes Berryman's art (29) and, arguably, characterizes most memorable articulations of the male gaze.

In Dream Song 4 this pressure includes the primal (and, many would argue, mythic) competition for women Freud postulated in both *Totem and Taboo* and *Moses and Monotheism* (see Chap. 6). This influential Freudian construct, among several Freudianisms that inform Berryman's poetry (Bloom, *Stock* 73), helps account for what "makes *The Dream Songs* an original book" (Vendler, "Poetry"). The primal foe Henry faces appears mid-poem, in the middle distance of the confined restaurant space Berryman pictures. This rival, rather than Henry, commands this space, so that the gaze object at a nearby table "might as well be on Mars." This rival has not only the advantages of proximity and attachment; he also has the numbers on his side: "the fact of her husband and four other people kept me from springing on her." The thwarted gazer's sole recourse entails rhetorically degrading his rival, a total stranger, turning him into "the slob beside her." Kept at a distance and denied a seat at the table where "the slob beside her feasts," Henry has, as a gazer, only the paltry compensations of speculative imagining. "What wonders is she sitting on, over there?" Henry asks before admitting failure and reproaching himself by suggesting, "there ought to be a law against Henry" and concluding, plausibly, that "there is." While "a law against Henry" may seem needed to constrain Henry's wayward desire, the need for such a law may rest as much on what Henry says and on how he says it as it does on his errant gaze and on what he claims to want. When Larkin links the beginning of sexual intercourse with the end of state censorship of *Lady Chatterley's Lover* he heralds—grudgingly to be sure—an era of candor. Such candor is reflected both in Henry's profession of desire and in the self-disciplining self-condemnation it occasions.

Berryman's call for a "law against" only "Henry," rather than for restrictions on all male gazers, implicitly frees other gazers, including Berryman's readers, from feeling bound by such "laws." Unlike Keats' 1820 Grecian Urn speaker or Anderson's 1919 *Winesburg, Ohio* suitors, male-gazing poets in 1963 and beyond were free to consider and call attention to whatever "wonders" they imagined their gaze objects to be sitting on. Translated from Latin, "Annus Mirabilis"—Larkin's title for this announcement of a new age of sexual intercourse and frank writing about it—means "wonderful year" or "year of wonders." Such wonders might plausibly include the "wonders" invoked but never specified in Dream Song 4. Helen Vendler identifies the poem as Berryman's "picture of the Id at work, checked in its lust by Conscience ... a poem unthinkable in American poetry before the postwar Freudian era" ("On 'Dream Song 4'"). Vendler's *Zeitgeist* emphasis in praising Berryman's 1964 poem indicates why readers might readily recall Larkin's proclamation of 1963 as the dawning of a new age of wonders and delights for male gazers, a transformation heralded in *Time* magazine, at the beginning of 1964 (the year the *Dream Songs* first appeared), as the "second sexual revolution" ("Morals"). Such newly emancipated male gazers included readers and writers inspired by this much-hyped revolution and finally permitted to give free reign to their inquisitiveness by asking, along with Henry, "what wonders"?

OBJECTS

What Vendler refers to as the "postwar Freudian era" glibber observers, more broadly and more loosely, sometimes sanguinely and often querulously, simply call "the sixties" (Perlstein; Farber). Just as the liberation as a male gazer Berryman showed Henry pursuing met with resistance from his "slob" rival in Dream Song #4 and met, according to Vendler, with resistance from "Conscience," throughout the Dream Songs, the broader liberation Larkin heralded has also faced resistance ever since the 1960s. However influential, Mulvey's critique of male gazing has been one of many contributions to this ideological and conceptual resistance.

What many feminist critiques of male gazing shared was an aversion to what countless critics typically rebuke as the objectification of women. Such censures became an indispensable, invaluable trope in the broader egalitarian agitation that still distinguishes the 1960s and its enduring legacy. Consequently, the very noun objectification has itself become, according to philosopher Martha Nussbaum, "a pejorative term, connoting a way of speaking, thinking, and acting" that whoever uses the word "finds morally or socially objectionable" (249). Nussbaum attributes this stigmatizing simplification to one tendency in "feminist thought," which "has typically represented men's sexual objectification as ... a central problem in women's lives, and the opposition to it as the very heart of feminist politics" (249–250).

As Nussbaum explains, reflexively stigmatizing objectification has discouraged attention to the ambiguities as well as the morally and political neutral inevitability of objectification. Perhaps the starkest, most rigorously materialist recognition of Nussbaum's postulate was voiced by the Marxist theorist and polemicist, Frantz Fanon, when he acknowledged "here I am an object among other objects" (89). More recently Paula Rabinowitz has argued that

> objects tell stories. In the 1960s when feminists argued
> against women's position as sex objects, demanding
> subjectivity, objects acquired a lousy reputation [even
> though] they have something to say (21).

In this light and in its historical contexts, Berryman's "law against Henry" represents an effort to deflect, if not legitimate, such rebukes, which came to include by the early 1970s Mulvey's avowedly polemical male-gaze essay along with Kate Millett's *Sexual Politics*. This surprise 1970 bestseller remains one of the most influential critiques of the literary objectification of women (Freedman 318).

In recent years a counter-critique has emerged as women writing about the gaze object's experience after the millennium have set out to remedy the oversimplifications that Nussbaum and Rabinowitz have challenged. In her 2014 novel *The Wallcreeper*, for example, Nell Zink talks back to the feminist censures of objectification that have become reflexive over the past generation. Zink shows her narrator invidiously subdividing the male gazer's foci to explain why she experiences traditional objectification as preferable to a more insidious form of objectification. Thus, recalling her Montenegrin lover, Zink's narrator concludes that "objectifying my body saved him from objectifying my mind" and thus from exercising any control over her "thoughts" (22–23). Vendela Vida's 2015 novel *The Diver's Clothes Lie Empty* captures, from a gaze-object's perspective, the contradictorily edifying and diminishing experience of objectification. Vida's narrator observes how her blind date is "looking at your face," how "he leans over and softly takes your chin in his large hand, and tilts your head to the side. With the fingers of his left hand he brushes the bangs of the wig out of your face so that he can see you more clearly" (167). Whatever else may motivate the male gazer in this exchange, Vida's narrator precisely and with sardonic appreciation registers the effort this gazer had made to her see clearly.

In recent works of fiction, perhaps no gaze object has relished her objectification as enthusiastically as one of the filmmaker narrators of Dana Spiotta's 2016 novel *Innocents and Others*. Eulogizing her much older lover, an *a-clef* Orson Welles avatar, she recounts how he

> ... wrote love letters to me. I found them in my books ... I would read about my lips ... my long legs in shorts and loose socks. Yes. They were about my body, but a body is part of you and there's no getting around it even if you want to. Besides, I liked the attention to my body details ... I hadn't had that before. (22)

In this recollection the pleasures of reading itself converge with the adolescent satisfactions of realizing the limits of received wisdom, including traditional moralists' and post-Mulvey feminist vilifications of men's "attention to" women's "body details."

More discursively, in her 2010 memoir *Possession*, Elif Batuman set out to repair the damage this multi-generational animus toward objectification has inflicted (Hawkesworth 83–84). Grappling with the oversimplifications that continue to burden gazers and their objects, Batuman speaks as a proponent of what she calls "interdisciplinary materialism" (247). Adapting this doctrine (with tongue in cheek) from the Frankfurt School of critical theory, Batuman argues *for* the necessity of objectification because it provides a means of conceptualizing sensory stimuli, of integrating love and learning, affection and curiosity, and of overcoming the "alienation" that so vexed the Frankfurt school (Wheatland 344):

> Walking back to my apartment, I passed the laundry room. Warm, detergent-scented air gusted from vents near the floor and a stereo in the open window was playing Leonard Cohen's 'First We Take Manhattan': *I love your body and your spirit and your clothes.*

> What is it you love, when you're in love? His clothes, his books, his toothbrush. All of the manufactured, formerly alienated commodities are magically rehabilitated as aspects of the person—as organic expressions of actions, of choice and use. (Batuman 80)

Batuman compares this aesthetic contemplation of inanimate objects to the passion with which "scholars … pore over articles that once belonged to" the figures from the past whom they study. As Batuman dialectically frames the concept of objectification, it can reflect both the oppressive power play typically attributed to male gazing *and* some more aspirational and edifying curiosity-driven motives for erotic gazing.

In her 1955 story "Good Country People," Flannery O'Connor ascribes such feelings, the sense of wonder and the desire for cognitive enhancement Batuman describes, to an itinerant bible salesman named Manley Pointer. At first O'Connor casts him as a stock-figure con man, a sexual predator intent on seducing Joy Hopewell, a prospective customer's daughter. Throughout the story O'Connor repeatedly stresses Joy's lack of conventional attractiveness and in describing Manley Pointer's first glimpse of Joy, O'Connor also intimates that Manley Pointer may be motivated by impulses other than lust or even the will-to-power that preoccupied Mulvey:

> He was gazing at her with open curiosity, with fascination, like a child watching a new fantastic animal at the zoo (*Stories* 283).

Manley Pointer's objectifying seems to be motivated by morally neutral materialist curiosity—at once childlike and quasi-scientific. But as in much of O'Connor's fiction, as the narrative unfolds, the gazer's motivations prove arguably far more sinister than those ascribed to stock, lecherous gazers. This seducer doesn't crave his gaze object's body. He fixates instead on the prosthesis she wears in place of the leg she lost in childhood. Manley Pointer absconds with this wooden leg at the end of "Good Country People," adding to a collection he boasts of that includes another prosthetic body part, a glass eye (291). In the course of insinuating a possibility of morally neutral "open curiosity" gazing, before revealing both Manley Pointer's stereotypical exploitiveness and his atypical curiosity, O'Connor articulates a more severe, more graphic, more literal, and more sophisticated critique of the objectifying gaze than our prevailing male-gaze conversation usually affords us. By pairing Joy Hopewell, an intellectually imperious hubris-driven gaze object, with Manley Pointer, O'Connor introduces a gaze object as morally compromised as her assailant. Thus O'Connor extends her understanding of male gazing beyond reassuring gender binaries. And by ultimately disclosing the object of Manley Pointer's gaze as literally an *object* detached from Joy Hopewell O'Connor dispels the considerations of sexual attraction that male gazing supposedly rests on.

Writing, as always, as a rigorous Catholic moralist ("Church"), O'Connor also exposes the ground on which all critiques of objectification inevitably rest, including the prevailing antagonism toward objectification that 1960s progressive politics has made axiomatic among social critics and scholars. In censuring sexual objectification, many post-1960s academics and intellectuals—or "innerleckchuls," as an earlier O'Connor character calls them (*Wise Blood*, 159)—often neglect the reactionary contradiction implicit in their reflexive antagonism to objectification (see the discussion of *Wise Blood* in Chap. 2).

This antagonism made for an especially odd coupling for emerging "new left" movements and the emancipatory rhetoric pervading the 1960s. Antipathy to acknowledging the object-hood of other humans reflects thinking mired in pre-enlightenment (religious and Platonist) mystifications and in the platonic transcendentalisms that survived the skepticism of the French *philosophes* and the materialism of the Scottish Enlightenment. This obscurantism, widespread among late twentieth-century radicals and counter-culturati, reflects what Susan Sontag condemned in 1966 as "the platonic devaluation of the world (and of its heir, that 'popular Platonism' known as Christianity)" (*Against* 262). The 1960s Left's anti-objectification legacy harkens back, ironically, to the most influential post-Enlightenment transcendentalist, Immanuel Kant, who denounced "objectification" so vehemently that his denunciation devolved into call for renouncing sexual desire altogether:

> sexual love makes of the loved person an Object of appetite; as soon as that appetite has been stilled, the person is cast aside as one casts away a lemon which has been sucked dry ... as soon as a person becomes an Object of appetite for another, all motives of moral relationship cease to function, because as an Object of appetite for another a person becomes a thing and can be treated and used as such by every one. (163)

While touted as "new" and "revolutionary, much about the radical critiques associated with the 1960s turned away from the Enlightenment "materialist tradition" (Meeker 20), the matrix of three centuries of progressive thinking. Such critiques disavowed the "desentimentalizing" and "somaticization of the human subject" that shaped "emergent modernity" (19) and with it the philosophical materialism that nineteenth-century radicals and liberals (Marxists, Benthamites, Comteists) adapted from the Enlightenment, from Paris physiocrats and Edinburgh skeptics alike. To refuse to recognize that, most fundamentally, humans are objects, whatever else we try to make of our humanity, is to deny this legacy. The wholesale stigmatizing of objectification verges on advocating a return to an "age of faith" in intangibles, a reactionary repudiation of one of modernity's fundamental insights as characterized by Terry Eagleton:

> Human beings are among other, more glamorous things natural material objects, and if they were not so there would be no possibility of relationship between them. Objectification is by no means always a vice (563).

The very durability of this faith in what's unseen, unproven, and undemonstrable may account for Emily Dickinson's derisively "praising" faith as a (verbal) "invention," which men and women turn to when the evidence of our senses disturbs and provokes us. From this perspective, contemporary objectors to objectification can be said to have joined a long line of transcendence affirming, immanence-resisting believers: Christians, Platonists, many but not all capital-R Romantics, and small-r romantics—sentimentalists and the euphemizers of all stripes who still dominate our public conversations. When they balk at treating bodies as objects, critics of objectification leave little choice but to conceive of human subjects as being *more than* our bodies, as belonging to some super-phenomenal realm—an absolute or higher realm beyond quotidian matter and sense perception (Abrams 184–185). This is the view that the Left's most prominent intellectual ancestors, Karl Marx and Friederich Engels, mocked as the German ideology. This "ideology," which descends from heaven to earth" rather than "from earth to heaven," has traditionally legitimated the power of "phantoms in the human brain" and sustained "the nonsense which ... may hold men together" by compelling us to believe that "'spirit' is afflicted with the curse of being 'burdened' with matter."

The case *for* objectification, a legacy of this venerable materialist critique of the coercive mystifications long promoted by both religious authorities and philosophical idealists, usually figures in the political and economic controversies engendered by Marxist and post-Marx social critiques. These materialist arguments also have an aesthetic dimension, which legitimates the thinking now so often reflexively discredited as male gazing. As Susan Stewart explained in *On Longing*, objectification needs to be understood as morally neutral and perhaps even psychologically inevitable. All objectifying entails removing what we take to be "natural ... from the present flow of events" (150) with "our attention ... continually focused upon boundaries and limits of the body ... as an object" (104). With this objectifying knowledge, Stewart continues "adult desire" transforms "the body" into "a pure object" (125). This argument, that "adult desire" *requires* objectifying, seems to relegate idealizing the body, denying or mystifying its status as an object, to children—and to intellectually underdeveloped "grownups."

An edgier argument for mature objectifying, in Shulamith Firestone's *The Dialectic of Sex*, appeared at about the same time as Kate Millet's more influential *Sexual Politics*. Firestone, subtitling *The Dialectic of Sex* as "The Case for Feminist Revolution," opened with an epigraph quoting that arch-materialist Engels and argued throughout her critique against abstraction and idealization (148–150). Rather than disavowing objectification itself (177–178), as did many influential feminists of her generation, Firestone observed that objectification in and of itself isn't inevitably an instrument of oppression. Treating objectification as synonymous with (the politically and aesthetically fraught noun) "representation," Firestone called for freeing the "objectification" of women's experience from the "male bias" that "saturates" it and for the end of uni-directional objectification (167). As if warily and even admonitorily anticipating what Mulvey would argue a few years later, Firestone warns against stigmatizing objectification:

> Sex objects *are* beautiful. An attack on them can be with an attack on beauty itself. Feminists need not get so pious in their efforts that they feel they must flatly deny the beauty of the face on the cover of *Vogue* (175).

Male gazing, according to Firestone's reasoning, needn't be an instrument of command or an assertion of control.

This argument speaks to the aesthetic Wallace Stevens articulated in 1945 in "Esthetique du Mal" (313). He warned that "the greatest poverty is not to live in a physical world" and thus allow "one's desire" to become "too difficult to tell from despair." Stevens' warning echoes in Firestone's admonition against "attacking beauty." Such thinking makes a case for male gazing as a variegated aesthetic experience rather than as the crude political move that Mulvey (at least early in her career) vilified.

FROM WINDOWS 0.0 TO KALEIDOSCOPY

What such arguments suggest is that as an effort to engage with material "beauty" male gazing requires aesthetic cultivation. In light of the countless opportunities for gazing now available, the kaleidoscope, or even the "kaleidoscope eyes" once blazoned by the Beatles (see below), may now seem like a more supple instrument for gazing than the microscopes and telescopes, the spyglasses and binoculars discussed earlier in this chapter. Almost two centuries ago Søren Kierkegaard spelled out the value of gazing kaleidoscopically or vertiginously, as he described this practice, upon the "multitudinous variety" that kaleidoscopes bring into focus. In the "Diary of a Seducer" section of *Either/Or*, where Kierkegaard writes in the voice of his "seducer" title character, the philosopher recalls Shakespeare's infinitely various Cleopatra; recounts what happens "when I have gazed and gazed again, considered and considered again this multitudinous variety ... then gather fragments into unity"; and goes on to proclaim that "the man who feels no impulse toward the study of women is no aesthetician" (72–73).

Such a figure, the male gazer as aesthete and would-be seducer, serves as the focal point of Edith Wharton's Pulitzer Prize-winning novel *The Age of Innocence* (see Chap. 2). Wharton's gazer, Newland Archer, comes to appreciate, without ever fully attaining it, the modern ideal of seeing kaleidoscopically. This story, which spans some fifty years starting in the 1870s, begins by introducing opera glasses as Archer's preferred means of gazing as he undergoes his "masculine initiation" into the tribe Wharton designates "masculine New York."

Wharton first shows Archer as "he scanned the opposite side of the house"—along with the novel's omniscient narrator—as part of a clique of male gazers. "The house" refers to the theater where these gazers, who presage the moviegoers Mulvey would envisage, have gathered to watch an opera. Instead of watching the opera on the stage, Gounoud's *Faust*, these gazers direct their attention elsewhere. They've all "turned their opera-glasses critically on the circle of ladies" seated in "the box which was ... attracting the undivided attention of masculine New York." The eye-catching box includes two young women: the would-be society matron May Welland and her prodigal cousin, the exotic "Europeanized" Countess Olenska. May first appears as "a young girl in white with eyes ecstatically fixed on the stage-lovers" as "a warm pink mounted to the girl's cheek, mantled her brow to the roots of her fair braids, and suffused the young slope of her breast to the line where it met a modest tulle tucker fastened with a single gardenia." Gazing on "this miracle of fire and ice" inspires in Archer "a thrill of possessorship in which pride in his own masculine initiation was mingled with a tender reverence for her abysmal purity." By following her detailed catalog of May's physical attributes with the adjective "abysmal," Wharton insinuates a dissonant note into Archer's reverie. Modifying the idealizer's desideratum, "purity," this adjective serves as an early warning to readers that Archer's impulse to idealize rather than objectify may end badly—or at least sadly.

Archer's fellow gazers, with whom he shares a (men's) "club box," direct his attention away from May and from "the young slope of her breast" to the "theatrically" displayed "bosom" of the slim young countess.

> ... a little less tall than May Welland, with brown hair growing in close curls about her temples and held in place by a narrow band of diamonds. The suggestion of this headdress, which gave her what was then called a 'Josephine look,' was carried out in the cut of the dark blue velvet gown rather theatrically caught up under her bosom by a girdle with a large old-fashioned clasp. The wearer of this unusual dress, who seemed quite unconscious of the attention it was attracting, stood a moment in the center of the box.

What Archer experiences as he gazes on May with a sense of "possessorship," an attitude akin to male gazers' supposed sense of command, differs sharply from what he focuses on when he looks at the countess. Gazing on her, he sees the empress to whom Wharton alludes: Bonaparte's consort Josephine, who reigned with him at the peak of his power and who was, by many measures, a woman in "command." Struck by the countess's imperial aura, Archer becomes bemused at her air of indifference to the social authority of "masculine New York"—on matters of pedigree and taste—which Wharton's narrator ascribes to two of the senior club-members in Archer's box.

As the plot unfolds, both May and the countess continue to be subjected to Archer's gaze. Even after his marriage to May, Archer intermittently woos the countess until she returns to Paris to live out her days with a once-and-future lover. Widowed at the end of his story, Archer persists in gazing at an image of the absent May. His early idealizing, though, has subsided into prosaic objectification. Her tree-like body has become in retrospect a knickknack like the inkstand beside it or at best an *objet d'art*, on which to hang the clothes that enabled her to have once seemed so "abysmally pure":

> His eyes, making the round of the room … came back to the … first photograph of May, which still kept its place beside his inkstand. There she was, tall, round-bosomed and willowy, in her starched muslin and flapping Leghorn, as he had seen her [during their engagement] so she had remained.

Posthumously, according to Wharton's narrator, it's the adornment of May's bosom and May's head, rather her "purity," that lingers in her husband's memory.

Though less inclined to relinquish "abstract" idealizing entirely, Newland has also transformed the countess into a two-dimensional object by the end of *The Age of Innocence*:

> When he thought of Ellen Olenska it was abstractly, serenely, as one might think of some imaginary beloved in a book or a picture: she had become the composite vision of all that he had missed. That vision, faint and tenuous as it was, had kept him from thinking of other women.

In this final chapter Archer learns from his son what readers had learned much earlier—that it was May, as a member of "a conspiracy of mothers and aunts and grandmothers," and not the countess, who plotted effectively to keep Archer monogamous and to keep him (as he had imagined his bride) "pure." Rather than gazing to establish and maintain command of the stage of action, according to Mulvey's view of gazing, Archer comes to realize that his gazing has worked to restrain him. Wharton underscores this view of Archer as a subdued gazer in the last paragraph of *The Age of Innocence*. On a trip to Paris, Archer demurs when offered an opportunity to visit once more with and to gaze once more at the countess. Archer opts to gaze instead at what obstructs his living gaze, at a "shadow of reality."

> Archer sat down on the bench and continued to gaze at the winged balcony … Then he tried to see the persons already in the room … among them a dark lady, pale and dark, who would look up quickly, half rise, and hold out a long thin hand with three rings on it … He thought she would be sitting in a sofa-corner near the fire, with azaleas banked behind her on a table. 'It's more real to me here than if I went up,' he suddenly heard himself say; and the fear lest that last shadow of reality should lose its edge kept him rooted to his seat as the minutes succeeded each other. He sat for a long time on the bench in the thickening dusk, his eyes never turning from the balcony. At length a light shone through the windows, and a moment later a man-servant came out on the balcony, drew up the awnings, and closed the shutters. At that, as if it had been the signal he waited for, Newland Archer got up slowly and walked back alone to his hotel.

This passage subjects Archer to someone else's control of the stage of action that, in Mulvey's view, gazers supposedly dominate. The "signal" Archer reacts to also marks the culmination of many such moments throughout *The Age of Innocence* showing Archer making the stage-management efforts akin to those of the countess' "man-servant." Such passages show Archer manipulating windows, shades, the opera glasses that seemed *de rigeur* among members of Archer's club, and other optic frames, so as to control what's "real" to him. One of Archer's most decisively manipulative moves to control and regulate his own gaze—and perhaps evade the matriarchal conspiracy he unknowingly faced—takes place in one of the novel's few traditionally "masculine" domestic spaces and as Archer practices the only "abiding occupation" his home afforded:

> He had insisted that the library curtains should draw backward and forward on a rod, so that they might be closed in the evening, instead of remaining nailed to a gilt cornice, and immovably looped up over layers of

lace, as in the drawing-room; and he pulled them back and pushed up the sash, leaning out into the icy night. The mere fact of not looking at May, seated beside his table, under his lamp, the fact of seeing other houses, roofs, chimneys, of getting the sense of other lives outside his own, other cities beyond New York, and a whole world beyond his world, cleared his brain and made it easier to breathe.

Perhaps attuned to if not aware of the conspiracy he faced, Archer finds this refuge threatened and feels the perspective it provides completely overturned by an innocuous request from May: "Do shut the window."

> He pulled the sash down and turned back … and he felt like adding: 'But I've caught it already. I *am* dead—I've been dead for months and months.' And suddenly the play of the word flashed up a wild suggestion. What if it were *she* who was dead! If she were going to die—to die soon—and leave him free! The sensation of standing there, in that warm familiar room, and looking at her, and wishing her dead, was so strange, so fascinating and overmastering, that its enormity did not immediately strike him. He simply felt that chance had given him a new possibility to which his sick soul might cling. Yes, May might die—people did: young people, healthy people like herself: she might die, and set him suddenly free … as he passed he laid his hand on her hair. 'Poor May!' he said. 'Poor? Why poor?' she echoed with a strained laugh. 'Because I shall never be able to open a window without worrying you,' he rejoined, laughing also. For a moment she was silent; then she said very low, her head bowed over her work: 'I shall never worry if you're happy.' 'Ah, my dear; and I shall never be happy unless I can open the windows!' 'In THIS weather?' she remonstrated; and with a sigh he buried his head in his book.

By allowing May the last word, a reproach, Wharton emphatically, if implicitly, establishes the extent to which May remains in command of Archer's gaze as well as his stage of action.

Wharton, however, depicts Archer as reluctant to abandon his search for a serviceable optic by ascribing to him an interest in a more complex vision-enhancing instrument than a window. When he moves beyond May's domestic sphere, Archer explores "the New York of literary clubs." At "first shake," Wharton's narrator observes, this worldly milieu began to "seem [to Archer] more of a kaleidoscope." Once Archer became familiar with it, though, literary New York "turned out, in the end, to be a smaller box, with a more monotonous pattern." Taking a broader view, aiming to "look at his native city objectively," Archer's gaze falters. Trying out a more straightforward and traditional perspective, Archer ends up gazing "through the wrong end of a telescope" and turns his gaze to his immediate foreground where he finds the countess

> ... bent over the fire, stretching her thin hands so close to it that a faint halo shone about the oval nails. The light touched to russet the rings of dark hair escaping from her braids, and made her pale face paler.

Over the course of the decades that *The Age of Innocence* encompasses, the kaleidoscope—etymologically, a tool for observing beauty—wins out over opera glasses, telescopes, and windows. In a closing rhetorical question, Wharton has Archer acknowledge, without entirely accepting its implications, the life around him as a "huge kaleidoscope where all the social atoms spun around on the same plane."

Thus appreciating the twentieth-century's emerging kaleidoscopic sensibility Wharton decisively refutes the position voiced by the narrator of the 1920s' most durably popular novel, *The Great Gatsby*. Early on in *Gatsby* Wharton's young friend F. Scott Fitzgerald has his less-than-reliable narrator complacently assert that "life is much more successfully looked at from a single window, after all." The rest of the narrative proceeds to discredit this claim with proliferating perspectives, often the perspectives of male gazers, including those of the Dutch sailors who first espied "the green breast of the new world" invoked at the end of *The Great Gatsby*.

The plots in both *The Great Gatsby* and *The Age of Innocence* leave their gazing heroes stymied—notwithstanding their manifest material advantages. Wealth, leisure, and status all fail to secure for them that commanding mastery Mulvey ascribes to male gazers. Archer's defeat may have proved less dire and less dramatic than Gatsby's murder on the estate he purchased as a vantage point for gazing on his ever-elusive Daisy. Nevertheless, the failure of Archer's gaze holds more implications for the politics of gazing. This failure extends beyond the way he looks at women. It encompasses his willful withdrawal from modernity, which Wharton couples with his preference for windows over the emerging kaleidoscopic perspective she describes.

Echoing D.H. Lawrence's "allotropic" understanding of fictional characters' ego-instability (*Letters* 78), Philip Kitcher has characterized this modernist perspective as the tendency of supposedly fixed characters to dissolve and fuse with kaleidoscopic rapidity" (5). This perspective would enable Archer to examine, perhaps even appreciate his immediate material circumstances. This attentiveness seems to motivate Archer to accompany his son Dallas, whom Archer associates with modernity, in visiting the countess. The impending face-to-face reunion between Archer and the countess would promise, in turn, to renovate, complicate and enrich— add new dimensions—to Archer's gaze. Thus his last-minute demurral at seeing the countess marks conclusively his withdrawal from and his disa-vowal of the distinctly modern kaleidoscopic perspective Kitcher cites.

This view of single objects from varied perspectives and the concomi-tant understanding of character as containing multiple reflections pro-duces the effect that Theodore Dreiser delineated *in Jennie Gerhardt* (see Chap. 3). While Wharton described Archer resisting this "glitter," Dreiser positioned Archer's contemporary, the *Jennie Gerhardt* protago-nist Lester Kane, in the center of modernity's kaleidoscopic turbulence.

Unlike Kane, a commanding gazer and seducer, Archer declined to accept and perhaps even embrace the promise of an emerging epistemo-logical paradigm. As Wharton finally depicts him, Archer stands between the "two iconographic ages" that Roland Barthes anatomized in his ana-lytic homage to Greta Garbo (56–57). For Barthes, how a man gazes corresponds to how he lives in history. The encounter, the opportunity, Archer eschews when he turns away from the countess's flat constitutes what Barthes designated "an Event." "An Event" Barthes identified with the gaze-experience Audrey Hepburn's screen image provides in contrast to the more Platonic gaze-experience Barthes identified with the "Idea" of Greta Garbo.

> the face of Audrey Hepburn, for instance, is individualized, not only because of its peculiar thematics (woman as child, woman as kitten) but also because of her person, of an almost unique specification of the face, which ... is constituted by an infinite complexity of morphological func-tions ... The face ... of Hepburn [is] an event. (57)

In *The Age of Innocence* "an event," an experience of "infinite com-plexity," can include both a face-to-face visit to the contentedly settled countess and, more broadly, the kaleidoscopic experience of modern cities. When Archer opts to remain "lost in" and fixated by the resid-ual "Platonic Idea of the human creature [as] an essence ... not to be degraded," he refused the multi-dimensional, time-lapse gazing so many of his contemporaries were discovering and articulating, Wharton and among them.

Among early twentieth-century gazers, Dreiser's and Wharton's contemporary William Butler Yeats articulated such discoveries in two poem sequences that allow gaze objects to speak on their own behalf. In his "Crazy Jane" sequence and his "A Woman Young and Old" sequence, Yeats presents women who speak and are spoken about during various phases of their lives, in an array of circumstances, recalling their relationships and their experiences as gaze objects.

The speaker in "A Woman Young and Old," for example, appears to be interrogating an off-stage gazer.

> Why those questioning eyes
> That are fixed upon me?

This interrogation targets artists as well as lovers and addresses the gaze object's recognition of her central place as an art object:

> All stately women ... seemed a
> Quattrocento painter's throng,
> A thoughtless image of Mantegna's thought—
> Why should they think that are for ever young?
> Till suddenly in grief's contagion caught,
> I stared upon his blood-bedabbled breast
> And sang my malediction with the rest.
> That thing all blood and mire ...
> Half turned and fixed a glazing eye on mine,
> And, though love's bitter-sweet had all come back,
> Those bodies from a picture or a coin
> Nor saw my body fall ...
> Nor knew ...
> That they had brought no fabulous symbol there
> But my heart's victim and its torturer.

These lines rehearse an incessant contest between gazers claiming the command Mulvey ascribes to them and an object of this gaze as she learned to resist. This never-to-be-resolved push-and-pull turns gazing itself kaleidoscopic: a catalyst for amplifying and enhancing vision rather than a definitive instrument of any man's or any men's command.

WAREHOUSE EYES

The so-called counterculture associated with the 1960s encapsulated this catalytic reciprocity in a single phrase: "kaleidoscope eyes," which appeared in 1967 as a track on what's arguably the single most important rock album ever produced, even the most important "popular event of the era" (Lytle, 218): *Sgt. Pepper's Lonely Heart's Club Band*. In his pioneering 1967 essay "Learning from the Beatles" Richard Poirier singled out one song on this album, "Lucy in the Sky with Diamonds," as enacting the band's signature agenda: to resist reductive monolithic conclusions about what the Beatles and their listeners see and hear (*Performing* 133). The song's "kaleidoscope eyes" metaphor underscores this resistance by endowing the gaze object, Lucy, the elusive muse who "calls" upon the singers to "answer" *her* question in the opening verse, with the power to summon rather than simply be summoned like traditional muses:

> Somebody calls you, you answer quite slowly/
> A girl with kaleidoscope eyes.

The attention to *her* eyes and to how *she* sees, moreover, transforms Lucy from the gaze object in the "picture" that the opening line cites into a gazer gifted with the power to see kaleidoscopically—to reshape, shake up, and expand what we get to see—and with whatever advantages and authority this endowment affords her.

Among rock performers during these years, kaleidoscopy became an appealing trope. In the year that *Sgt Pepper* was released Bob Dylan released his first greatest hits collection. As an insert, this LP featured a now iconic poster of Dylan. Designed by the 1960s' era-defining illustrator Milton Glaser, the poster bore the title "Bob Dylan with the Kaleidoscope Hair."[2] Glaser depicted Dylan's head (his hair and/or his brains) gorgon-like in profile. Most vividly, this allusion to the gorgons of Greek mythology recalls the power of the best-known Gorgon's—Medusa's—scourging counter-gaze and argues for the unisex availability of Medusa's power (in keeping with the spirit of the age—or at least with the spirit of its sartorial fads). This image also emphasizes Dylan's stylistic extravagance and what many of us fans then regarded as his intellectual

---

[2] Glaser, "Bob Dylan with the Kaleidoscope Hair." http://www.sweetbooks.com/pictures/SKB-14607.jpg.

depth, while Glaser's own style testifies to an apparently popular belief in kaleidoscopy's powers of penetration. In many of his songs of the sixties, Dylan promoted this view and tested these powers. He set out, like the Beatles, to "infuse the imagination of living with other possibilities" (Poirier, *Performing* 139).

In large part, this agenda is reflected in Dylan's emergence during the 1960s as perhaps popular culture's most versatile and kaleidoscopic male gazer. This seems to have required a concerted effort on his part, since, when he first came East in 1961, he viewed himself more as a *telescopic* male gazer. As he recounts in a 2004 memoir:

I gazed ... across the street to an office building where I could see a blazing secretary soaked up in the spirit of something ... scribbling busy, occupied at a desk in a meditative manner. There was nothing funny about her. I wished I had a telescope (*Chronicles* 8).

Three years, later, Dylan performed a song that helps explains his evolving motives and increasingly complex epistemology as a gazer. Singing "I'd be curious to know if you can see yourself as clear as someone who has had you on his mind," Dylan adds another perspective to the uni-directional gazing his memoir describes ("Mama You've Been on My Mind"). He also embraces as motives for gazing both curiosity and the same need for clarity that Emily Dickinson avowed in asserting a preference for microscopes over faith.

Dylan's 1966 double LP *Blonde on Blonde* marks a culmination of this transformation. Pride of place on *Blonde on Blonde* belongs to "Sad Eyed Lady of the Lowlands," at the time the longest uninterrupted rock-album track ever. This track takes up an entire side on *Blonde on Blonde* and serves, according to Dylan's most eminent scholarly critic, Christopher Ricks, as a palimpsest of approaches to male gazing (107). The song's refrain repeatedly calls attention to the singing gazer's own "warehouse eyes." Ricks plausibly hears the phrase "warehouse eyes" ambiguously. These ambiguities call to mind some of the tritest ways of referring to eyes metonymically in characterizing how men look at women. These ambiguities include "whorehouse eyes" and (more obliquely) a timeworn description of how women and men look at one another with "bedroom eyes." Dylan's warehouse metaphor, though, might also stand alone as a fundamental trope for many gazers' point of departure. Call it the storage function of male gazing that Kierkegaard's diary-writing seducer seemed to have in mind, boasting in his diary that "women will always offer an inexhaustible fund of material for my reflection" (72).

This attitude among seducers, among empowered gazers, may have seemed as applicable to Dylan's contemporaries as to Kierkegaard's and even perhaps to Dylan himself at the peak of his celebrity during the mid-1960s. Repeatedly offering his "warehouse eyes" to the "lady" in the song, though, cumulatively seems to transfer—or smuggle—the prerogatives of gathering, storing, and owning the gaze object's image across gender boundaries. Consequently, "Sad-Eyed Lady of the Lowlands" ends without establishing the gazer's commanding position. Instead of emerging empowered, the singer depicts his gaze object as defiant and perhaps unassailable and indestructible, asking "Who among [your suitors] do you think could destroy you?" In repeating this refrain throughout the song, Dylan keeps changing the verb in each verse so that verses with verbs such as "impress," "resist," and "persuade" all precede the verse featuring "destroy." Cumulatively, this pattern renders the male gazers' motives more diffuse and less compelling. Before reiterating the supplicant's question, "Or sad-eyed lady should I wait?" Dylan's resounding sexual pun, the reference in each refrain to "the sad-eyed prophet [who] says that no man comes," empowers the song's titular gaze object to deny her beholders sexual pleasure—the satisfaction of *coming*—and shows her presiding over a realm in which she commands prophecy and repels all comers.

Several other tracks on *Blonde on Blonde* also explore the anxieties vexing male gazers while testing the artistic opportunities male gazing seems to afford. One of the LP's lesser-known songs, "Temporary Like Achilles," announces this weakness with its very title. This title allusion to Homer's *Iliad* and to its hero, arguably the fiercest warrior and the most tenacious gazer known to literature, identifies the song as a meditation on weakness, for which Achilles (thanks to the myth of his "Achilles heel") may be even more famous than for his courage and passion. The opening verse, moreover, doubles down on this preoccupation with male weakness with the singer fretting about "feeling so harmless." The singer's preoccupation with unmanning weakness resonates punningly as a distinctly phallic weakness in a plaintive refrain importuning the singer's beloved not to be "so hard." Addressing his gaze object in the second person, he positions himself as "standing by your window trying to read your portrait." This verb sequence—*stand, try, read*—stresses both the difficulties and the temptations of gazing. With the double mediation—a framed window and a presumably framed reproduction—Dylan evokes both the will to gaze in action and some familiar, literally structural, inevitably mediating obstacles to gazing. Showing the gazer "reading" instead of *watching* or *viewing*, moreover, accentuates the intellectual or conceptual dimension of gazing. This view of male gazing as an act of "reading" also recalls Kierkegaard's seducer's description of the male-gaze object as integral to an "aesthetician's" "fund for reflection" (72). Like Kierkegaard, whose seducer ultimately preferred—as the god "Neptune did for a nymph"—to turn his gaze object "into a man" (80), Dylan repeatedly sabotaged such moves to aestheticize the women characters on *Blonde on Blonde*. For example, in one of the verb-shifts in the "Sad-Eyed Lady of Lowlands" refrain he positions the gazer at a cognitive impasse as he confesses his intellectual failure, asking "Who … can think he could outguess" the gaze object who obsesses and bewilders him?

The kind of gender-bending or gender-blending sabotage that Kierkegaard envisioned distinguishes the *Blonde on Blonde* track that Dylanologists continue to find notoriously perplexing. "Just Like a Woman," released as a 45-RPM single and one of only a handful of Dylan songs to become a top-40 radio hit, has earned a reputation as both a "complete catalogue of sexist slurs" (Meade) *and* as a "feminist ballad" (Marz). This divergence of reactions may rest in part on the title simile. The phrase "just like a woman" implies at first glance that the singer has *command* over his subject and enjoys the authority that legitimates the generalizer's certainty. But doubts about this authority proliferate as this simile changes with each reiteration in the song's refrain. This reverberation cumulatively deflects the reductive certainty that the adverb "just" often aims to establish, since in the top-40 version the accent in this refrain fell mostly on "like," an indication that the speaker is guessing. Thus, increasingly, the entire song functions like a series of guesses about what women are *like*. The singer gestures at explaining this lack of command over himself, his thoughts, and his "woman" by interrupting this series of guesses with a flashback to a time a when he was "hungry," dependent on or subservient to his gaze object. During this break, the singer finally concedes to his gaze object that, despite harping on her fragility, or "breakability," where they first came together was in "your world" rather than in a space, on a "stage," that was his to "command," as Mulvey would argue almost a decade later.

In the LP's other radio hit, a raucous plaint importunately titled "I Want You," the singer surrenders command even more decisively. One verse begins with the singer introducing a woman he "talks with," perhaps a lover too, as a "chambermaid," a woman traditionally treated as a subordinate employee and all-too-often disrespected as a powerless sex object, subject to each hotel guest's "command." The sexual charge in the verse rests on the singer's boast that he's "not afraid to look at her." But he follows this boast with a concession. Revealing his insecure position in this relationship, he surrenders the gazer's power to see panoptically—his command of the stage of action in Mulvey's paradigm—to his gaze object. In a decisive power inversion, the singer acknowledges losing the power that gazing supposedly affirms, when he admits that "there's nothing she doesn't see."

Such perceptual and cognitive failures becomes most pronounced on *Blonde on Blonde* in "Visions of Johanna." One of the album's longest, most narratively suggestive, and character-laden tracks, its very title identifies it as a meditation on looking at a woman. Recalling the other gazers and stymied inquirers on *Blonde on Blonde*, this gazer finds himself pressed to ask "how can I explain?" What makes this song a more complex meditation than most of the album's other tracks is the introduction of several alternate or surrogate gazers. The most thwarted of these may be the figure who's supposed to be exceptionally attentive and who's officially authorized—and paid—to gaze: "the night watchman." Despite or perhaps because of his commanding position, this unseen night watchman, in what Dylan stages as a moment of illumination, ends up questioning his own sanity and apparently that of whomever he "watches": "We can hear the night watchman click his flashlight ask himself if it's him or them that's insane." The watchman's question unanswered, the singer's perspective shifts to a view of the singer's gaze object—to one vision of Johanna—as an elusive, intangible apparition: "a ghost of 'lectricity" who "howls in the bones of her face." In electrifying his gaze object, characterizing a woman's face as charged with electricity, the singer has literally empowered Johanna, attributing to her the power that enables and controls modern life. Singing the noun electricity with two brusque trochees as "'lectricity," Dylan may be highlighting the threat of electricity rather than the civilizing comforts the electric industry has traditionally promised. As Dylan envisions it, electrical power appears, moreover, to be emitting the intimidating noise of an animal traditionally personified in referring to a *male* sexual predator: the "howling" of a wolf.

In between the watchman anecdote and the electrical ghost image Dylan counterpoints the fear and bemusement male gazers face, by introducing Joanna's surrogate, Louise, to the scene:

Louise, she's all right, she's just near/

She's delicate and seems like the mirror[3]/

But she just makes it all too concise and too clear/

That Johanna is not here.

A powerful—articulate and cognitively competent-gaze object in her own right—Louise serves as a reminder of Johanna's conceptual elusiveness as well as of her physical unavailability, her absence from the very stage that Mulvey's male gazers supposedly command.

"Visions of Joanna" also recalls one the most venerable traditions in European poetry and painting, the conflation between spiritual aspiration and sexual yearning, the practice among poets and painters of spiritualizing their own lust. When the singer frets that "Madonna still has not showed" he expresses his longing but leaves open the question of what exactly it is that he desires. Dylan doesn't specify what the singer actually wants from or wants to see in Madonna. Is it divine inspiration or carnal comfort? In an earlier verse, with a reference to Johanna's "farewell kiss," the singer signals that the likely answer is the latter.

This answer echoes William Blake. One of English poetry's most forthright champions of carnal desire and of trusting our senses, Blake warned that the failure to act on one's desires "breeds pestilence" and urged readers to "cleanse the doors of perception" (*Marriage*). The Blake allusion in "Visions of Johanna" introduces yet another troubled gazer, a character called "Little Boy Lost," who shares a sobriquet with the title character of one Blake's brief lyric monologues in *The Songs of Innocence* and the title of an anti-clerical protest in Blake's *Songs of Experience*. In both poems, the title character—the little boy—weeps helplessly. Though Dylan's "little boy" is a grown man, he, too, appears overwhelmed by abjection and so inured to it that "he

---

[3] "the mirror": sometimes sung as "veneer".

brags of his misery" and associates his thwarted desire with "living dangerously." Though not weeping, this adult "little boy" also voices his inconsolability. The loss of his lover—the departure of his gaze object—has reduced him to dwelling on "her farewell kiss" and "muttering small talk" to which no one listens except "the wall"—and the generations of listeners who have eavesdropped on Dylan's meditations on male gazing.

Even though the "Visions of Johanna" singer misses Madonna and Little Boy Lost longs for a missing body and an absent listener, the song does offer listeners a glimmer of comfort and consolation or "salvation," as Dylan calls it. "Voices echo this is what salvation must be like after a while," he sings as he identifies "salvation" with a smiling gaze object, the most famous gaze object European art has produced—Leonardo DaVinci's *La Giocanda*: "Mona Lisa musta had the highway blues you can tell by the way she smiles." Thwarted gazers need to look, Dylan seems to argue, "inside the museums" and turn for salvation and consolation to Europe's secular aesthetic heritage, the "inexhaustible fund," available to male gazers (Kierkegaard 72). Distinguishing her from the *cinquecento* original, Dylan provides his twentieth-century Mona Lisa with a voice of her own ("the blues") and brings her into his own conversation as a fellow singer whose words, like Dylan's own, belong to an artist who "musta had the highway blues" as source and inspiration. As in the Beatles' "Lucy in the Sky" Dylan's modernizing and complicating of the gaze experience and his refiguring of gaze objects voices the growing understanding that Lorrie Moore has elucidated of "women not so much as sex objects but as sex subjects" for whom "men were the actual objects" ("Singular"). This turn may account for the co-incidence in 1966 of *Blonde on Blonde*'s various abasements of male gazers with the Mamas and Papas' top-10 hit "Words of Love," which warned that "longing gazes and worn-out phrases won't get you where you want to go."

On *Blonde on Blonde*, Dylan doesn't turn only to museums and Madonnas to depict and at times sabotage efforts to aestheticize gazing. He also turns, like Edith Wharton, to the most tangible and visibly ubiquitous form of popular aesthetics, fashion, especially fashion at its most glamorous. "Leopard Skin Pillbox Hat," another *Blonde on Blonde* track also released as a 45-RPM A-side, featured the signature millinery product of the 1960s, a product celebrated for its association with the decade's most celebrated and perhaps its most sympathetic gaze object, US First Lady Jacqueline Kennedy.[4]

The song opens with the singer bluntly identifying himself as a male gazer, informing his gaze object "I see you've got your brand new leopard skin pillbox hat." In spite of this forthright opening and the singer's apparent bona fides as zeitgeist reader, as at least a would-be fashionista, the bulk of his musings entangle him in uncertainty and disorientation, imploring his erstwhile lover that she "*must* tell" him how her "head feels under something like that." Subsequently this apparent empathy modulates into curiosity with the singer insisting that he just wants to "see if" her hat is "really that expensive kind" before shifting his curious gaze away from the hat to his ex's "new boyfriend," about whom he frets, "I never seen him before." The unfamiliarity of this "new boyfriend," a token of the primal competition among men Freud theorized, restores the singer's blunt certainty about what his successor "really loves" her for. What he "really loves her for," the singer concludes, is her "brand new leopard-skin pill-box hat." But as in a traditional dramatic monologue, where poets often make sure that the speaker reveals damning information about himself, Dylan shows the cocky singer, who "really knows" the score, entirely losing sight of his gaze object. He focuses on what he can't see and hasn't seen or has seen only at distance: through "the garage door." He admits to excluding from his cognitive range, from his field of vision, all that he purports to know, except for his gaze object's pillbox hat. By 1966 this product had become yet one more bit of pop ephemera in a decade teeming with them, rendering this gazer's elective myopia all the more pronounced.

During his 1960s career peak Dylan's interest in male gazing extended beyond his songs. The jacket design on some of his mid-1960s LPs repeatedly called attention Dylan's male-gazer persona. Like Anthony van Dyck, who moved in the 1630s to bring the gazing painter into the frame in *Titian's Mistress*, Dylan used his album jackets to similar effect (see Chap. 2). In 1963, the cardboard sleeve for *The Freewheelin' Bob Dylan*, Dylan's second album, shows the singer on a

<hr />

[4]Leopard-Skin Pillbox Hat. http://farm3.static.flickr.com/2378/2039227838_ef98ee4307.jpg?v=0.

Jackie Kennedy Pillbox Hat. http://lisawallerrogers.files.wordpress.com/2010/01/jackie-k-arrives-paris-may-31-1961.jpg.

windy city street clinging arm-in-arm to his longtime lover Suze Rotolo. His head tilts toward hers, hers rests on his shoulder, and their torsos overlap, leaving no daylight between them. Not only does the pose nearly close the distance between the gazer and his muse and gratefully acknowledged mentor (*Chronicles* 268, 277, 288). With his feet set a few inches further from the vanishing point than his companion's, Dylan seems intent on shielding her from the wind and perhaps from the invisible authorized gazer beyond the frame, Columbia Records' photographer Don Hunstein. Dylan's posture may also signal some resistance to what he regards as a threat to his exclusive gazing privileges.

Two years later, on the jacket of *Bringing It All Back Home*, Dylan's stance as a gazer, several feet in front of the woman with whom he shares the frame, appears decidedly less "freewheeling." A camera-lens iris eye superimposed inside a rectangular frame encloses a living room two-shot: Sally Grossman, wife of Dylan's manager, lounges in a scarlet sheath dress before a status-affirming neoclassical "great house" fireplace. Holding a cigarette vertically, like a teacher's chalk, she glares at both the photographer (Daniel Kramer) and at Dylan in the foreground. Surrounded by reading matter, Dylan looks up as if the camera has caught him at moment of uncertainty as to where to cast his gaze and as to where to position himself culturally amidst a mélange of words and images—LPs, magazines, a painting, a pamphlet, a fallout shelter sign—from which to choose. Amidst all the cultural bric-a-brac, the color of Sally Grossman's dress makes her the most eye-catching point in the frame. Her preeminence inside the frame seems to intimate that Dylan's own gaze will, like that of his album's buyers, turn in the direction that artistic convention demands and fix on Sally Grossman so that, despite his apparent wariness, he'll recover his position as the male gazer in the picture.

As a double LP requiring double album sleeves, *Blonde on Blonde* allows for a book-like open folio design. The front cover shows a full-color head shot of Dylan solo. Inside, a black and white photo montage includes Dylan offstage in command of his entourage—his manager, a photographer, an unidentified woman bending over to whisper to a seated Dylan. The long top-to-bottom center panel shows a medium shot of a woman entirely unconnected with this apparent backstage scenario. The photo shows the Italian movie star Claudia Cardinale in a dark blouse with some of its top buttons open, biting her lower lip.

During the 1960s Cardinale came to be associated with a cohort of European movie beauties—Sophia Loren, Brigitte Bardot, Jeanne

Moreau, Ursula Andress, Melina Mercouri, Anna Karina, Virna Lisi—who conquered US art houses over the course of the decade. In an early song, hopefully titled "I Shall Be Free," Dylan identified this group compositely with *his* American Dream by objectifying them, in a decidedly commercial vein, as America's most inspiring import. The singer in "I Shall Be Free" fantasizes about President Kennedy "callin' me up" and asking his "friend Bob" about what America needs "to make the country grow?" Bob replies by sharing with "my friend, John" the names of three of these Continental movie stars: "Brigitte Bardot, Anita Ekberg, Sophia Loren." In appropriating an image of one of these marketable European beauties for the centerpiece of the *Blonde on Blonde* montage (illegally, it turns out, since the photo appeared without Cardinale's permission and had to removed from subsequent reissues), Dylan staked his claim as a both a conventionally lecherous and an aspirationally cosmopolitan gazer. He also promoted himself as the equal of the most "commanding," the most powerful and most notoriously glamorous gazer in American history: JFK. At least JFK's equal in this anecdote, the singer may even be claiming to outrank the president of the USA by showing himself positioned to satisfy a "need" JFK acknowledges but can't satisfy on his own and to satisfy it in a way likely to prove especially gratifying to (heterosexual) male gazers across America.

The very extravagance of this conceit, of course, mocks the megalomaniacal chutzpah it voices, serving as yet another move by Dylan to ridicule male gazing and many male gazers' presumptuous, often self-sabotaging overreaching. Dylan recounts one such humbling realization in recollecting a discovery he made soon after moving to Manhattan in the early 1960s. While pondering "the kind of songs they played on the radio," he realized that he "had no ambition to stir things up" because "whatever you were thinking could be dead wrong" (*Chronicles* 34–35). This admission calls to mind tensions between *Blonde on Blonde*'s images of Dylan in command—the iconoclast star pictured on the LP's jacket—and the emotional unease of the various male gazers heard and heard about in the songs on the album. This tension indicates how much Dylan's work, like that of artful male gazers everywhere, argues with and challenges the artist's inclinations to gaze, objectify, and "command." Yeats imputed this tension to poetry itself, which he defined as the poet's argument with himself ("A Dialogue of Self and Soul").

Nearly a decade after *Blonde on Blonde*, in his phantasmagoric torch-song odyssey "Tangled Up in Blue" Dylan encapsulated, voiced, and pictured the endless unease of the male gazer by staging the kind of "argument" Yeats envisioned. The song appears on the album *Blood on the Tracks*, which Dylan released in the same year, 1975, that Mulvey introduced her male-gaze argument.

The singer in "Tangled Up in Blue" identifies himself as a seasoned male-gazer who's "seen a lot of woman." The song's narrative recounts an unexpected encounter with one of these women, an ex-lover who "never escaped my mind." Since they last met, she has become a professional gaze object now working "in the spotlight," "at a topless bar." The singer recounts watching her perform and then waiting till "the crowd thinned out" as he prepares "to do the same" until she approaches him, asking, "Don't I know your name?" The singer recalls having "muttered something under my breath as" the object of his gaze "*studied* the lines on" *his* "face" before bending down to tie his shoelaces, leaving him feeling "a little uneasy." This unease seems attributable to the transformation of the gaze object into the gazer and of the gazer into a gaze object. While the gazer can only mutter "something" indecipherable, his gaze object speaks forthrightly and keeps him from gazing exploitatively (at her breasts rather than her "face") as the unwritten rules of "topless bar" establishments direct. Both the gazer and his object, in effect, sabotage the establishment's fundamental business practice: the objectification of women's breasts. Within the space of this verse, the "uneasiness" that would normally afflict the gaze object shifts to the gazer. Dylan also turns the gaze object into the more actively engaged gazer or spectator in this encounter. While the gazer only "kept looking," without any apparent change of focus, the performer "studied" him, with near microscopic intensity, and seeing something amiss with what she saw took action to correct it. The poise and command with which this narrative endows the supposed gaze object become more pronounced in the verse that follows in which the gaze object becomes a source of transcendent wisdom when she hands the gazer a book filled with "words [that] rang true like burning coal." "Tangled Up in Blue" closes by insisting that the difference between gazer and gaze object has less to with the power and command that the gazer never claims and may rest on more on their conflicting commitment to see "from ... different point[s] of view".

One of Dylan's early songs about loving, losing, and gazing voices this conclusion more colloquially. In "One Too Many Mornings," on his *The Times They Are a-Changin'* album, Dylan expressly refers to the act of seeing as gazing and recounts literally losing sight of his gaze object on their "doorstep." Conjuring their parting and its setting, "where my eyes start fade," as a "room where my love and I have laid" [sic], the singer apostrophizes his "love" and concedes that "you're right from your side and I'm right from mine." Hardly the words of a commander, these lyrics reflect the relegation of this gazer, incapacitated with his "fading eyes," to the ranks of the countless chastened and thwarted gazers who populate so much modern writing.

CHAPTER 5

American Fiction After Mulvey

In his 2012 novel *Billy Lynn's Long Halftime Walk* Ben Fountain observes a soldier watching NFL cheerleaders at work. Intent on ensuring that these gaze objects receive "a considered look" (130), the novel's eponymous hero settles into the stands at the Dallas Cowboys' former home, Texas Stadium, and begins "walking his gaze down the row of women" and treating this gazing as "an experiment." As a result of this experiment gazing becomes for Billy an expression of intimate equality, "not a leering perv look but more like" the gaze "of a childhood friend" (147). The acclaim Fountain's novel garnered, including a National Book Award nomination, indicates the extent to which both appreciating and taming the male gaze has become a staple of American fiction since Laura Mulvey first coined the concept. In telling a millennial love story, Fountain treats as inextricable Billy's avidity as a gazer and his urgency to begin his sexual adulthood (26).

Billy's candor and scruples as a gazer recall the legacy (discussed earlier) that the British poet Philip Larkin commemorated about a decade before Mulvey's intervention, when he reminisced that "sexual intercourse began in nineteen sixty-three" (Larkin, 34). Though not a literal historical statement (Roth, *Reading* 16), the chronological exactitude of Larkin's stanza—"Between the end of the Chatterley ban/And the Beatles' first LP"—prompts readers to treat this "*annus mirabilis*" as a discursive watershed. It seems to mark the widespread acceptance of "sexual intercourse" (already a widespread practice) as discursively unremarkable.

© The Author(s) 2017
J.D. Bloom, *Reading the Male Gaze in Literature and Culture*, Global
Masculinities, DOI 10.1007/978-3-319-59945-8_5

The early careers of novelists Robert Stone and Philip Roth, both cel-ebrated and rebuked for making the most of this opportunity, roughly coincided with this discursive sea change. For Stone, this change author-ized writers "to value the Dionysian" (*Prime* 228). Roth valued this watershed for "legitimizing obscene preoccupations" and "intimate sexual revelations" as "usable and valuable" literary resources (*Reading*, 41, 16–17). Ever zeitgeist-sensitive, both novelists came to be associated with writing about the pursuit of "sexual intercourse." Both belonged to the "cohort" that Katie Roiphe, writing in 2009, praised for "reporting from a new frontier of sexual behavior ... all of [which] had the thrill of the new, or at least of the newly discussed."

Larkin's proclamation of 1963 as the "beginning" of "sexual inter-course" didn't appear in print until over a decade after the transforma-tion it heralded. Larkin's publisher released *High Windows*, the volume that includes "Annus Mirabilis," in 1974, just as a younger British writer, Laura Mulvey, was poised to enliven Anglophone sex discourse and make "the male gaze" a watchword for generations to come: a ready concep-tual tool for disclosing the way men writers have traditionally skewed their accounts of women characters to sustain traditional forms of male dominance and to affirm the primacy of heteronormative male desire. The ubiquity of Mulvey's insurgent insight among academics and intel-lectuals and its diffusion throughout mass culture (Burger) provided an opportunity for novelists with reputations like Roth's and Stone's as masculinity-obsessed (Amidon, *Guide*; S. Anderson; P. Smith), as "phal-locentric divas," or "old goats" (Kipnis, *Men*, 3; Max), to demonstrate their "keen ability to adapt" to the zeitgeist shift Mulvey instigated (Max).

Early in the administration of President Barack Obama, one of his advisors encouraged his team to treat the financial crisis they faced as "an opportunity." Roth's and Stone's work beginning in the 1970s reflects a similar reaction to the zeitgeist shift Mulvey helped catalyze, which Sally Robinson has characterized as the "crisis of white male authorship" (105). According to Robinson, this crisis inspired several prominent male writers to "work to remap the cultural and interpretive terrain" (105).

The titles of Roth's and Stone's novels from the late 1970s and early 1980s indicate how these novelists earned these reputations, how each became, as a Roth biographer describes his reputation, "a foil for femi-nists" (Pierpont 237). Roth's 1970s novels sport such titles as *My Life as a Man* (1974) and *The Professor of Desire* (1977). The less prolific

Stone's 1981 novel, *A Flag for Sunrise*, takes its title from an Emily Dickinson poem (#461) in which the poet seems to voice a woman's submission to her "Sire." Both novelists went on to complicate the ideological implications of such titles and the reputations their earlier fiction earned them by adapting to the critique implicit in the emerging attention to male gazing and by meeting the challenge this emergence presented.

One of Roth's late-career novels reveals how long and how intently this challenge preoccupied Roth. In *Exit Ghost*, the last of his many novels narrated by his favorite alter-ego and first-person narrator, Nathan Zuckerman, Zuckerman recalls a life- and career-defining moment and feels himself "transported ... nearly fifty years back, when gazing upon an exotic girl ... seemed to an untried boy to answer for everything" (150). The persisting primacy of gazing for Zuckerman crystallizes in the septuagenarian's realization, as he chats with the thirty-ish writer who beguiles him and who "provided the usual visual jolt" (84), that "I might have been gazing upon young womanhood for the very first time. Or the last. All-enveloping either way" (122). A year earlier, in *Everyman*, a successful Madison Avenue advertising executive (and formerly promising painter) looks back posthumously on his life as a failed spouse, estranged parent, and thwarted male gazer. Recalling a late-life stroll along the Jersey shore, he reminisces about a young "ad agency" employee he chatted up.

> She would have to be in her twenties...with her long crinkly hair tied back and her running shorts and tank top ... small as she was she might have been fourteen. He tried repeatedly to prevent his gaze from falling to the swell of her breasts that rose and fell with her breathing. This was torment to walk away from. (131)

This evocation of the never-to-be-resolved tension between the impetus to gaze and normative strictures against gazing may be the bluntest of many passages in Roth's work illustrating the pressure that the crisis Robinson analyzed, particularly the ongoing male-gaze conversation Mulvey inaugurated, exerted on Roth.

The title of Robert Stone's last novel, *Death of the Black-Haired Girl*, published two years before his death in 2015, tersely underscores the durability of his preoccupation with women's appearances. Stone repeatedly distinguishes this title character as a gaze object notable for her dazzling hair and astonishing skin (2, 54), though the narrative begins with her roommate's impression of her as a "white captive" (1), an anticipation of the fate that awaits her as a dazzling and astonishing gaze object. As this narrative unfolds Stone holds fast to the fascination impelling his narrator's gaze while crediting the basis for increasingly critical views of male gazing. Like Roth, Stone raises only to leave unresolved questions about what it means to live as a male gazer and to live with the consequences of male gazing.

Both Roth's and Stone's critical fascination with male-gazing became especially striking in 1998 with the publication of novels featuring women performing in public, soliciting male gazes and making a living as gaze objects. The narrator in each novel looks askance at the "traditional exhibitionist role" in which "women are simultaneously looked at and displayed, with their appearance coded for strong visual and erotic impact so that they can be said to connote to-be-looked-at-ness" (Mulvey, "Visual Pleasure"). Roth's *I Married a Communist* documents the career of a star of stage and screen, a woman whom Roth's narrator "hadn't been able to stop looking at… a beauty hovering between the darkly exotic and the softly demure… beauty that must have been spellbinding at its height… A beautiful woman with pathos and a story to tell" (53). Roth ironically ends this crescendoing hyperbole with a deflating sentence fragment and on a caustic fashion note by characterizing this "spellbinding" performer as "a spiritual woman with décolletage" (55). In a similarly wary vein, Stone's 1998 novel *Damascus Gate* features a cabaret chanteuse whose career began with her "wriggling into the black thing that hung in her tiny dressing room" and who learns over the course of her career to sport "a sweet professional smile" (93–95).

In both these descriptions, Roth and Stone seem at once to accept and to question Mulvey's provocation, staking out for themselves what Jennifer Glaser characterized, in reference to Roth, as an "ambiguous place" in the late-century "culture wars" (1465). Their fiction over the past three decades consequently shares a recognition that educated audiences will embrace both gender equality and sexual candor, even though these practices have often and influentially been treated as incompatible, thanks to much-breached, awkwardly and anxiously policed boundaries between candor and exploitation, erotica and pornography.

Addressing this problem, Stone and Roth, both of whom have, as part of the "cohort" Roiphe extolled, steeped their work in Eros, more notably in forthright lust verging on lechery. But they have also increasingly sharpened the gaze of their narrators by incorporating the critical edge that has made the male gaze a linchpin of feminist theory. Mulvey's influence seems to have made it virtually obligatory to recognize how desire operates as an instrument of power. As novelists keen to "adapt" (Max) to such conceptual turns, Roth and Stone have, over the past thirty years, increasingly confronted readers with the troubling implications of male gazing. In exploring the male gaze, moreover, both novelists also allow for a plurality of male gazes, demonstrating the limitations that subsequent theorists came to ascribe to Mulvey's "monolithic" account of the male gaze as "invincible" (Modleski 9–11).

By incorporating this recognition of Mulvey's influence and its limitations into their work, both novelists pique the passionate curiosity that drives the "higher order" male gazing documented throughout this book, while discrediting the will-to-dominance that Mulvey and critics following her have often associated with male gazing, and the desire it supposedly legitimates. As a result, Roth's and Stone's novels have come, more and more, to dwell on conflicts between regulated libido and the "sense of omnipotence" that male gazers, in Mulvey's view, characteristically crave.

In Stone's *Children of Light* and *Outerbridge Reach* and in Roth's *Sabbath's Theater* and *The Human Stain*, the novelists transform the male gaze from an index of a perennial power differential into an instrument for investigating the possibilities and limits of mutual recognition between men and women. These narratives also reflect on the promise and vicissitudes of heterosexual intimacy and on the challenges of representing heterosexual male desire without sanctioning the sexism or misogyny implicit in the male gazing theorized by Mulvey and her followers. The website "Reading Guide to Mulvey" (Harris) characterizes this misogyny as a power play for subordinating "female figures" to "appear in accordance with male fantasies," for "deliver[ing] the main female character into the hands of the main male protagonist," and for "deliver[ing] pleasure to the gazer with 'an illusion cut to the measure of [male] desire.'"

In Roth's oeuvre, the late-century preoccupation with male-gazing, from both the gazer's and the gaze-object's perspective, became most pronounced in his 2002 novel *The Dying Animal*. Presumably in consultation with the book's jacket designer, who incorporated a supine Modigliani nude into the cover design, Roth made a point of framing *The*

Dying Animal as a study in male gazing.[1] (Roth's sale of the film rights to the novel seems to have furthered this agenda. The 2008 Hollywood adaptation, retitled *Elegy*, features Ben Kingsley as the aesthete gazer and Penélope Cruz as his dying, eloquent and intellectually sophisticated love interest and gaze-object.) Allying this agenda with yet another gaze tradition, portrait painting, Roth's narrator ponders in the novel's final pages "a painting of Stanley Spencer's… a double nude portrait" of the artist and his wife, which depicts not only the object of male gazing but the gazer himself, inside the frame, in the act of "looking ruminatively down at her from close range through his wire-rimmed spectacles" (142–143).[2]

Published a year later, *Bay of Souls*, Stone's first post-millennium novel, encapsulates how male-gazing at once inspires and confounds the gazer, at once deepening and impoverishing his gaze. Stone's English professor protagonist in *Bay of Souls* cultivates the persona for which students honor him and the traits they ascribe to him: "the beauty that you have absorbed, the poetry and wisdom" (238). Throughout the narrative, this absorption takes the form of male-gazing. One Sunday after Mass, for example, the professor envisions his mistress, an accomplished scuba diver, as "a picture… among coral arches, her long body gliding past luminous tendrils or against the silky surface" and then watches his wife as she "took off her church clothes and put on a pair of tight jeans that caught his attention" (115). After depicting the gazer framing his lover as a "picture," Stone shows him framing his wife through "the front window" where he "stood… watching her rake winterkills in the yard." Stone's attention to framing here illustrates the control-seeking deliberateness of customary male gazing and recalls how male gazing requires gazers to "adjust our visual apparatus," ever trying and always failing to reconcile the mutually exclusive "incompatible operations" of seeing the object of our gaze and its mediating frame, as José Ortega y Gasset influentially explained in "The Dehumanization of Art," one of the charter documents of European modernism (9–10).

According to Walter Benn Michaels' explanation of "Modernist work," such framing has become a distinguishing characteristic of

---

[1] *The Dying Animal* front cover. http://upload.wikimedia.org/wikipedia/en/archive/6 /63/20130711205753!DyingAnimal.jpg.

[2] Stanley Spencer, *Double Nude Portrait.* http://c300221.r21.cfl.rackcdn.com/stanley-spencer-double-nude-self-portrait-with-second-wife-1348764039_org.jpg.

modernism and a seminal modernist trope. Its implication for male gazing rests on the extent to which framing "excludes" the beholder from
what he beholds and from being "absorbed into" the framed "site" (90).
Ortega's insight has colored Stone's work since the narrator of his first
novel, *Hall of Mirrors* (1966), described a "little window" as "quite
piece of show business" (87). The "incompatible operations," the vicissitudes of the "different adjustments" that Ortega registered, surface in
Bay of Souls, where Stone's gazer edits out the foreground frame, a television, which he had consciously planned on observing in the first place.
Stone follows this editing-out by showing the gazing professor divided
between a here-and-now gaze and a mind's-eye male gaze:

> Those warm curves at the hip and the choice ones at the seat. The center
> seam cut taut, deep in. It was strange, ever since Lara had come into his
> life he had been in a state of sexual tension that focused itself equally on
> the two women. He was in different ways besotted with both of them. The
> high-pitched ache of desire was *always one sensation away*. (115, emphasis
> added)

The narrator's conclusion stresses the extent to which male-gazing dis-
tances what it sees instead of closing in on it. Stone thus highlights how
male gazing defers, instead of gratifying, desired "sensations."
    Stone aligns this gazer with the perennial Romantic longing that at
once ennobles and thwarts male gazing. This gazer's failure to live the
"life of sensation," the failure that John Keats lamented in an 1817 letter
and reflectively enacted in his odes, leaves Stone's gazer "endlessly waiting
for the consequences" of his desire (Stone, *Bay* 237). Leaving him powerless, "passive and numb," and enduring "paroxysms of anxiety," this failed
career as a gazer produces a frame of mind that in Keats' phrase "perplexes
and retards," a "fugue" state according to Stone (*Bay*, 235) reminiscent
of Keats' "dull-brained" Nightingale Ode speaker. Though the status of
the male gaze as a literary commonplace has a long and varied pedigree
among Romantics and modernists, this sequence in *Bay of Souls* highlights
how much Mulvey's late twentieth-century coinage enhanced its availability as a conceptual tool and the challenge its waywardness poses for male-
gazing novelists, for their narrators, and for other male characters.
    The emergence, out of early Film Studies, of the male gaze conver-
sation coincides suggestively with the emphasis in Stone's fiction on
moviemaking and with the interest among moviemakers his narratives

prompted, beginning with the adaptation of Stone's *Hall of Mirrors* into *WUSA* (1970). Published within a year of Mulvey's essay, Stone's second novel, *Dog Soldiers*, also became a movie three years later.

Starring Tuesday Weld, an actress by then renowned (or notorious) as a popular object of the male gaze, director Karel Reisz's adaptation of *Dog Soldiers*, as *Who'll Stop the Rain*, confounded the consensus about Weld that the popular male gaze helped sustain. Reisz achieved this effect by casting Weld against type as Marge Converse, a heroin addict and drug smuggler on the lam. Reisz's move challenged a generation of male gazers accustomed to viewing Weld as an implicit and consistent on-screen enforcer of gender boundaries—the star of every gazer's dream—in such movies as *Sex Kittens Go to College* and the Elvis Presley vehicle *Wild in the Country* or as the relentlessly nonplussing temptress Thalia Menninger in the early sixties hit sitcom *The Many Loves of Dobie Gillis*. In *Dog Soldiers*, Stone's prose darkens the dream Weld popularly incarnated by depicting Marge's allure as a luminous gaze-object as entirely dependent on her heroin fixes "instead of sex." After Marge shoots up:

> The glow had come back to her skin the grace and suppleness of her body flowed again. The light came back, her eyes' fire. Hicks marveled. It made him happy... Hicks touched her breast. (Stone *Dog*, 171)

The coming-and-going of "the light" that illuminates what male gazers see became—as its title indicates—Stone's foremost concern in his most movie-centered work, his 1986 novel: *Children of Light*. Mulvey's understanding of movies as the master medium for the male gaze, the site where the gaze preeminently transforms desire into power, reverberates throughout *Children of Light*. Stone's plot places the male gazer both in and at the movies, among the men who make movie and the gazers who watch them.

Children of Light takes place mostly on a movie set along Mexico's Pacific coast. Stone's characters are working on—or sabotaging—a long-delayed screen adaptation of *The Awakening*, Kate Chopin's 1899 account of a young New Orleans matron's fatal accommodation and resistance to the male gaze. Stone's treatment of *The Awakening* prompted one feminist critic, Elaine Showalter, to single out *Children of Light* for broadening her perspective as a critic because Stone's novel provided, in Showalter's view, "the most significant contemporary rewriting of *The Awakening*" (84). Underscoring Showalter's observation, *The Awakening* surfaces again as a prominent intertext for Stone and as an object of disdain for "class feminists" twenty years later in *Bay of Souls* (49). What Showalter calls Stone's "dialogue with Chopin" focuses on one of his signature male gazers, Gordon Walker, the screen-writer who adapted Chopin's novel and then waited nearly a decade for production until "the book was discovered by academics and declared a feminist document" (Stone, *Children*, 11).

After sketching in Walker's solitude and his sex life, his writing and acting careers, Stone turns his attention to what happens during the *Awakening* shoot. As Walker approaches the filming location along a mountainous coast road, he stops his car on a promontory within bin-ocular-viewing distance of the cast and crew at work. Walker watches as they shoot the end of Chopin's novel, where Chopin's heroine drowns herself off the Louisiana coast. As he does throughout his novels, Stone operates here as a limited omniscient narrator and ascribes to his protag-onist a decidedly "male gaze," directing Walker's and the reader's atten-tion not so much to what Walker sees but to what Walker wants to see.

> He saw a woman in an old-fashioned gray bathing suit walking toward the water... saw her... remove her bathing suit and stand naked and golden in the sun. He was seeing, he supposed, what he had come to see... tiny distant figures at the edge of an ocean, acting out a vision compounded of his obsessions and emotions. He had never been so in love, he thought, as he was with the woman who stood naked on the beach before the cam-eras and several dozen cold-eyed souls. It was as though she were there for him, for something that was theirs. He felt at the point of understanding the process in which his life was bound, as though the height on which he stood was the perspective he had always lacked. Will I understand it all now, he wondered, understand it with the eye, like a painting? The sense of discovery, of imminent insight excited him... that's poetry, he thought. (129)

Stone's narrator's reiterated tentativeness, "he thought" and "he sup-posed," signals questions about whether or not what Walker sees legiti-mately passes for "poetry" or constitutes an epiphany (see Chap. 2). Or does this "revelation" foster cruder fantasies of ownership and control? The question of whether Stone and the reader side with Walker and Stone's narrator speaks directly to this narrative's investment in or resist-ance to male gazing and the prerogatives it customarily legitimates.

On reflection, Walker's conviction wavers as he worries that "per-haps it wasn't poetry" but "only movies": a purely sensory, largely visual apprehension of "the coming and going of light," a preemptively mediated mass gaze. As an instrument of male gazing and as an image magnifier (like movie projectors and movie cameras), Walker's binoculars prompt him to treat his vision as "only movies." These binoculars thus become a rudimentary analogue for seeing cinematically, like Mulvey's hypothetical male gazer (see Chap. 4). With his first binocular glance, Walker believes that he's looking at Lu Anne Bourgeois Morgen, the star of *The Awakening* and a former (equivocally relinquished) love of his life; however, with a second gaze Walker realizes he was mistaken. "The naked figure he saw" turns out to be Lu Anne's body double. "A younger woman who somewhat resembled" the star (130), she bears the name Joy. In calling attention to Hollywood's practice of dividing, between actresses and their doubles, the "traditional exhibitionist role" that Mulvey ascribes to women on screen, Stone calls into question both Mulvey's lumping together of "spectacle and narrative" and male gazers' tendency to fuse carnality and the Romantic idealism reflected in Stone's allusively naming Lu Anne's body double "Joy." As an allegorical tease, Stone's allusion prefigures Walker's temptation to treat Joy as "poetry," recalling Wordsworth's sonnet on "faithful love" and "grievous loss," "Surprised by Joy." This allusion also nods, salaciously, to Keats' "Ode on Melancholy," in which the poet voices a longing to savor the sensation of "burst[ing] Joy's grape."

The initial resemblance between Joy and Lu Anne fools Walker again when, later on the same day, he sees Joy up close (130, 147). Stone's description of these unsettling gazes highlights the extent to which a male gazer, even when technologically assisted, often ends up seeing what isn't there and substituting desire for perception. Finding at once a muse and an object of desire and investing a nameless woman spied prosaically at work and at a distance with "poetry" has long been a staple of male gazing, at least since the speaker in Wordsworth's "Solitary Reaper" hailed "yon highland lass" and seized her "music" as his exclusive possession over two centuries ago (see Chap. 3).

Walker's second look at the star's body-double highlights the tenacious appeal of such Romantic substitutions:

> Walker saw the figure of a woman... The sight brought him to his feet...
> She was wearing her hair as she had worn it fifteen years before, he
> thought. He knew her silhouette, her moves, her aura... 'I'm not her,' said
> a small antipodean voice. (147)

Though a literal reference to Joy's Australian nationality, "antipodean" also indicates that the body double has become more distant from Walker when seen close-up and when speaking with a voice of her own— for herself—than when viewed from a distance as the mute object of Walker's gaze. The interjected "he thought" further impeaches the credibility of what Walker's male gaze has constructed without diminishing its authority, his certainty about what he "knew," which apparently obliges Joy to be answerable to him before he even speaks.

Having thus highlighted both the groundless authority and dubious cognitive reliability of male gazing, Stone begins in the interval between these two encounters to differentiate Walker's critical, disenchanted gazing from that of the other gazers in the novel. Arriving on the set, Walker finds himself at a meeting in the director's trailer and part of an entourage of professional male gazers. In addition to Walker, the group consists of the director of *The Awakening*, Walter Drogue, Jr., and his father, a curmudgeonly (John Huston-like) Hollywood eminence grise. As they "watch tapes of Joy undressing… her stripping" stuns "the group" into "a reverent silence" (130). For all its seeming force here, though, the male gaze proves to be a precarious means of control, "a big fuss… wild, unpredictable" (130–131), because the body double has refused to play the scene entirely naked. She resists the demands of the male gaze imposed by the director. She claims to understand male gazing better and with more nuance than do her bosses: "She had the nerve to tell me her problem was with the Mexicans" on the crew who would "take it wrong."

Joy's resistance also discredits the assumption implicit in the very concept of the body double: the understanding that, visually at least, the star and her body double share a single identity. Consequently, Joy rejects pleas from the director who reminds her that the star herself would "show her ass." The ensuing exchange ends up swaying "the group" to concede that gazing at the star, Lu Anne, and gazing at Joy differ radically: "With Lu Anne, you might have her bare breast and it's tragic," but with Joy "it's weird and it turns you on." Their resistance notwithstanding, both Joy and Lu Anne struggle and fail to free themselves from the demands of the various male gazers who strive throughout the novel to "command" various "stages" (Mulvey, "Visual Pleasure"). Soon after dramatizing her fleeting, carnal star turn, Stone shows Joy mercenarily ("careerwise") succumbing to a familiar "boring" showbiz cliché by "like, balling" the most celebrated Hollywood player on the set, the senior Drogue (148).

In contrast to Joy's casual capitulation to the this alpha gazer, Lu Anne's excruciatingly protracted collapse occupies much of the rest of the novel as various male gazers—Walker, the Drogues, various studio functionaries, and her patronizing husband (a prominent physician with "a stare" that "made him seem cruel and unfeeling") who briefly visits Lu Anne on location (26)—claim her. One such gazer, a reporter writing a feature on the making of *The Awakening*, "watched her hungrily... gazed at her with drunken ardor," prompting Lu Anne to "return his look, pitying... his fecal eyes" (217, 204). Embodying the male gaze at its most mercenary and predatory, this professional gazer ends up blackmailing the production company with photos snapped though Lu Anne's bedroom window (182–183, 189–190).

Walker, by contrast, appears intent on differentiating himself from these stock gazers and on rescuing Lu Anne from the constraints to which a lifetime of being gazed upon have subjected her. Lu Anne, however, resists Walker's chivalrous designs. First, she chides Walker to "stay home and fuck your fecund imagination" (176). Finally, the narrative culminates with her decisively censuring the hackneyed romance rhetoric with which Walker voices his unwelcome ardor (231–232). Just as Walker melodramatically proclaims "I would die for you," he understands that, though "true," this sentiment isn't "really helpful." With Lu Anne's riposte, "I don't need dying for," Stone shows the counter-gaze with which she subdues Walker's ardor becoming intellectually as well as sensually omnipotent: "She had grown so thin" during filming (in other words, as a professional gaze object) "that her face contracted to its essential lines, which were strong and noble and lit by her eye with intelligence, generosity, and madness."

LuAnne's resistance confounds Walker's romanticizing, his shopworn view that an actress's face radiates her star quality. Lu Anne's contrariness also lends credence to Drogue senior's earlier disdain for such mystifications. Citing Janet Gaynor in *A Star is Born* as the consummate instance of such stellar radiance, Drogue scoffs at judging actresses at face value, declaring that Gaynor's "face looks like a cunt" and "makes you think of her pussy" (180). Lu Anne's face, by contrast, "represented" to Walker's idealizing, sublimating, mythological, oxymoronic gaze "a Juggernaut" of comforting "philosophy" (232). This juggernaut takes charge during the protracted bout of ecstatic, masochistic love-making that follows Walker's physiognomic revelation. Playing the "juggernaut" Walker has conjured, Lu Anne at once takes charge of both seeing and of sex:

"standing naked over" Walker as "a great thunderclap echoed" and "the earth shook under him like a scaffold" (234). These storm images at once associate Lu Anne with Zeus and a state executioner. Walker, by contrast, appears physically subdued, "unable to gain his feet" while facing Lu Anne, who appeared "raised up, as though she hung suspended between the trembling earth and the storm. Her hair was wild, her body sheathed in light. Her eyes blazed amethyst."

The remainder of this spectacle increasingly obscures her nudity, the coupling bodies, and the Shakespearean storm in the background (Cartelli 171–172). Instead, Stone's narrator focuses exclusively on the force of Lu Anne's gaze. Lu Anne commands Walker to attend to her "secret eyes." Then, "marking a line between his eyes and hers," she ascribes to her gaze the powers of "hunting and recognition," the capacity to "see the things you never saw," including "eighty-two thousand colors" (235–237).

This ceremony of intimacy, whereby Lu Anne exorcises Walker's gaze, sets the stage for a final escape from the male gazing of Hollywood's alphas and moviegoers everywhere. In drowning herself, like the heroine of *The Awakening*, Lu Anne escapes, once and for all, from all male gazing (255). Finally, Stone shows Walker challenging the Hollywood gazers' posthumous claims to Lu Anne's missing body. When a studio publicist laments the lack of a corpse and a coffin he pronominally equates Lu Anne with her body and carps "that she wasn't found." Walker counters that "it was better" not to have found a corpse—a visible body—so as not to encourage further male-gazing.

Nevertheless, Lu Anne does become, posthumously, a contested object of male gazing. In a barroom conversation, a corpse-less wake, two of her colleagues reminisce about her greatest stage performance (258). As Rosalind in *As You Like It*, Lu Anne played a heroine who foiled the male gaze with "a swashing and a martial outside" (1.3) by cross-dressing and retreating to the forest of Arden. Only by means of disguise and tactical retreat from male gazing courtiers could Rosalind attain the heterosexual intimacy she sought. *Children of Light* seems to culminate in the argument that if Hollywood's and Hollywood-inspired male gazers "poisoned" Lu Anne, as one of these reminiscers suggests, then *becoming* Rosalind (not simply playing her) might promise an antidote or at least a bold challenge to oppressive male gazing.

Featuring a renowned documentary maker as its prime gazer, Stone's next novel, *Outerbridge Reach* (1992), also aligns the corrosive force of oppressive male gaze with moviemaking. Though "not from Hollywood" (313), Strickland, the documentary maker and the story's "phallocentric foil" (Kipnis, *Men* 3), exhibits a gaze like Walker's. Strickland's gaze compounds his vocation with concupiscent obsession, along with a dominator's affect. Stone initially presents this gazer as both more professional and more effective than Walker. A self-confessed male-gazer (256), a typical male filmmaker in Mulvey's schema (Walters, 57), Strickland boasts of his gift for reducing his subjects to powerlessness—getting them "to piss all over themselves" (30) and to "feel violated" (325).

As the object of his gaze, Strickland fixes on Anne Browne, the wife of a solo circumnavigating yachtsman whose voyage Strickland has been commissioned by Anne's husband's corporate sponsor to film. On first seeing Anne, Strickland pegs her as "a big creamy bitch" (137). Strickland revises this image as Anne's resistance to his gaze spurs an "impatient" determination to gaze on her more intently, which in turn provokes further resistance: "it seemed to Strickland that she avoided his eye," an "interesting sign" he decides (173). Gazing at Anne along the seat of a darkened car, Strickland "managed a secret look at her" and finds himself bemused at "how she had worked her way into the scheme of his senses" (173–174). At this juncture, Strickland alters his view of Anne as "creamy"—soft, smooth, milky, maternal—deciding rather that she seems "wary of him... her face... strong, willful and austere, wonderfully softened by her smile." Anne's "brazen, faintly androgynous, pre-Raphaelite beauty" proves "daunting, almost more than he thought he could handle" in contrast to his habitual preference for "mysterious and perversely turned" women, like Pamela, the suburban demimondaine and part-time hooker Strickland keeps on retainer and whom he films obsessively (31–36). What differentiates Anne from Strickland's "type," the sexually and visually ever-available Pamela, emerges as Strickland gazes on Anne and concludes:

> No one had ever instructed her in concealing her intelligence or moderating her enthusiasm. Nothing about her spoke to his particular desires. But somehow everything about her did (174).

Strickland's gaze, with its concluding revelation that "everything about" Anne "spoke to his particular desires," follows the typical gaze scenario parsed by Suzanne Danuti Walters: having "sexualized" his object, the gazer proceeds to subject her "under the scrutiny of" an "ideal" (56). As the narrative unfolds, though, this move to subordinate Anne fails. Stone turns Strickland into a troubled, less than "invincible" gazer (Modleski 9). Once Anne starts reeducating Strickland and managing his gaze and his desire, he phones Pamela, "asking her to come over... dialed her again and said, 'Forget about it.'" As this reeducation takes hold, Stone elaborates the realignment of Strickland's perspective on both sex and seeing, his growing awareness that "his penetration" as a moviemaker and his "readiness to fuck" might rest entirely on "what he failed to see" (326). Such reflections on his failures to see prompt Strickland to view himself as others see him, as "the average asshole in the street... just another asshole" (326, 330). "All at once," as this chapter concludes, Strickland finds himself, his gaze redirected, "afraid of losing" his hold over Anne.

Spurning Strickland, Anne reduces him to "a child" and denies him all "proprietary rights," all "hope," to such an extent that she disarms his gaze and so obliges him to resort to forms of expression over which he has no mastery (379–381). He first resorts to language, "vain words," which leaves him "stammering" and unable "to explain." As words fail him, Strickland resorts to violence. In league with her father, a powerful shipping tycoon, Anne retaliates. She commissions the theft of Strickland's footage and production notes, his copies of her husband's navigation logs, and even his cherished Manhattan parking space. Adding injury to insult with a savage, bone-breaking beating that renders him "bloody-faced, bent double at the waist, his crippled, broken left hand supported by his right," Anne has reduced the gazer to the object of others' callous gaze, to fleeing his assailants "under the unseeing gaze of busy passers-by." By depicting Anne as more resourceful and more ruthless in defeating Strickland's gaze than Lu Anne was in disengaging herself from Walker's gaze in *Children of Light*, Stone shows Anne triumphing over what Strickland embodies: artful visual exploitation, purportedly "in the service of truth" (22), as a vehicle for sexual domination.

Stone's novels of the 1980s and 1990s register both perennial vindications of male gazing and the emerging imperative to censure it. Questions about whether to thwart or reward gazing, whether to celebrate or humiliate the gazer, became even more pronounced four years after the publication of *Outerbridge Reach*, in Philip Roth's fifteenth novel, *Sabbath's Theater*. *Sabbath's Theater* all at once acknowledges, repents for, and vindicates Roth's controversial reputation as a "phallocentric diva" (Kipnis, *Men* 3). This reputation is mirrored, magnified, and mortified in the adventures and ordeals of *Sabbath's Theater*'s title character, Mickey Sabbath. Though the phallocentric diva has probably never appeared as vividly as in this 1995 novel, Roth's reputation for playing and capturing this role rests on the candor with which Roth's male protagonists and narrators have indulged in voyeurism, masturbatory fantasizing, and unreconstructed fascination with women's bodies throughout his career.

These characteristics of Roth's work date back to his first book, especially its title novella, *Goodbye, Columbus*, in which the first-person narrator speculates about how he might have acquitted himself had the Judgment of Paris been his to make (76) (see Chap. 2). This identification with Greek mythology's arch-gazer follows a reminiscence about how as a boy this narrator, Neil Klugman, had to lie in order to gaze. This Ur-gaze milestone consisted of "lying about my age in order to see Hedy Lamarr naked" in the movie *Ecstasy* (31).[3]

Goodbye Columbus opens with Neil unabashedly gazing, reminiscing about "the first time I saw Brenda." The long paragraph that follows first homes in on Brenda's eyeglasses and her dependence on them, which limits her power to see, despite her accomplished intellect, her sharp wit, and her "knack for asking practical infuriating questions" (27). With this stress on her myopia, Neil overstates her susceptibility to being seen (as opposed to seeing) and thus objectified. After registering Brenda's "clipped" coif and her bathing suit, Neil "watched her move off," noticing how "she caught the bottom of her suit between the thumb and index finger and flicked what flesh had been showing back where it belonged." This gazer peers microscopically at his gaze object's "thumb and index finger" in contrast to the features that drew looks from Stone's more conventionally lecherous male gazers. Still more contrary to male gazers' customary foci, the squeamishly qualifying appeal to propriety, the relative clause "where it belonged," apparently reflects Neil's preference for the concealment, rather than the exposure, of Brenda's "flesh." Whatever faint erotic charge this paragraph sparks lies in the vaguely clinical, and remotely biblical noun "flesh" and the recollection that this glimpse stirred the gazer's "blood" to "jump."

---

[3] *Ecstasy.* https://s-media-cache-ak0.pinimg.com/736x/2a/d0/eb/2ad0ebe540a27f1d 2ca5a9bbf7658e14.jpg.

Neil has his next opportunity to fix his gaze on Brenda when he gets to observe her as an animated competitor, playing tennis at twilight. In contrast to the "poetry" in motion Walker found in looking across a rugged coastal landscape in *Children of Light*, Neil preoccupies himself with Brenda's sweat. Even before seeing her he hears her shouting "deuce again" and "sounding as though she was sweating considerably." His first sighting of her during this encounter fixes on her tennis "racket... spinning up in the air" and her catching it "neatly" as the narrator "comes into sight" (9). With Brenda standing still in gazing range, "she ceased being merely a voice and turned into a sight again" (11). Noting this reversion of Brenda to a silent object, Neil permits himself to gaze at will, recalling that "I let myself appreciate her." The zoom lens of this gazer's appreciation fixes again on sweat, "on the wet triangles on the back of her tiny-collared white polo shirt," and the ensemble "she wore to complete the picture, a tartan belt, white socks, and white tennis sneakers." With his appreciation of her "polo shirt" and "tartan belt," the narrator (in a move reminiscent of Cole Porter's famous animadversion to "a glimpse of stocking" or "a Bendel's bonnet") leavens his interest in Brenda as a purely bodily object with his cognizance of her as a social construct and an economic product, as a socially located consumer. Despite these status- and fashion-conscious refinements, Roth repeatedly shifts the gazer's focus away from the local to the exotic, from the suburban princess to nude-filled landscapes by the once notorious, now canonic male gazer Paul Gauguin (37, 47, 59), reproductions of whose work Neil finds to be a popular item in the public library where he works. References to Gauguin's paintings reverberate throughout the novella as a utopian subtext, a narrative about a gazer in paradise for whom gazing became completely unconstrained by custom or clothing, a gazer whose artistic works became priceless treasures in museums throughout the "civilized" world. Beyond museums and the library, Neil encounters the ubiquity of male gazing in the "illustrations of women so dreamy" in calendars found on countless walls in American workplaces (92). With this attention to pervasive visual representations by and for male gazers, Roth embeds Neil as a critical and sympathetic participant in both the elite and lowest-common-denominator cultural markets (for pin-up calendars and Gauguin oils) that sustain male-gazing.

Roth's male gazer again played the socio-cultural participant-observer a decade later in his most famous—and infamous—novel, *Portnoy's Complaint*. Though "chasing cunt... roaming the streets with eyes popping," Roth's eponymous narrator can't picture himself as a gazer without scrupulously lifting his gaze to take in the socially produced milieu of his gazing "as he makes his way across the major arteries of Manhattan" (100–101). Even *Portnoy*'s notorious "whacking off" reveries fix the adolescent Portnoy's gaze on language and narrative, by "pretending that the cool and mealy hole" carved into an apple core "was actually between the legs of that *mythical* being who always *called* me Big Boy" (18, emphasis added). However much Portnoy plays the deranged satyr, he never falters as a narrator in the obligation to embed his crude, solitary, and generic vision of womanhood culturally and economically in a family picnic, a butcher shop, a billboard (108, 134), even in the literary canon, in Dostoyevsky's St. Petersburg: "So galvanic" did Portnoy find "the word 'panties'" that he became "the Raskolnikov of jerking off" (18–20).

Like Raskolnikov, Portnoy ends up being punished (for gazing rather than homicide), humiliated by the final woman upon whom he casts his gaze: "a hardy, red-headed, freckled... ideological hunk of a girl" (258). (As another instance of Roth's signature impetus to treat male gazing as unavoidably *meta*-physical, his anomalous adjective sequence, which groups "ideological" with Portnoy's impressions of his gaze object's hair and skin, accentuates both Portnoy's derangement and his sophistication.) This *meta*-physical description refers to an Israeli soldier named Naomi with "work-molded legs" in "utilitarian shorts" (269). With "utilitarian" Roth refines Naomi's "ideological" profile and stresses how Naomi represents as much a cultural as a corporeal construct for Portnoy. Thus appearing to Portnoy as an "ideological" embodiment, Naomi reduces him to the object of her withering female gaze. "Unmanning" Portnoy (Roth, *Reading* 119), this gaze-reversal compels him to see himself "quivering under the disapproving gaze of his mother" (*Portnoy* 267) instead of sexually mastering a "hardy hunk of a girl."

A generation later, in *Sabbath's Theater* (1995), Roth explored the penalties for and the pleasures of gazing still more excruciatingly and more tenderly. Roth's rhetorical agenda in *Sabbath* seems to coincide with its "phallocentric diva" hero's agenda, at least to the extent that both Roth and his protagonist understand "art" as a way "to unshackle" an audience from the "habit of innocence" (213) and "teach estrangement from the ordinary" (27). Both narrator and protagonist, moreover, cultivate "the artistry... to open up... the lurid interstices of life" (213).

As a bereaved sexagenarian whose "many farcical, illogical, incomprehensible transactions" and insights "are subsumed by the mania of lust" (233), Mickey Sabbath begins his odyssey against the backdrop of the late-century shift from mute acquiescence to male gazing and its association with sexual freedom and candor to the growing influence of feminist critiques, many-Mulvey-inspired, of the male gaze as an instrument of sexual oppression (163, 165, 237) and of sexist humiliation. A puppeteer who implemented his sexual fantasies and imposed his desires through his performances (122–123), Sabbath found himself forced into retirement from puppet making by arthritis and as a result of sexual harassment charges, banned from working at the college where he had taught theater arts.

Thwarted by the emerging zeitgeist, Sabbath's male gazing proves even more marked by social and cultural commentary than the gazing in *Portnoy's Complaint* and *Goodbye Columbus*. *Sabbath's Theater* thus opens by turning the object of the hero's gaze into "a mythical being." In conjuring Mickey Sabbath's "firmly made" paramour, Roth's narrator cites "those clay figurines molded circa 2000 B.C.… unearthed all the way from Europe down to Asia Minor and worshipped under different names" (5). Even making the conventional male gazer's move, conjuring the gaze object's "uberous breasts," Sabbath hearkens back to the etymology of "uberous" and to Tintoretto's portrait of yet another "mythical being," Juno (13) in his 1570 painting *The Origins of the Milky Way*.[4]

In Sabbath's extravagantly microscopic application of male gazing, he reflectively rhapsodizes in his mind's eye about his estranged wife's clitoris (431–434). Roth sustains this microscopic, clitoris-conjuring male gaze over three pages. Sabbath's gaze here encompasses a lifetime of desire, both thwarted and gratified. These lecherous musings also recuperate Sabbath's crippled artistic calling, the passion that Stone ascribed to Strickland in *Outerbridge Reach*. Echoing Puccini's Tosca, who "lived for art, lived for love," Strickland voices this "*vissi d'arte*" imperative importunately, in order to "ensure that" his "definitions prevailed" (326–327). Sabbath's clitoral rhapsody represents his last effort to "prevail" according to Strickland's precept. Proposing an array of outlandish "definitions," Sabbath pronounces that clitorises offer "much to be compared

---

[4]Tintoretto, *The Origins of the Milky Way*. https://s-media-cache-ak0.pinimg.com/736x/34/68/5b/34685b53522c72f908fad030fe5ed9b5.jpg.

with: Bernstein conducting Mahler's eighth"; "ecstatic machinery" that would have "dazzled Aquinas" with "its economy"; "an argument for the existence of god"; "the mother of the microchip, the triumph of evolution, right up with the retina and the tympanic membrane"; a "Cyclops' eye"; "the toy at the bottom of the Cracker Jack box" (431–434). Visualizing the clitoris so grandiloquently casts a transcendent spell on Sabbath. This ecstatic conjuring convinces Sabbath that, "entering" a "fairy tale, freed at last," he's found "a home" and a "reason to go on."

This transcendence proves short-lived. Like *Portnoy's Complaint*, *Sabbath's Theater* closes punitively, with the hero transformed from a gazer into the humiliated object of a gaze, subjected to the commanding disciplinary gaze of the state. This gaze belongs to a state trooper, the son of Sabbath's final and most beloved sex-mate. He catches Sabbath gazing upon, urinating on, and masturbating over his mother's grave in the beams of his flashlight and cruiser's headlights. "Lighting up Sabbath's face," these beams make him a "star," "the feature attraction" of his last performance (446–450). Amplifying Portnoy's allusive, hyperbolic confession—as "the Raskolnikov of jerking off"—Sabbath, in his finale, pleads, suicidally, to be allowed to "purge myself publicly of my crimes and accept this punishment that's coming to me." "With his eyes just inches from Sabbath's," the trooper kills this performance by unlocking the handcuffs that mark Sabbath as a criminal gazer. This move seals Sabbath's fate: an incorrigible male-gazer—at once punished and liberated—who has lived doggedly by the gaze, now trying and failing to die cathartically under a far colder traditionally male gaze: the disciplinary gaze of the state.

The gazer's comeuppance proves more irrevocable, his transgression more venial, and his liberation more conclusive in Roth's millennial novel *The Human Stain* (2001). Like *Sabbath's Theater*, *Portnoy's Complaint*, and Stone's 1997 story "Bear and His Daughter," *The Human Stain* limns and probes what Roth calls "transgressive audacity" (*Stain*, 31). Like Stone's *Dog Soldiers*, *The Human Stain* also extended its gazing into to that Mecca of male-gazing, Hollywood. As with Tuesday Weld's star turn in the screen version of *Dog Soldiers*, Hollywood piqued the male gaze in *The Human Stain* by casting—miscasting, according to some reviewers—the "mesmerizing" screen beauty Nicole Kidman, all "porcelain skin and... tousled ringlets," as the female lead, Faunia Farley, in Robert Benton's 2003 screen adaptation of the novel (Abeel; Travers; Taylor).

Roth's narrator—his go-to alter-ego—Nathan Zuckerman, recounts first gazing on Faunia, while she was working as a milkmaid. With this bucolic turn, Roth echoes Wordsworth's "Solitary Reaper," and recalls Stone's Wordsworth-echoing move in *Children of Light*—his account of Walker being surprised by Joy. In contrast to Stone, Roth defiantly acknowledges the feminist critique of male gazing as well as calling to mind, forty years into his prolific career, many of the reasons "why feminist critics have consistently made Roth such a target" (Taylor). In both *Sabbath's Theater* and *The Human Stain*, Roth continues to expose himself to such targeting, notwithstanding his accommodations to the prevailing Mulvey-generated critique. In *Bay of Souls* (2003), Stone similarly melds accommodation and provocation. Stone and Roth both dwell on the alleged excesses of what sociologist Neil Boyd decries as an ascendant, "quaint and reactionary," "big sister" ethic that belittles both "Eros and Thanatos" (Warner; Snider; Moore, "Wrath"; Shechner). Described by Roth's omniscient *Sabbath's Theater* narrator as "clinical … lawerly with palpable hatred" and as "intellectually unstimulating" and "pedestrian" (213–215), this ethic penalizes what Stone calls "solitary acts of personal liberation" (Stone, *Bay* 50). In *The Human Stain*, Zuckerman at first reviles the guardians of this ethic as "unsurpassable social obstacles" (47) to the liberation sought by this novel's ill-fated protagonists.

Although Zuckerman initially characterizes the couple's relationship as mutual by citing the mutual intensification of "their pleasure" (47), whatever transcendence this pair's mutual gazing promises increasingly redounds to Faunia's gazing lover, a septuagenarian classicist named Coleman Silk. As a classicist, Silk gazes as a connoisseur, a learned authority who identifies Faunia, in Latin, as "his Voluptas," pitting his established intellectual credentials against those of the academic guardians who set out to sabotage his enchantment and involvement with Faunia.

All he ever did there was watch her work… looking in and let her get on with the job without having to bother to talk to him. Often they said nothing, because saying nothing intensified their pleasure. She knew he was watching her; knowing she knew, he watched all the harder—and that they weren't able to couple down in the dirt didn't make a scrap of difference… it was enough to have to maintain the matter-of-factness of being separated by unsurpassable social obstacles, to play their roles as farm laborer and retired college professor, to perform consummately at her being a strong, lean working woman of thirty-four, a wordless illiterate, an elemental rustic of muscle and bone who'd just been in the yard with the pitchfork cleaning up from the morning milking, and at his being a thoughtful senior citizen... an accomplished classicist, an amplitudinous brain of a man replete with the vocabularies of two ancient tongues. It was enough to be able to conduct themselves like two people who had nothing whatsoever in common, all the while remembering how they could distill to an orgasmic essence everything about them that was irreconcilable, the human discrepancies... There was, at first glance, little to raise unduly one's carnal expectations about the gaunt, lanky woman spattered with dirt, wearing shorts and a T-shirt and rubber boots, whom I saw in with the herd that afternoon and whom Coleman identified as his Voluptas. (Roth, *Stain* 47–51)

Zuckerman sounds as transfixed as Silk himself. Nevertheless, in reconsidering Silk's gaze, Zuckerman denies Faunia the status of "enticing siren" and transforms her into "something virile" (50). Zuckerman's characterization of Faunia as virile may rest on what he gleaned earlier when Coleman confided in him his appreciation of Faunia's carnal acumen as a gazer in her own right: "Her flesh has eyes. Her flesh sees everything. In bed she is a powerful, coherent, unified being whose pleasure is in overstepping boundaries" (31). Zuckerman's memory and his discovery that the "controlling" and initiating gaze no longer belongs exclusively to men (Kaplan 29) seem to herald an emerging wariness towards unreconstructed, uni-directional male gazing on the part of this narrator, if not his older, smitten protagonist.

This wariness, Zuckerman quickly reveals, rests on his retrospective foreknowledge of the repercussions of Silk's desire and Faunia's potency. Roth abruptly follows the novel's early idyllic gaze passage by flashing forward to Faunia and Coleman's burial four months later and, in the same paragraph, flashing back to describe Silk's "sexual longing" as "brought to a boil" (Roth, *Stain* 51). Casting himself as a mourner, Zuckerman recollects "the milking session as... a theatrical performance," confesses complicity in Coleman's "greedy fascination," and concedes that he "had played the part of an extra... observing the scene flawlessly performed... of an enamored old man watching at work the cleaning woman-farmhand who is secretly his paramour: a scene of pathos and hypnosis and sexual subjugation" (51). This recollection and the epiphany it inspires telescopes an entire history of male gazing from classical Greece and Rome, lifelong preoccupations of the classicist,

Voluptas-worshipping Coleman Silk, to 1998: "the year of America's presidential impeachment" (51).

Clinton's impeachment and the orgy of collective voyeurism it provoked, which Zuckerman reflects on as the novel opens, pitted the "stupefying power" of the male gaze and the desire it represents (51), in Zuckerman's view, against a national "ecstasy of sanctimony" (2). With the Clinton "scandal" as its point of departure, *The Human Stain* marks the decline of the hegemonizing male gaze and in turn its diminishment as a credible target of polemics (Paglia, "Ivory Tower"). Roth's narrative implicitly constitutes a recuperative argument for sustained appreciation of male gazing as a cognitive instrument and as an esthetic impetus. Roth's rhetorical agenda points to restoring to Mulvey's concept its "dialectical" edge, which, Laura Kipnis argues, has come to be "repressed in common usage" (*Ecstasy* 8–9). The prevailing male-gaze conversation had, in this view, grown increasingly "stupefying." It had become undialectical in an intellectual climate subject to the discursive policing that D.A. Miller described a generation ago in *The Novel and the Police*. Treating novels as disciplinary instruments, Miller identifies "the sheer pettiness of coercion… the policing power that never passes for such, but is either invisible or visible only under cover of other, nobler or simply blander intentionalities" (17). In *The Human Stain* Roth illustrates—and contests—the tendency of this "policing power" to become absolute. It becomes so absolute that Roth's plot punitively kills both the gazer and the object of his gaze, both overcome by "the powerful gaze of disciplinary" prying which, "fixed on the individual," imposes "conformity" and ensures that "everyone at all times is visible, known and controlled" (Lentricchia 76). Miller's theory of the novel echoes in Roth's account of fiction writing itself at the end of *The Human Stain*. Fiction writing, according to Zuckerman, simultaneously reveals and conceals "secret spots" (349–350, 360), such as those likely to harbor both gazers and gaze objects. Thus in *The Human Stain* Roth investigates forces that both enable and curb male gazers. Throughout the narrative Roth weighs the justness of the protagonists' particular punishment (violent death) and the motives of the authorities (Silk's colleagues) who claim the prerogative of disciplining Silk's gaze. Finally, Roth illustrates how the novel as a genre resists such policing and protects "the right to" keep "a secret" and offers in the process an antidote to "totalitarian" encroachment (Z. Smith 8).

According to Roth, this "encroachment" threatened what Silk and Faunia represent from opposing sides, from witch hunters on the Republican right, like those who dogged Bill Clinton, and from Silk's professedly progressive colleagues, whose "prestigious academic crap" (191) legitimated their disciplinary apparatus. To be sure, as a matter of historical fact, this "crap," more temperately characterized by feminist historian Wendy Brown as "denatured...theoretically incoherent and tacitly conservative... moralism" (33–35), often originated in legitimate demands for inclusion. (Roth's interest in Americans' struggles for inclusion and against tyranny has reverberated throughout his work, in early stories such as "Defender of the Faith" and "Eli, the Fanatic" and in this century in *The Plot Against America*.)

Stone's third novel, *A Flag for Sunrise* (1992), memorably grappled with such struggles. It featured a heroine who serves as both the narrator's gaze object and his moral compass. An Irish nun working in Central America, she appears variously as an arresting, "honey-haired" object of "predatory" lust, "an illusion of fulfillment" (377–378), a martyred champion of liberation theology, and a police-defying "radical of some kind" (341, 411, 413–416). Roth's and Stone's gaze-minded, police-challenging fiction honors such "radical" imperatives while showing male gazing as a liberating egalitarian instrument and as a constraining oppressive force. Their fiction demonstrates its power and limitations, its appeal and the harm it can do. As curators of the male gaze, both novelists characteristically treat it as a valuable literary resource while exposing the oppressive politics that the male gaze has too often underwritten. The verbal density and literary pyrotechnics both writers often invest in their accounts of gazing testify to the durability of the gaze, as a bountiful legacy that can sunder as well as bind women and men, as a rhetorical move that can diffuse as well as bolster power, as an esthetic stance, and as a heuristic for probing desire and the incessant construction, deconstruction, and reconstruction of gender.

CHAPTER 6

British Invasions Post-Bar Mitzvah

The last five chapters have demonstrated numerous ways in which (to paraphrase scripture) the male gaze has always been with us. In the beginning of male gazing, God presented Lilith, and then Eve, to Adam. Among the many lessons I've learned through my life-long exposure to Bible stories, a few stand out for both the hope they inspired and the despair they occasioned. Long ago God (or at least God's ghostwriters) seemed intent on assuring me that gazing was my birthright.

In *The Sun Also Rises*, his sequel to the Jewish Bible (to the book of Ecclesiastes, which the novel's title echoes), Ernest Hemingway explained Jewishness to gentile America by presenting his story's Jewish foil, Robert Cohn, not simply as a superlatively ambitious male gazer, exhibit A in The Mamas & the Papas' 1966 warning that "longing gazes won't get you where you want to go"(see Chap. 4). Hemingway aligns Cohn's gaze with the very origins of Jewish law (Torah) and Jewish nationhood. In recounting Cohn's infatuation with the story's Lost Generation *femme fatale*, Brett Ashley, Hemingway's narrator observes that "when I saw Robert Cohn looking at her, he looked a great deal as his compatriot [Moses] must have looked when he saw the promised land" (29). Hemingway leaves unmentioned what most of his readers (at least readers who recognized his title's biblical antecedent) already knew: that Moses never got to enter the Promised Land upon which he gazed from the summit of Mount Nebo (Numbers 20:12; Deuteronomy 34:1).

The Jewish Bible, the only scripture I knew during my first decade, repeatedly presented many of its prophets, patriarchs, and warriors as male gazers.

© The Author(s) 2017   189
J.D. Bloom, *Reading the Male Gaze in Literature and Culture*, Global
Masculinities, DOI 10.1007/978-3-319-59945-8_6

Unlike Moses, these gazers not only got to behold but also ended up actually holding and embracing what they gazed upon: Isaac and Rebecca, Jacob and Rachel, David and Bathsheba (see Chap. 2). When the comic pundit Stephen Colbert objected to a hotel's substitution of bedside Gideon bibles with copies of *Fifty Shades of Grey* he reminded viewers that the Bible is "a steamy read" full of "strong domineering patriarchs ordering women to perform some truly freaky acts, including one woman Ezekiel denounced for 'dot[ing] upon her paramours.'"[1]

My first intimation of scriptural "steaminess" hit me at the movies. Long before the "New York poet" Frank O'Hara instructed me, in "An Image of Leda" (see Chap. 4), that I was supposed to have my "first sexual experience" at the movies, my family took me to see Cecil B. DeMille's 1956 remake of *The Ten Commandments*. This family outing marked a milestone as the only time I remember we brought a grandmother to the movies with us. Flanked by parents at the Embassy theater on Main Street (really), I turned to my mother to ask her to tell me what Dathan (played by a snarling Edward G. Robinson) meant by the word "fleshpot." Dathan used this unfamiliar noun to provoke an uprising against Moses' leadership, urging his fellow Israelites to return with him to "the fleshpots of Egypt." My mother (mis)informed me that fleshpots were like burger joints or steakhouses, meat-serving establishments.

But the stories of Isaac and David as gazers couldn't be euphemized so readily. Thanks to all this early exposure to god-sanctioned carnality, when Bar Mitzvah time rolled nearly a decade after my introduction to fleshpots, I had some idea about what all the Bible's references to concubines and handmaids might promise. The most profound impression my religious training made turned out to be inspiring the hope that by "becoming a man" and a full-fledged alpha member of a "chosen people" I might get a piece of the same action enjoyed by the monarchs and patriarchs among my forbears. In retrospect, I'm relieved to have been disillusioned.

About a decade later, as post-Bar Mitzvah disenchantment took root, Sigmund Freud almost reassured me that this disillusionment is a universal norm rather than a divinely ordained bait-and-switch reserved only for "chosen people." In *Moses and Monotheism*, Freud postulated that that human history and eons of mammal life has consisted of males

---

[1] Colbert. http://www.frequency.com/video/colbert-report-bibles-swapped-for/55144110/-/5-316869 'date accessed' [9th May 2017].

battling other males to possess and control and females (see Chap. 4). In Freud's view, most men could only "provide themselves with wives," seldom with handmaids and concubines, "by stealing them from others" (102). Men of my background often flatter ourselves as being beyond all this deadly primal contention and in turn we hope to be flattered by the women around us for having "evolved" beyond such objectifying impulses. Still there must be some reason Major Renault's warning in *Casablanca* to the movie's alpha hero, Humphrey Bogart's Rick Blaine, sticks in men's minds: "How extravagant you are, throwing away women like that. Some day they may be scarce."

LONDON CALLING

As I exited the synagogue after my induction into concubineless manhood, two much-ballyhooed and intertwined cultural transformations were in full swing: the "British invasion" and what *Time* magazine had recently dubbed the sexual revolution.[2] While *Time* warned that "each man and woman" faced a perilous "walk through ... sexual bombardment," it also held out—biblically—a promise of "*covenants* of intimacy" (emphasis added).

What such "covenants" would look and sound like might have been left to my imagination. But my imagination wasn't up to the job—at least not without the help of the popular songs and screen entertainment, movies and TV, that suffused most of my waking hours. Early 1964 marks not only *Time*'s declaration of a sexual revolution and of my own manhood. The first half of 1964 also saw the first US tours by the Beatles and the Rolling Stones. Hence I entered upon manhood torn between reassurance from the Beatles that a loss of love and presumably its tactile comforts is likely to prove illusory because "she loves you and you know that can't ba-ad" and the Rolling Stones' repeated realization, dire enough to send correct grammar to the winds, that young men "can't get no satisfaction" (see Chap. 2). Since I have only anecdotal evidence to rely on, I'll refrain from venturing a guess as to which of these states of mind the teenage "men" of my generation (or of any generation) have found most apt.

---

[2] *Time* cover 1964: Sex in the US. http://img.timeinc.net/time/magazine/archive/covers/1964/1101640124_400.jpg.

As a younger child I fell under the sway of college-age siblings who dreamed of becoming cosmopolites. Sometimes, I looked up to them. More often, I mindlessly aped them. In aping, I learned about a second, more rarefied British invasion, which took place in a handful of metropolitan-area movie theaters and a bit later on late-night television. Consequently, throughout the 1960s, the movies of John Schlesinger and Lindsay Anderson added some grit, some disturbing and illuminating density, to the influence of the Brits who dominated the airwaves with their accounts of lads and birds, mods and rockers. For me, the darker sides of these narratives resonated mostly in the Zombies' 1964 and 1965 hits, "She's Not There" and "Tell Her No," the refrain of which is the plea of a Beta or Zeta male to an Alpha winner of the incessant struggle Freud described: "Don't hurt me now for her love *belongs* to me."

The same year another export from the UK's Home Counties fleshed out and indelibly etched these fables of longing and losing in my roiling consciousness and introduced me to one of the most astute explorers and critics of male gazing, English director John Schlesinger. Both his 1965 hit *Darling*, which won Academy Awards for its screenplay (with an uncredited assist from novelist Edna O'Brien) and for Julie Christie's portrayal of the title character, and *Midnight Cowboy*, winner of the best picture Oscar for 1969 (becoming the first X-rated movie to do so), vivified more memorably than any of the movies I've seen subsequently the tensions and nuances of male gazing (Pirnia). In both movies Schlesinger and his collaborators make male gazers out of their audience and of most of the movie's on-screen spectating characters, regardless of sex, gender, and sexuality. His expansive, inclusive, and dialectical accounts of the male gaze at once celebrated and exposed male gazing as a source of both pleasure and trouble for gazers and gaze objects alike.

In between Schlesinger's two transatlantic Oscar-winning 1965 and 1969 hits, *Darling* and *Midnight Cowboy*, MGM released an adaptation by Schlesinger and *Darling* screenwriter Frederic Raphael of a literary classic, Thomas Hardy's 1874 novel *Far from the Madding Crowd*. Schlesinger's adaptation allusively recalls one of the erotically charged biblical stories that had fascinated—and misled—me. *Far from the Madding Crowd* features *Darling* star Julie Christie as the heroine Hardy named Bathsheba (after the fatal object of King David's gaze in 2 Samuel) (see Chap. 2). In chapter three of *Far from the Madding Crowd*, "A Girl on Horseback—Conversation," Hardy introduces a latter-day

Bathsheba as a masterful, free-spirited "performer"—as much a male-gaze *subject*—as an object of male gazing:

Lingering and musing ... he heard the steps of a horse at the foot of the hill, and soon there appeared in view an auburn pony with a girl on its back, ascending by the path leading past the cattle-shed. She was the young woman of the night before. Gabriel ... returned to his hut. Here he ensconced himself, and peeped through the loophole in the direction of the rider's approach ... Gabriel was about to advance ... when an unexpected performance induced him to suspend the action for the present ... The girl, who wore no riding-habit, looked around for a moment, as if to assure her-self that all humanity was out of view, then dexterously dropped backwards flat upon the pony's back, her head over its tail, her feet against its shoulders, and her eyes to the sky. The rapidity of her glide into this position was that of a kingfisher—its noiselessness that of a hawk. Gabriel's eyes had scarcely been able to follow her. The tall lank pony seemed used to such doings, and ambled along unconcerned. Thus she passed under the level boughs.

The performer seemed quite at home anywhere between a horse's head and its tail, and the necessity for this abnormal attitude having ceased with the passage of the plantation, she began to adopt another, even more obvi-ously convenient than the first. She had no side-saddle, and it was very apparent that a firm seat upon the smooth leather beneath her was unat-tainable sideways. Springing to her accustomed perpendicular like a bowed sapling, and satisfying herself that nobody was in sight, she seated herself in the manner demanded by the saddle, though hardly expected of the woman, and trotted off ... Oak was amused, perhaps a little astonished ... She came, the pail in one hand, hanging against her knee. The left arm was extended as a balance, enough of it being shown bare to make Oak wish that the event had happened in the summer, when the whole would have been revealed. There was a bright air and manner about her now, by which she seemed to imply that the desirability of her existence could not be questioned; and this rather saucy assumption failed in being offensive because a beholder felt it to be, upon the whole, true, Like the exceptional emphasis in the tone of a genius, that which would have made mediocrity ridiculous was an addition to recognized power. It was with some surprise that she saw Gabriel's face rising like the moon behind the hedge.

As this passage unfolds, Hardy associates Gabriel Oak, a local farmer and one of Bathsheba's suitors, with a general group of "observe[rs], per-sons who go about the shires with eyes for beauty," and with a tradition of gazing dating back at least as far as ancient Greek mythology (with its legends of Paris and Zeus) before shifting attention from Bathsheba's physical attributes to "the girl's thoughts," which "hovered about her face," troubling Gabriel's—and Hardy's narrator's—"critical" judgment:

> Without throwing a Nymphean tissue over a milkmaid, let it be said that here criticism checked itself as out of place, and looked at her proportions with a long consciousness of pleasure.

Without expanding his cast of characters in the passage beyond the gazing Gabriel and the gazed-upon Bathsheba, Hardy transforms male gazing from a single, private encounter into a social practice and artistic tradition by describing "the girl" becoming "the performer." Hardy's solo gazer, Gabriel, becomes a stand-in for all Englishmen "who go about the shires with eyes for beauty." Gabriel's simple sensory perception prompts reflection sustained enough to undermine Gabriel's "saucy assumption" about the apparent gender identity of a gaze object whose equestrian deportment could be "hardly expected of the woman." Finally, Hardy highlights how gazing often occasions tensions between untroubled sensory indulgence and troublingly reflective "criticism."

In *Darling* these tensions suffuse Christie's Oscar-winning portrayal of the title character, a fashion model ironically named Diana (after the chaste Roman hunter goddess) and nicknamed Darling. To call Christie's role that of a male gaze object isn't simply an academic figure of speech. One of Darling's modeling assignments early in the movie shows photos of Diana being vetted at an ad agency's client meeting to see if "she'll do" as the face of the client's new-product rollout. When the German client expresses his interest in hiring Diana as his cosmetics company's "Happiness Girl," an English agency executive asks if he's willing to "buy her," both for her "Aryan look" and for having "a face men will see too much of." Even before anyone speaks a line in *Darling*—as the credits role—the title character appears as the most familiar kind of sex object with her face going up on a London billboard and, we soon find out, on magazine covers throughout the kingdom. With these two scenes, Schlesinger establishes early on Diana's pan-European appeal as a gaze object. The opening credits roll over a team of billboard-painters pasting an extreme close-up of Christie's face, that of "the ideal woman," over an ad soliciting "World Relief" for emaciated Africans. As the movie ends, Diana has become undeniably the face the public "has seen too much of" and even more of a universally available gaze object. Ultimately, the trophy wife of an adulterous Italian *principe* and chatelaine of his Tuscan estate, Diana has settled—grudgingly—into the role of a tabloid celebrity and a newsstand staple.[3]

Contrary to the widespread, ideologically straitjacketing assumption that male gazing is a heterosexual practice, the movie's most avid male gazer turns out to be Diana's gay confidante, Malcolm, the fashion photographer who knows better than anyone how to "capture" her look. With Malcolm, Diana shares her misery, and, during the holiday in Amalfi where she meets her *principe*, Malcolm and Diana also share at least one lover. Schlesinger's treatment of male gazing as a social practice unbound by any particular gazer's sexuality occupied the foreground four years later in *Midnight Cowboy*. As an exploration of male gazing, *Midnight Cowboy* proved even more prescient than *Darling* in anticipating *and* complicating Mulvey's unidirectional command-and-control subject–object model of male gazing.

Screenwriter Waldo Salt's adaptation of a 1965 novel by James Leo Herlihy, *Midnight Cowboy* tells the story of Joe Buck (a breakout role for Jon Voight), a Texas dishwasher and, thanks to having grown up around his grandmother's beauty shop, a birth-right male gazer. The narrative begins with Joe's decision to change careers. Determined to move to Manhattan to become a high-end gigolo, Joe boards a northbound Greyhound. Approaching the city, its skyline in the background through the bus windows, Joe picks up a New York AM station on his transistor radio and thrills to "hear New York talkin'." The enthralling broadcast consists of woman-in-the-street interviewees responding to the question "What is your ideal in a man?" As various interviewees speak, the screen shows Joe Buck imagining what they look like. These shots feature close-ups of thirtyish and fortyish soigné-looking blondes replying "Gary Cooper but he's dead," "a Texas oil man," "someone I can talk to in bed," "not afraid of sex," "a rebel," "young." Introduced comically, these questions about masculinity become increasingly consequential and disturbing after Joe Buck hits the midtown streets in a black Stetson, a fringed buckskin, and stitched cowboy boots. As the narrative unfolds, Schlesinger backgrounds Joe's sexual experiences–passionless sex

---

[3] *Darling* billboard. https://thebestpictureproject.files.wordpress.com/2011/03/darling1.jpg.

for money and passionate sex for pleasure—by recalling the affectionate consensual intimacy and the sexual violence Joe and his girlfriend experienced in Texas. A wordless flashback shows them gently making love before being gang-raped by a group of young men who caught them *in flagrante*. For all the movie's on-screen sex, Schlesigner and Salt deprived Joe Buck of any committed or even sustained sex life. What sustains the plot is the transformation of Joe Buck's sex-free relationship with Enrico "Ratso" Rizzo (played by Dustin Hoffman)—a polio-lamed Times Square hustler, whose fecklessness exceeds Joe's own—from mutual exploitation into fraternal love.

Despite the movie's chaste core, Schlesinger maintains the movie's erotic charge by stressing throughout the story how integral Joe's ambitions to play the "stud" are to his self-image and self-esteem. Schlesinger achieves this erotic frisson by highlighting the pleasure Joe Buck takes in gazing and by making this gazing the focus of an inquiry by the camera and on behalf of the audience. Joe's gaze not only encompasses a kaleidoscopic variety of women. Schlesinger pictures Joe's gaze with such a wide range of poses from varied camera angles in a number of locations—interior and exterior, light and dark—and introduces and dismisses these gazes with such an array of edits that the movie's *mise-en-scène* becomes inseparable from Schlesinger's implicit but emphatic brief on behalf of male gazing. This brief rests on Schlesinger's rendering of Joe's gaze as at once innocent and promiscuous, avid and ineffectual.

With these contradictions, Schlesinger challenges masculine ideals of sexual mastery and domination that Joe Buck voices, embodies, caricatures, and is betrayed by near the beginning of *Midnight Cowboy*. Joe Buck's first line of dialogue encapsulates this acute, fraught but often comic sensitivity to prevailing understandings of masculinity. The line begins with the conditional clause, "if you ain't man enough to do it yourself." With this imagined parting shot to his boss, Joe makes a suggestion about what to do with–and where to stick– the unwashed dishes he's leaving behind. Before and during his actual departure, Joe explains his high hopes for success in his new career by observing that "the men" where he's heading "are mostly tutti-fruttis." Gazing on women throughout *Midnight Cowboy*, Joe and perhaps many 1969 moviegoers found such facile understandings of manhood becoming increasingly subjected to oblique but cumulative and durable pressures.

Joe Buck's first foray in search of clients takes him to Manhattan's traditional luxury shopping zone around 5th Avenue and 57th Street.

In a speechless sequence, during which Harry Nilsson sings "Everyone's Talking at Me "on the soundtrack, the camera watches Joe stepping briskly and standing tall among the New York women whom he imagined describing their ideal man on the radio during his bus ride north. Long shots of these women, most of them in tailored beige, pink, or coffee-brown suits, some in hats and most in low heels, alternate with close-up and medium shots of Joe weaving through the throng at a brisk pace. Shots of luxury store logos and shop windows equate the allure of the goods on sale and on display in these shops with the mystique these exotic women embody for Joe. Joe's reconnaissance mission ends with a plot turn that compounds this confusion when his first "client" turns out to be a Park Avenue call girl. After marveling at her "goddamned penthouse" he ends up paying *her* for their tryst or rather "lending" her twenty dollars.

The next sustained heterosexual encounter in the movie, a far more protracted, intimate, and gaze-centered encounter, takes place downtown in the aftermath of a Warhol Factory-like party to which Joe Buck's out-of-context "freaky" cowboy garb apparently earned him an invitation. The slowness with which Joe Buck wanders gazing through this loft party, after unwittingly smoking an entire joint by himself under the impression it's a cigarette, recalls and inverts his uptown outdoor stroll in bright midday sunshine. When Schlesinger shows Joe Buck looking at a woman party guest, it's often her hair that occupies the center of the frame. In contrast to the emphasis on clothing and tailoring uptown, Joe Buck's most sustained pause to gaze during this party focuses on women's bodies: a naked woman who passes in front of him, followed by several dressed women, shadow-dancing in front of a white and purple strobe-lighted screen. In a rose-lighted scene, Joe and Shirley—the party-guest who first turned him on to pot—meet in a side room. A series of close-up two-shots shows them alternately touching fingers, kissing, and laughing. When Ratso interrupts their stoned idyll, arguably the first earnestly erotic encounter in the movie, Shirley half-derisively conjectures, "Don't tell me you two are a couple," obliquely acknowledging an alternative to the understanding of manhood implicit in Joe Buck's reference to tutti-fruttis and Ratso's repeated slurs about "faggots." When Ratso promotes Joe's hyper-hetero credentials as "a very expensive stud," Shirley agrees to play along and offers "twenty bucks," essentially to send Ratso packing and bring Joe Buck back to her apartment.

Back at Shirley's place, though, Joe's "thing quits on" him, for "the first time," he claims. Nevertheless, Shirley and Joe share a generic (if unearned) post-coital moment. Shot from above and sharing a bright gold bedspread, as they each smoke a cigarette, they chat calmly and candidly, like familiar friends rather than like one-night-stand accomplices. Admitting "I may be making it worse," Shirley teases him back into a state of arousal by suggesting he stop calling her "m'am" and by introducing Joe to a Scrabble-like game called Scribbage. Joe leads off by spelling out *man*, which leads to a rhyming game that moves from *say*, *pay* and *lay* to *gay* and *fey*. This wordplay allows Joe to play other roles and try on other identities in addition to or instead of simply insisting on remaining "one hell of a stud."

While Joe's Park Avenue encounter was shot from the bedroom doorway and showed Joe on top, his encounter with Shirley consists of a series of extreme close-ups. Cutting between various body parts, including the lovers' faces, these shots show them assuming numerous positions in relation to each other's bodies. In a morning-after shot Shirley appears suited-up like one of the prosperous uptown shoppers Joe espied on 57th Street, talking on the phone and recommending Joe's services to a friend. Though Joe's virility seems secure and his career seems launched, this morning-after becomes a false happy ending. When he finds Ratso dying in the condemned building they share, Joe has to hustle a middle-aged man, whom Joe roughs up and robs, in order to take Ratso somewhere safe and warm. Repeated pauses to show Joe's agonized, horrified expression during this assault accentuate the out-of-character anomalousness of Joe behaving like the assailants who raped him and his girlfriend in Texas. Joe's solicitude for Ratso and his willingness to abandon the career path Shirley had opened for him further accentuate the anomalousness of Joe's violence.

Rather than censuring Joe's delusional career aspiration and rather than punishing—or redeeming—him, *Midnight Cowboy* allows for his character to leaven his sense of himself as "one hell of a stud" and his on-screen appearances as a compulsive male-gazer with the geniality and gentleness he displayed early in movie toward his restaurant co-worker, toward his fellow travelers on the bus to New York, toward the call girl he allowed to shake him down, and mostly toward Ratso. Laura Mulvey's famous disparagement of male-gazing notwithstanding, this "male protagonist" discovers over the course of *Midnight Cowboy* how little freedom gazers have "to command the stage … in which he articulates the look and creates the action" ("Visual Pleasure").

The London provenance of *Darling* and *Midnight Cowboy* and many American moviegoers' enthusiasm for these Schlesinger works anticipate the geographical coordinates of Mulvey's indelible introduction of the phrase "the male gaze" a decade after the release of *Darling*. Mulvey's argument grew out of her engagement with the conceptual and attitudinal changes we've come to call "the sixties" and her own responses to the work of the film industry's first influential London–Hollywood crossovers director, Alfred Hitchcock. Mulvey pinpoints the "sixties" context her male gaze essay "Visual Pleasure and Narrative Cinema" in recounting how her male-gaze thesis emerged from her "women's liberation reading group" at St. Martin's College of Art, which served as an impetus for her to reconsider Hollywood movies from a feminist perspective (Kelly).

Keeping both her own Britishness and Hollywood's seemingly unassailable hegemony in view, Mulvey singles out Hitchcock—Hollywood's most renowned British director and one of its earliest auteurs—as her prime example of gaze-promoting cinema. Narrowing her data base, she limits her evidence to the movies Hitchcock made in the later, Hollywood phase of his career, for Universal and Paramount, in the 1950s and 1960s. In Mulvey's account, Hitchcock's typical American hero is a consummate hegemon. Voyeurs whose "perversion" hides "under a shallow mask of ideological correctness," Hitchcock and the gazers he empowers occupy a position of authority from which to objectify women: that site of "command and control" in which Mulvey positioned her male gazers. In her view, Hitchcock achieves this effect so consummately as to "draw the spectators deeply into his position, making them share his uneasy gaze."

BIRDWATCHING AND STARGAZING

While Hitchcock was popularizing this narrative of hegemonic gazing for Hollywood, British movies from younger directors began to present gazing as an expression of discontent, alienation, and rage, rather than as a prerogative and expression of power, and to present gazers themselves as heirs to the "angry young men" who occupied London stages during the 1950s. A memorable instance of this subgenre is director Lindsay Anderson's and screenwriter David Sherwin's anti-empire coming-of-age polemic *If ....* Released several months before *Midnight Cowboy, If ...* won the 1969 *Palme d'Or* at Cannes. Anderson's title echoes and, with its ellipsis, registers the inadequacy of one of English poetry's most familiar mainstays, "If—" by Rudyard Kipling. Drummed into schoolchildren throughout the English-speaking world during much of the twentieth century "If—" served the empire as the definitive lesson in imperial manhood. After a series of anaphoric "If—" clauses, the poem ends by promising, "yours is the Earth and everything that's in it, and—which is more—you'll be a Man, my son!"

Indian-born like Kipling himself, Anderson rebelled against having Kipling thrust upon him "as one of our ... great poetic geniuses" and more generally against Kipling's "nauseating sentiments, and vulgar, blatant, superficial versification" (L. Anderson 38). As a naval intelligence trainee during World War Two, the conflict Hitchcock patriotically championed in *Foreign Correspondent, Lifeboat, Notorious,* and *Saboteur,* Anderson reacted against what many critics have come to regard as Kipling's "imperial hysteria" (Gopnik). While in service, Anderson told his commanding officer that he "did not like Kipling and mentioned with disfavor his jingoistic imperialism" (Sutton 6–7). Accordingly, in *If ...* Anderson depicts a group of teenage schoolboys' passage to manhood as a hopeless but perilously aggressive adolescent fantasy (like empire itself according to familiar anti-imperialist arguments). In aligning this critique with a group of male gazers' "youthful yearnings," Anderson turned gazing itself into a radical political argument. To characterize his agenda Anderson took as his motto "*imagination au pouvoir*" (idiomatically translated as "power to the imagination"), a slogan coined by insurgent French students during their May 1968 protests (Ehrenstein).

Early on, the movie establishes its hero, Mick (played by Malcolm McDowell), as an arch male gazer. Anderson drives home this point in a scene in which Mick's only studious friend shares his treasured high power telescope and explains the sidereal phenomena visible through their dormitory window. When Mick takes his turn viewing the heavens, he immediately shifts his focus from his astronomy lesson to his girlfriend (Christine Noonan) as she stands in chiaroscuro black and white at a window that seems to float free in the black space surrounding it.

During a conversation with his roommate about their summer vacation, Mick recounts carousing in East End pubs and watching young women—"birds" whom he describes as dancing and "showing their knickers." In a subsequent dorm room exchange Mick and his mates pass around a centerfold about which Mick asks rhetorically "isn't she beautiful?" and then concludes that there's "only one thing you can do with a girl like that." Midway through *If ...* Anderson accentuates this view of gazing as a group activity and as a bonding ritual. While dining with Mrs. Kemp, the young theatrically prim wife of one their school's masters, Nick and his friends subject her to incessant staring, sarcastic politesse while turning the food on the table into phallic visual puns. Anderson validates the desire underlying this hazing by literally visualizing the cliché about men "undressing women with their eyes," a phrase typically introduced to disparage male gazing.

In Mrs. Kemp's last on-screen appearance, she appears entirely nude in a long silent black-and-and-white interlude. This sequence begins with a long shot down a school corridor, filmed at such a distance that the approaching blonde remains anonymous, even as she moves into the smaller space of the school kitchen where, shot from behind, she remains unidentifiable, until she turns and faces the camera to steal a bun from a baking table. Earlier in the movie Mrs. Kemp had savagely scolded one of her husband's students for exactly the same transgression. Alone, naked, and frankly hungry—presumably no longer repressed and repressive—Mrs. Kemp emerges, in the words of a Carole King song then recently popularized by Arethra Franklin, as a "natural-born woman." The editing in this sequence spotlights Mrs. Kemp's liberating solitude. As a stately nude promenading deliberately through the school building, she assumes a dignity not previously afforded her. This stark naked dignity contrasts sharply with the scenes that alternate with Mrs. Kemp's nocturnal foray: the bright color exterior shots of all the faculty and students drilling and war-gaming, chasing one another across the countryside with rifles.

The most memorable gaze sequence in *If…* also relies on sharp contrasts between color and black and white, between a bright countryside exterior and the dim interior of the narrow sparsely furnished café where Mick's girlfriend works as a waitress. Upon entering the café and approaching the counter at the far end of the shot, Mick begins ogling his girlfriend, *the* "mythic' girl" according to screenwriter David Sherwin (Ehrenstein), from across a café counter. After a rebuff—a slap—that launches Mick across the room, the scene turns imperceptibly into a reverie: a sexual fantasy. Growling like a tiger, the "girl" approaches Mick and, threateningly, demands: "go on look at me" (pause) "I'll kill you." Then "the girl" falls on Mick. So suddenly that "'reality' and 'fantasy' converge" (Ehrenstein), they're both naked on the floor. With Mick underneath her, the "girl" bites his arm. Just as suddenly, they're sitting a table, with one of Mick's schoolmates, fully clothed, playing rock–paper–scissors.

Anderson follows this fantasy *en plein air*, with a brightly colored exterior crowd scene, apparently another "fantasy." In this scene, Anderson ends *If* ... with Mick and his schoolmates massacring their school's staff and its benefactors during its annual Founder's Day cele-bration. The café waitress or "the girl" (as the credits call her in an hom-age to Veronica Lake in *Sullivan's Travels*) (Ehrenstein) has joined Mick and his schoolmates and fires the revolver shot that kills the headmas-ter as he seeks to quell the rebellion by peaceably asserting his authority. Rather than identifying with authority, the pattern Mulvey finds recur-ring throughout Hitchcock's Hollywood work, Anderson's gazer allies with his gaze object, the "girl," to flout—or at least imagine violently defying—what Mulvey calls "the "symbolic order and the law" and the "ideological correctness" on which male gazing rests and which it helps maintain.

Anderson's more expansive, more catholic, understanding of gazing is also evident in his attention to *male* same-sex gazing. With the same kind of interplay between busy color and the loosely restrained black and white with which he pictures female nudity, Anderson pictures men look-ing erotically at other men: Anderson follows a color nude crowd shot of the schoolboys' hectic morning shower ritual with a black and white slow-motion shot of three first-year students gazing raptly at an upper-classman performing a high-bar gymnastic routine. Framed as a gazer in a medium shot, one of the boys lingers worshipfully. He appears no less intent on what he sees than Mick appears soon after locating "the girl" through a friend's high power telescope.

The commandingly heteronormative gazers Mulvey imagined in "Visual Pleasure and Narrative Cinema" might find the act of gazing empowering, enabling the gazer to "subject another to [his] will," as did the biblical patriarchs and autocrats. But for the young gazers in *If...* and *Midnight Cowboy* and for the plaintive gazers in countless songs of the same era gazing usually serves as reminder of the distance, often a growing distance, between young gazers and what we looked at—and looked for.

WORKS CITED

Abeel, Erica. *"The Human Stain."* *Film Journal International.* http://www.
filmjournal.com/human-stain. Web. 2003.

Abrams, M.H., *Natural Supernaturalism: Tradition and Revolution in Romantic Literature.* New York: W.W. Norton, 1973. Print.

Abur-Rahman A. "'Simply a Menaced Boy': Analogizing Color, Undoing Dominance in James Baldwin's *Giovanni's Room.*" *African American Review,* 41:3 (2007): 477–486. https://www.brandeis.edu/departments/english/faculty/docs/articles/abdurrahman/MenacedBoy.pdf. Web.

Adams, S. *"Giovanni's Room*: The homosexual as hero", in H. Bloom (ed.), *James Baldwin Modern Critical Views,* New York: Chelsea House, 1986. Pp. 131–139. Print.

Als, Hilton. "Cate Blanchett and Blanche Dubois." *New Yorker* 23 December 2009. http://www.nybooks.com/blogs/nyrblog/2009/dec/23/cate-blan-chett-and-blanche-dubois/. Web.

Amidon, Stephen. "Frank O'Hara Provides the Poetry of Mad Men." *Sunday Times* 22 February 2009. http://www.thesundaytimes.co.uk/sto/culture/film_and_tv/tv/article151560.ece. Web.

———. "A Guide to Philip Roth." The *Times* (London) 23 September 2007. www.thesundaytimes.co.uk/sto/culture/books/article71930.ece. Web.

Anderson, Lindsay & Sutton, Paul. *The Diaries.* London: Methuen, 2004. Print.

Anderson, Sam. "Schlong of Myself." *New York* 2 Sept 2007. http://nymag.com/arts/books/reviews/37997/. Web.

Anderson, Sherwood. *Winesburg, Ohio.* 1919. http://archive.org/stream/winesburgohio005800mbp/winesburgohio005800mbp_djvu.txt. Web.

Austen, Jane. *Persuasion.* 1817. http://www.gutenberg.org/files/105/105-h/105-h.htm. Web.

© The Editor(s) (if applicable) and The Author(s) 2017
J.D. Bloom, *Reading the Male Gaze in Literature and Culture*, Global
Masculinities, DOI 10.1007/978-3-319-59945-8

Baldwin, James. *Collected Essays*, New York: Library of America, 1998. Print.
————. *The Fire Next Time*. 1963. New York: Random House/Vintage, 1993. Print.
————. *Giovanni's Room*. 1956. New York: Random House/Delta, 2000. Print.
————. *Go Tell it on the Mountain*. 1953. New York: Dell/Laurel, 1985. Print.
————. *Nobody Knows My Name: More Notes of a Native Son*, New York: Dell, 1963 Print.
————. *Notes of A Native Son*. 1955, Boston: Beacon Press, 1957. Print.
Ball, Edward. "Gone With the Myths." *New York Times* 19 December 2010. http://www.nytimes.com/2010/12/19/opinion/19Ball.html?_r=0. Web.
Banner, Lois. *American Beauty: A Social History Through Two Centuries of the American Idea Ideal, and Image of the Beautiful Woman*. New York: Knopf, 1983. Print.
Baraka, Amiri. *Dutchman & The Slave: Two Plays by Leroi Jones*. 1964. New York: William Morrow/Quill, 1979. Print.
Barthes, Roland. *Mythologies*. Tr. Annette Lavers. New York: Macmillan, 1972. Print.
Barzun, Jacques. *Race: A Study in Superstition*. New York: Harcourt, Brace, 1937. Print.
Batuman, Elif. *Possession: Adventures with Russian Books and the People Who Read Them*. New York: Farrar, Straus, Giroux, 2010. Print.
Bauman, Zygmunt *Legislators and Interpreters: On Modernity, Post-Modernity, and Intellectuals*. Ithaca: Cornell UP, 1987. Print.
Baxter, Charles. *Burning Down the House: Essays on Fiction*. St. Paul, Graywolf Press, 1997. Web.
Bell, Julian. "The Great & Singular Vallotton." *New York Review of Books*. 19 December 2012. http://www.nybooks.com/articles/archives/2013/dec/19/great-singular-felix-vallotton. Web.
————. "There, This Is Life." Rev. *Rendez-vous with Art* by Philippe de Montebello & Martin Gayford. *New York Review of Books*. 25 June 2015. www.nybooks.com/articles/archives/2015/jun/25/there-this-is-life/. Web.
Berger, John. *Ways of Seeing*. New York: Viking/Richard Seaver, 1973. Print.
Berryman, John. *The Dream Songs*. New York: Farrar, Straus & Giroux, 1969. Print.
Bishop, Helen Gary. "Winogrand Woman." Introduction to Winogrand, Garry. *Woman Are Beautiful*. Light Gallery Books/Farrar, Straus Giroux, 1975. Unpaged. Print.
Blackmur, R.P. *Eleven Essays in the European Novel*. Ed. Joseph Frank. New York: Harcourt Brace, 1967. Print.
Blake, William. *Songs of Innocence and of Experience*. 1789. http://www.gutenberg.org/files/1934/1934-h/1934-h.htm. Web

————. *The Marriage of Heaven and Hell.* 1793. http://www.gutenberg.org/files/45315/45315-h/45315-h.htm. Web.

Bloom, James. *The Stock of Available Reality: R.P. Blackmur and John Berryman.* Lewiston PA: Bucknell UP, 1984. Print.

"Books." *Boston Herald* 3 September 1995: 75. Print.

Booth, George. "Whistle, You Dumb Bastard." *New Yorker* 27 August 1973. http://www.art.com/products/p15063518123-sa-i6848715/george-booth-whistle-you-dumb-bastard-new-yorker-cartoon.htm. Web.

Borus & Feinstein, *Girls & Sports* 21 February 2008. Web. [NO LONGER AVAILABLE].

Bowen, Elizabeth. *The Heat of the Day.* 1948. New York: Penguin, 1962. Print.

————. "Why I Go to the Cinema." In Davy, Charles., ed. *Footnotes to the Film.* London: Lovat Dickinson/Readers Union, 1938. Pp. 202–220. Print.

Boyd, Neil. *Big Sister: How Extreme Feminism Has Betrayed the Fight for Sexual Equality.* Vancouver: Greystone Books, 2004. Print.

Brennan, Stephen. "The Sex Which Is One: Language and the Masculine Self in *Jennie Gerhardt* "in *Theodore Dreiser and American Culture: New Readings.* Ed. Yoshinobu Hakutani. Newark DE: U of Delaware Press, 2000. Pp. 138–157. Print.

Brody, Richard. "Movies: Mothers and Lovers." *New Yorker* 21 July 2014: 6. Print.

Brown, Wendy. *Politics Out of History.* Princeton: Princeton UP, 2001. Print.

Burger, Alissa. "Diamonds Are A Girl's Best Friend: Performances of Femininity in *Gentleman Prefer Blondes, Material Girl, and Moulin Rouge.*" *Americana* January 2006. http://www.americanpopularculture.com/archive/style/diamonds.htm. Web.

Burke, Edmund. *Philosophical Inquiry into the Origin of Our Ideas of the Sublime and Beautiful.* 1757. http://cnqzu.com/library/Philosophy/neoreaction/_extra%20authors/Burke,%20Edmund/Burke%20Edmund-Of%20the%20Sublime%20and%20Beautiful.pdf. Web.

Bush, Kate. *Sensual World.* Columbia, 1989. CD.

Butterfield, Andrew. "Venice: The Masters in Boston." *New York Review of Books* 16 July 2009: 13–14. Print.

Campbell, James. *Talking at the Gates: A Life of James Baldwin,* New York: Viking, 1991. Print.

Calvino, Italo. *Mr. Palomar.* 1983, Tr. William Weaver. Harvest/HBJ, 1985. Print.

Cartelli, Thomas. *Repositioning Shakespeare: National Formations, Postcolonial Appropriations.* New York: Routledge, 1999. Print.

Castle, Terry. *The Apparitional Lesbian: Female Homosexuality and Modern Culture.* New York: Columbia University Press, 1993. Print.

Cather, Willa. "Coming, Aphrodite!" 1920. http://www.online-literature.com/willa-cather/2115/. Web.

Chesnutt, Charles W. *The House Behind the Cedars*. 1900. http://www.gutenberg.org/files/472/472-h/472-h.htm. Web.
————. Charles W. Chesnutt: *Essays and Speeches*. Eds. Joseph R. McElrath, Jr., Robert C. Leitz, Jesse S. Crisler. Palo Alto: Stanford UP, 2001. Print.
Chiasson, Dan. "Bicentennial." *Paris Review* 206 (Fall 2013). https://www.theparisreview.org/poetry/6262/bicentennial-dan-chiasson. Web.
Clark, Kenneth. *The Nude: A Study in Ideal Form*. 1958. Princeton: Bollingen Series/Princeton University Press, 1990. Print.
Coetzee, J.M. *Diary of a Bad Year*. New York: Viking, 2008. Print.
Cope, Karin. "Painting after Gertrude Stein." *Diacritics* 24: 2–3 (1994): 190–203. Print.
Cotter, Holland. "Avant-Gardist in Retreat." *New York Times* 17 June 2010. http://www.nytimes.com/2010/06/18/arts/design/18renoir.html?pagewanted=all. Web.
Curtin, William M., ed. *The World and the Parish: Willa Cather's Articles and Reviews, 1893–1902*. Lincoln, NE: University of Nebraska Press, 1970. Print.
DeLillo, Don. *Great Jones Street*. 1973, New York: Penguin, 1994. Print.
DeWaal, Edmund. *The Hare With Amber Eyes: A Family's History of Art and Loss*. New York: Farrar, Straus, & Giroux, 2010. Print.
Dickinson, Emily. *Complete Poems*. Ed. Thomas Johnson. 1955. https://archive.org/stream/poemsofemilydick030097mbp/poemsofemilydick030097mbp_djvu.txt. Web.
Diehl, L. "A Toast to Miss Rheingold." *Daily News* 12 October 2000. http://www.materchristi.websitetoolbox.com/post?id=3468928&goto=nextoldest. Web.
Donne, John. "Elegy XIX. To His Mistress Going To Bed." 1669. http://www.eecs.harvard.edu/~keith/poems/Elegy19.html. Web.
Donoghue, Denis. *Speaking of Beauty*. New Haven: Yale UP, 2003. Print.
Dos Passos, John. *Three Soldiers*. 1921. http://www.gutenberg.org/files/6362/6362-h/6362-h.htm. Web.
Dreiser, Theodore. *Gallery of Women*. New York: Liveright, 1929. Print.
————. "Gloom." Revised ts. Box 229, folder 9469. Theodore Dreiser Papers. U of Pennsylvania, Philadelphia.
————. *Jennie Gerhardt*. 1911. http://www.gutenberg.org/files/28988/28988-h/28988-h.htm. Web.
————. *Jennie Gerhardt*. 1992. New York: Penguin, 1994. Print.
————. *Sister Carrie*. 1900. http://www.gutenberg.org/files/233/233-h/233-h.htm. Web.
DuBois, W.E.B. *The Souls of Black Folk*. 1903. https://www.gutenberg.org/files/408/408-h/408-h.htm. Web.
Dunbar, Paul Laurence. *The Sport of the Gods*. 1902. http://www.gutenberg.org/files/17854/17854-h/17854-h.htm. Web.

Dyer, Geoff. *Jeff In Venice, Death In Varanasi*. New York: Pantheon, 2009. Print.

Dylan, Bob. *Chronicles: Volume One*. New York : Simon & Schuster, 2004. Print.

Eagleton, Terry. "Bodies, Artworks, and Use Values." *New Literary History* 44: 4 (2013). 561–573. https://muse.jhu.edu/article/536122. Web.

Eby, Claire. "Dreiser and Women" in *The Cambridge Companion to Theodore Dreiser*. Eds. Leonard Cassuto & Clare Eby. Cambridge: Cambridge University Press, 2004. Pp. 142–159. Print.

Ehrenstein, David. "*If...: School Days.*" *The Criterion Collection*. http://www.criterion.com/current/posts/488-if-schooldays. Web.

Ellmann, Richard. *Oscar Wilde*. 1984. New York: Knopf, 1987. Print.

Emerson, Ralph Waldo. "Quotation and Originality." 1876. http://www.bartleby.com/90/0806.html. Web.

Eugenides, Jeffrey. *The Virgin Suicides*. New York: Picador/Farrar Straus Giroux, 1993. Print.

Fanon, Frantz. *Black Skin. White Masks*. Trans Richard Philcox. 1952. New York: Grove, 2008. Print.

Farber, David. "*The 60's: Myth and Reality.*" *Chronicle of Higher Education*. 7 December 1994. http://chronicle.com/article/The-60s-MythReality/84165/. Web.

Fiedler, Leslie. *Love and Death in the American Novel*. 1960. Normal, IL: Dalkey Archive Press, 1997. Print.

Firestone, Shulamith. *The Dialectic of Sex: The Case for Feminist Revolution*. New York: Morrow, 1970. Print.

Fitzgerald, F. Scott. *The Great Gatsby*. 1925. http://gutenberg.net.au/ebooks02/0200041h.html. Web.

———. *The Stories of F. Scott Fitzgerald*. 1955. http://archive.org/stream/storiesoffscottf030459mbp/storiesoffscottf030459mbp_djvu.txt. Web.

Florence, Ronald. *The Perfect Machine: Building the Palomar Telescope*. New York: Harper Collins, 1994, Print.

Foer, Jonathan Safran. "Love is Blind and Deaf." *New Yorker* 8 June 2015. http://www.newyorker.com/magazine/2015/06/08/love-is-blind-and-deaf. Web.

"For Those Who Think Young." *Mad Men*. Season 2, Episode 1. AMC. 27 July 2008. Television.

Fountain, Ben. *Billy Lynn's Long Halftime Walk*. New York: Ecco/Harpers, 2012. Print.

Freedman, Estelle. *No Turning Back: The History of Feminism and the Future of Women*. New York: Ballantine, 2003. Print.

Freud, Sigmund. *Moses and Monotheism*. 1939. Trans. Katherine Jones. New York: Random House/Vintage, 1967. Print.

———. *Totem and Taboo*. 1913. Trans. James Strachey. New York: W.W. Norton, 1990. Print.

————. *Three Essays on Sexuality*. 1905 Trans. James Strachey. New York: Basic Books, 1975. Print.

Frost, Robert. "The Bear." 1928. https://www.poemhunter.com/poem/the-bear/. Web.

Gallagher, Gary & Nolan, Alan. *The Myth of the Lost Cause and Civil War History*. Indianapolis: Indiana University Press, 2000. Print.

Gallop, Jane. "Precocious *Jouissance*: Roland Barthes, Amatory Maladjustment, and Emotion." *New Literary History* 43: 3 (2012). 565–582. Print.

Gamman, Lorraine & Marshment, Margaret. *The Female Gaze: Women as Viewers*. Seattle: Real Comet Press, 1989. Print.

Gammell, Irene. *Sexualizing Power in Naturalism: Theodore Dreiser and Frederick Philip Grove*. Calgary: University of Calgary Press, 1994. Print.

Garber, Marjorie. *Vice Versa: Bisexuality and the Eroticism of Everyday Life*. New York: Simon & Schuster/Touchstone, 1996. Print.

Glaser, Jennifer. "The Jew in the Canon." *PMLA* 123 (2008) 1465–1478. Print.

Golding, William. "Thinking as A Hobby." 1961. http://www.gmsdk12.org/Downloads/Thinking%20as%20a%20Hobby2.pdf. Web.

Gopnik, Adam. "The Comparable Max. *New Yorker*" 3 August 2015 http://www.newyorker.com/magazine/2015/08/03/the-comparable-max. Web.

Gordon, Brandon. "Physical Sympathy: Hip and Sentimentalism in James Baldwin's *Another Country.*" *Modern Fiction Studies*, 57: 1 (2011). http://muse.jhu.edu/journals/modern_fiction_studies/v057/57.1.gordon.html. Web.

Guthrie, James. "Darwinian Dickinson: The Scandalous Rise and Noble Fall of the Common Clover." *Emily Dickinson Journal* 16.1 (2007) http://muse.jhu.edu/journals/modern_fiction_studies/v057/57.1.gordon.html. Web.

Hall, Calvin S. *A Primer of Freudian Psychology*. 1954. New York: Signet, 1955. Print.

Hall, Stuart. "Old and New Identities, Old and New Ethnicities" in *Theories of Race and Racism A Reader*. Eds. Les Back, John Solomos. London: Routledge, 2000. Pp. 199–208. Print.

Hardy, Thomas. *Far From the Madding Crowd*. 1874. http://www.gutenberg.org/cache/epub/27/pg27-images.html. Web.

Harris, Dave et al. "Reading Guide to Mulvey on Cinema and Psychoanalysis: Essays, Papers and Courses." http://www.arasite.org/mulvey.htm. Web.

Hawkesworth, Mary. *Feminist Inquiry: From Political Conviction to Methodological Innovation*. New Brunswick: Rutgers UP, 2006. Print.

Hawthorne, Nathaniel. *The Scarlet Letter*. 1850. http://www.gutenberg.org/cache/epub/33/pg33-images.html. Web.

Hemingway, Ernest. "Soldier's Home." 1925. http://www.somanybooks.org/eng208/SoldiersHome.pdf. Web.

————. *The Sun Also Rises.* 1926. New York: Scribner/Simon & Shuster, 1954. Print.

Himes, Chester. *If He Hollers, Let Him Go.* 1946. Philadelphia: Da Capo Press/ Perseus, 2002. Print.

Holland, Sharon. "*(Pro)Creating Imaginative Spaces* and Other Queer Acts: Randall Kenan's *A Visitation of Spirits* and Its Revival of James Baldwin's Absent Gay Man in *Giovanni's Room*" in D. McBride (ed.), *James Baldwin Now*, New York: New York University Press, 1999. Pp. 265–288. Print.

Holden, Stephen. "What Kind of Fool Is Love? No Matter, the Search Is On." *New York Times* 28 September 2007. http://www.nytimes. com/2007/09/28/movies/28feas.html?_r=0. Web.

Holmes, Richard. *The Age of Wonder: The Romantic Generation and the Discovery of the Beauty and Terror of Science.* New York Pantheon, 2008. Print.

Hooks, bell. "The Oppositional Gaze: Black Female Spectators." 1992. www. umass.edu/afroam/downloads/reading14.pdf. Web.

Hurston, Zora Neale. *Their Eyes Were Watching God.* 1937. New York: Harper Perennial, 1998. Print.

Irving, Washington. "The Legend of Sleepy Hollow." 1820. http://www.guten-berg.org/files/41/41-h/41-h.htm. Web.

James, Henry. *The Ambassadors.* 1903. 1909. http://www.gutenberg.org/files/ 432/432-h/432-h.htm. Web.

————. "The Beldonald Holbein." 1903. http://www.gutenberg.org/files/ 2366/2366-h/2366-h.htm. Web

————. "Daisy Miller." 1879. http://www.gutenberg.org/files/208/208-h/ 208-h.htm. Web.

————. *The Europeans.* 1878. http://www.gutenberg.org/files/179/179-h/ 179-h.htm. Web.

————. *Hawthorne.* 1879. http://www.gutenberg.org/files/18566/18566-h/ 18566-h.htm. Web.

————. "In the Cage." 1898. http://www.gutenberg.org/files/1144/ 1144-h/1144-h.htm. Web.

————. *The Letters of Henry James.* Ed. Percy Lubbock New York: Scribner, 1920. Print.

————. "Preface to *The Golden Bowl.*" 1909. http://www2.newpaltz. edu/~hathawar/goldenbowl1.html. Web.

Joyce, James. *Stephen Hero.* 1944. New York: New Directions, 1963. Print.

————. *Ulysses.* 1922. http://www.gutenberg.org/files/4300/4300-h/4300-h.htm. Web.

Kalfus, Ken. "Coup de Foudre" *Harpers* April 2014: 65–80. Print.

Kant, Immanuel. *Lectures on Ethics.* Trans. Louis Infield. New York: Harpers & Row, 1963. Print.

Kaplan, E. Ann. *Woman and Film: Both Sides of the Camera*. New York: Routledge, 1988. Print.

Keats, John. *Letters of John Keats to His Family and Friends*. 1925. http://www.gutenberg.org/files/35698/35698-h/35698-h.htm. Web.

————. *Poems Published in 1820.*, Ed. M. Robertson. http://www.gutenberg.org/files/23684/23684-h/23684-h.htm. Web.

Kelly, Mary. "A Secret Agreement: An Era Defined by the Events of 1968." 26 March 2015. http://www.tate.org.uk/whats-on/tate-modern/talks-and-lectures/mary-kelly-conversation-hans-ulrich-obrist/secret-agreement. Web.

Kierkegaard, Søren. *A Kierkegaard Anthology*. Ed. Robert Bretall. Princeton: Princeton UP, 1946. Print.

Kipnis, Laura. *Ecstasy Unlimited: On Sex, Capital, Gender, and Aesthetics*. Minneapolis: U of Minnesota Press, 1993. Print.

————. *Men: Notes from an Ongoing Investigation*. New York: Metropolitan/ Holt, 2014. Print.

Kitcher, Philip. *Joyce's Kaleidoscope: An Invitation to Finnegans Wake*. Oxford UP, 2007. Print.

Klay, Phil. *Redeployment*. New York, Penguin Random House, 2014. Print.

Lane, Anthony. "The Current Cinema: Wouldn't It Be Nice?" *New Yorker* 1 June 2015: 80–88. Print.

————. "Lady Be Good; A centenary season of Barbara Stanwyck" *New Yorker* 30 April 2007: 42. Print.

————. "Names and Faces: The Portraits of Julia Margaret Cameron". *New Yorker* 2 September 2013. http://www.newyorker.com/arts/critics/atlarge/2013/09/02/130902crat_atlarge_lane?currentPage=all. web.

Larkin, Philip. *High Windows*. New York: Farrar Straus Giroux, 1974. Print.

Lavin, Suzanne. *Women and Comedy in Solo Performance: Phyllis Diller, Lily Tomlin and Roseanne Barr*. New York: Routledge, 2004. Print.

Lawrence, D.H., *Letters*. Ed. James Boulton. New York: Cambridge, UP, 2000. Print.

————. *The Lost Girl*. Ed. John Worthen. New York: Cambridge, UP, 1981. Print.

————. *Studies in Classic American Literature*. 1923. http://xroads.virginia.edu/~hyper/lawrence/dhlch05.htm. Web.

Lentricchia, Frank. *Ariel and the Police: Michel Foucault, William James, and Wallace Stevens*. Madison: U of Wisconsin Press, 1988. Print.

Levy, Ariel. "Dolls and Feelings." *New Yorker* 14 December 2014. http://www.newyorker.com/magazine/2015/12/14/dolls-and-feelings. Web.

Lewis, Sinclair. *Kingsblood Royal*. 1947. http://gutenberg.net.au/ebooks02/0200171.txt. Web

Li, Yiyun. "A Man Like Him." *New Yorker* 11 May 2008. http://www.newyorker.com/magazine/2008/05/12/a-man-like-him. Web.

Lipking, Lawrence. *What Galileo Saw: Imagining the Scientific Revolution.* Ithaca: Cornell UP, 2014. Print.

Lord, M.G. *Forever Barbie: The Unauthorized Biography of a Real Doll.* 1994. New York: Avon Books, 1995. Print.

Lyons, Margaret. "Mad Men's New Art Has Don Draper Between Mannequins." *Vulture* 27 February 2012. http://www.vulture.com/2012/02/mad-men-mannequin-ad.html. Web.

Lytle, Mark. *America's Uncivil Wars: The Sixties Era from Elvis to the Fall of Richard Nixon.* New York: Oxford UP, 2006. Print.

Madden, Deirdre. *Time Present and Time Past.* New York: Europa Editions, 2014. Print.

Mailer, Norman. *Advertisements for Myself.* 1959. New York: Putnam/Berkeley Medallion, 1966. Print.

Marx, Karl & Engels, Friedrich. *The German Ideology.* 1845. http://www.marxists.org/archive/marx/works/1845/german-ideology/ch01a.htm. Web.

Marz, Melissa "Chimes of Freedom: The Songs of Bob Dylan." *Entertainment Weekly* 27 January 2012. http://www.ew.com/ew/article/0,,20562450,00.html. Web.

Max, D.T. "The Twilight of the Old Goats." *Salon* 16 May 1997. http://www.salon.com/1997/05/16/goats/. Web.

Maxim Staff. "Sexy Beast: Sarah Silverman is the New King Kong of Comedy." *Maxim* June 2007. Print.

Meade, Marion. "Does Rock Degrade Women." *New York Times.* 14 March 1971: 2:3. Print.

Meeker, Natania. *Voluptuas Philosophy: Literary Materialism in the French Enlightenment.* Fordham UP, 2006. Print.

Meryman, Richard. *Andrew Wyeth: A Secret Life.* New York: Harper Collins, 1996. Print.

Michaels, Walter Benn. *The Shape of the Signifier: 1967 to the End of History.* Princeton: Princeton UP, 2004. Print.

Mill, J.S. *Dissertations and Discussions: Political, Philosophical, and Historical.* Vol. 3. London: Longmans, Green, Reader and Dyer, 1875. Print.

Miller, D.A. *The Novel and the Police.* Berkeley: U of California Press, 1988. Print.

Millet, Kate. *Sexual Politics.* Garden City: Doubleday, 1970. Print.

Modleski, Tania. *The Women Who Knew Too Much Hitchcock and Feminist Theory.* New York: Routledge, 1988. Print.

Moore, Lorrie. "Gazing at Love." Rev. *Blue Is the Warmest Color. New York Review of Books* 19 December 2012. www.nybooks.com/articles/archives/2013/dec/19/gazing-love. Web.

————. "A Very Singular Girl." Rev. *Not Pretty Enough* by Gerri Hirshey & *Enter Helen* by Brooke Hauser. *Nework Review of Books* 14 July 2016. http://www.nybooks.com/articles/2016/07/14/helen-gurley-brown-very-singular-girl/. web.

————. "The Wrath of Athena." *New York Times Book Review* 7 May 2000. http://www.nytimes.com/2000/05/07/books/the-wrath-of-athena.html. Web.

"Morals: The Second Sexual Revolution." *Time* 24 January 1964. http://www.time.com/time/covers/0,16641,1101640124,00.html?internalid=AC. Web.

Morrison, Toni. *Playing in the Dark: Whiteness and the Literary Imagination.* Cambridge: Harvard UP, 1992. Print

Mulvey, Laura. *Visual and Other Pleasures.* Bloomington: Indiana UP, 1989. Print.

————. "Visual Pleasure and Narrative Cinema." 1975. https://www.amherst.edu/system/files/media/1021/Laura%20Mulvey,%20Visual%20Pleasure.pdf. Web.

Munro, Alice. *The View From Castle Rock.* New York: Knopf, 2006. Print.

Nussbaum, Martha. "Objectification." *Philosophy and Public Affairs* 24: 4 (1995). Pp. 249–291. Print.

Oates, Joyce Carol. "Lovely, Dark and Deep," *Harpers.* November 2013. http://harpers.org/archive/2013/11/lovely-dark-deep. Web.

O'Brien, Tim. *The Things They Carried.* 1990. Boston: HMH/Mariner, 2009. Print.

O'Connor, Flannery. "The Church and the Fiction Writer." *America* 30 March 1957. http://americamagazine.org/issue/100/church-and-fiction-writer. Web.

————. Complete Stories. New York: Farrar Straus Giroux, 1972. Print.

————. *Wise Blood.* 1953. *New York*: Macmillan, 2007. Print.

O'Hara, Frank. *The Collected Poems of Frank O'Hara.* Ed. Donald Allen. Berkeley: U of California Press, 1995. Print.

Oliver, Paul. *Blues Fell This Morning.* New York: Cambridge UP, 1990. Print.

O'Nan, Stewart. *West of Sunset.* New York: Viking, 2015. Print

Ortega Y Gasset, José. *The Dehumanization of Art and Other Writings.* Tr. Willard Trask. Garden City, NY: Doubleday, 1956. Print.

Paglia, Camille. "Ivory Tower." *Salon* 7 October 1998. http://www.salon1999.com/it/col/pagl/1998/10/07pagl.html. Web.

————. *Sexual Personae: Art and Decadence from Nefertiti to Emily Dickinson.* 1990. New York: Vintage, 1991. Print.

Patchen, Kenneth. *Memoirs of a Shy Pornographer.* New York: New Directions, 1945. Print.

Pearce, Richard. "How Does Molly Bloom Look Through the Male Gaze." *Molly Blooms: A Polylogue on "Penelope" and Cultural Studies.* Ed Richard Pearce Madison: U of Wisconsin Press, 1994. Pp. 40–60. Print.

Perlstein, Rick. "Who Owns the Sixties." *Lingua Franca* May/June 1996. http://linguafranca.mirror.theinfo.org/9605/sixties.html. Web.

Pierpont, Claudia R. *Roth Unbound: A Writer and His Books.* New York: Farrar, Straus, Giroux, 2013. Print.

Pinsker, Sanford. "Philip Rahv's 'Paleface and Redskin'—Fifty Years Later." *Georgia Review* 43: 3 (1989): 477–489. Print.

Pinsky, Robert. *The Situation of Poetry.* Princeton, N.J.: Princeton UP, 1976. Print.

Pirnia, Garin. "15 Uncensored Facts About *Midnight Cowboy.*" *Mental Floss.* 22 January 2016. http://mentalfloss.com/article/74222/15-uncensored-facts-about-midnight-cowboy. Web.

Poirier, Richard. *The Comic Sense of Henry James.* London: Chatto & WIndus, 1960. Print.

————. *The Performing Self: Compositions and Decompositions in the Languages of Contemporary Life.* New York: Oxford UP, 1971. Print.

Pollak, Vivian. "Dickinson and the Poetics of Whiteness." *Emily Dickinson Journal* 9.2 (2000): 84–95. https://muse.jhu.edu/journals/emily_dickinson_journal/v009/9.2pollak.html. Web.

Rabinowitz, Paula. *Black & White & Noir: America's Pulp Modernism.* New York: Columbia UP, 2002. Print.

Rahv, Philip. "Paleface and Redskin." *Kenyon Review* 1:3 (Summer, 1939): 251–256. Print.

Ricks, Christopher. *Dylan's Vision of Sin.* New York: Ecco, 2004. Print.

Robinson, Paul. *The Freudian Left: Wilhelm Reich, Geza Roheim, Herbert Marcuse,* Ithaca: Cornell UP, 1969. Print.

Robinson, Sally. *Marked Men: White Masculinity in Crisis.* New York: Columbia UP, 2000. Print.

Roiphe, Katie. "The Naked and the Conflicted." *New York Times Book Review.* 31 December 2009. http://www.nytimes.com/2010/01/03/books/review/Roiphe-t.html?pagewanted=all. Web.

Roth, Philip. A Conversation with Edna O'Brien." *New York Times Book Review* 18 November 1984. http://www.nytimes.com/books/00/04/09/specials/obrien-roth.html. Web.

————. *The Dying Animal.* Boston: Houghton Mifflin, 2002. Print.

————. *Everyman.* Boston: Houghton Mifflin, 2006. Print.

————. *Good-bye, Columbus* 1959. New York: Vintage, 1993. Print.

Salter, James. *Light Years.* 1975. New York: Vintage Books, 1995. Print.

————. *The Human Stain.* 2000. New York: Vintage, 2001. Print.

————. *I Married A Communist.* Boston: Houghton Mifflin, 1998. Print.

Schama, Simon. *Rembrandt's Eyes.* New York: Knopf, 1999. Print.

————. *The Plot Against America.* Boston: Houghton Mifflin, 2004. Print.

————. *Portnoy's Complaint.* 1969. New York: Vintage, 1994. Print.

————. *Reading Myself and Others.* New York: Farrar Straus Giroux, 1975. Print.

————. *Sabbath's Theater*. 1995. New York: Vintage, 1996. Print.

Sedgwick, Eve Kosofsky. *Epistemology of the Closet*, Berkeley: U of California Press, 1990. Print.

Shechner, Mark. "There's No Day of Rest For Roth's Voracious Sabbath." Rev. *Sabbath's Theater* by Phillip Roth. *Buffalo News* 3 September 1995: 6G. Print.

Showalter, Elaine. *Sister's Choice: Tradition and Change in American Women's Writing*. Oxford: Oxford U.P./Clarendon 1991. Print.

Shteyngart, Gary. *Little Failure: A Memoir*. New York: Random House, 2014. Print.

Smith, Patrick. "A Stone Unturned." *Nation* 14 April 2003: 30–34. Print.

Smith, Roberta. "Women, Art & Islam." *New York Times*. 20 August 2009. http://www.nytimes.com/2009/08/21/arts/design/21gall.html? pagewanted=all. Web.

Smith, Zadie. "That Crafty Feeling." *The Believer* June 2009: 5–12. Print.

Smyth, Nicola. "I Spy, with My Little Eye: Review of *The Male Gaze* by Joe Treasure." *The Independent*. 22 April 2007: 25. Print.

Snider, Norman. "Roth's Holy Fool Rages Against American Schlock." Rev. *Sabbath's Theater* by Phillip Roth. *Toronto Star* 9 September 1995: L15. Print.

————. *The Gulag Arichipelago: An Experiment in Literary Investigation*. Vol. 2. Tr. Thomas P Whitney. 1975. New York: Harper Perennial/Modern Classics, 2007. Print.

————. *The Gulag Arichipelago: An Experiment in Literary Investigation*. Vol. 3. Tr. Harry Willetts. 1978. NewYork: Harper Perennial/Modern Classics, 2007. Print.

Solzhenitsyn, Aleksandr. *The Gulag Arichipelago: An Experiment in Literary Investigation*. Vol. 1. Tr. Thomas P Whitney. 1973. New York: Harper Perennial/Modern Classics, 2007. Print.

Sontag, Susan. *Against Interpretation*. New York: Macmillan, 2013. Print.

————. "Persona." *Sight and Sound*. Autumn 1967. http://thomas-hersey. wiki.uml.edu/file/view/Sontag+on+Persona.pdf. Web.

Spiotta, Dana. *Innocents and Others*. New York: Scribner, 2016. Print.

Stein, Gertrude. *Wars I Have Seen*. New York: Random House, 1945. Print.

Stevens, Wallace. *The Collected Poems of Wallace Stevens*. New York: Knopf, 2011. Print.

Stewart, Susan. *On Longing: Narratives of the Miniature, The Gigantic, The Souvenir, The Collection*. Baltimore: Johns Hopkins UP, 1984. Print.

Stone, Robert. *Bay of Souls*. Boston: Houghton Mifflin, 2003. Print.

————. *Bear and his Daughter*. Boston: Houghton Mifflin, 1997. Print.

————. *Children of Light*. 1986. New York: Vintage, 1992. Print.

————. *Damascus Gate*. Boston: Houghton Mifflin, 1998. Print.

————. *Death of the Black-Haired Girl*. Boston: Houghton Mifflin Harcourt, 2013. Print.

————. *Dog Soldiers* 1974. Boston: Houghton Mifflin/Mariner, 1994. Print.

————. *A Flag for Sunrise*. 1981. New York: Random House/Vintage, 1992. Print.

————. *Hall of Mirrors*. 1966. New York: Penguin, 1987. Print.

————. *Outerbridge Reach*. 1992. New York: Harper/Perennial, 1993. Print.

————. *Prime Green: Remembering the Sixties*. New York: Ecco/Harper Collins, 2007. Print.

Sutton, Paul. *Turner Classic Movie/British Film Guide If*. London: I.B. Tauris, 2005. Print.

Swanberg, W.A. *Dreiser*. New York: Scribner, 1965. Print.

Taussing, Michael. "The Corn-Wolf: Writing Apotropaic Texts" *Critical Inquiry*. 37: 1. (2010): 26–33. Print.

Taylor, Charles. "The Human Stain." Rev. *The Human Stain* (movie). *Salon* 31 October 2003. http://www.salon.com/2003/10/31/human_stain/. Web.

Teres, Harvey. *The Word on the Street: Linking the Academy and the Common Reader*, Ann Arbor: U Michigan Press, 2010. Print.

"The Male Gaze in Retrospect." *Chronicle of Higher Education* 13 December 2015. http://chronicle.com/specialreport/The-Male-Gaze-in-Retrospect/20. Web.

Traister, Bryce. "The Wandering Bachelor: Irving, Masculinity, and Authorship." *American Literature* 74: 1 (2002). https://muse.jhu.edu/article/1797. Web.

Travers, Peter. "The Human Stain." Rev. *The Human Stain* (movie). *Rolling Stone* 25 September 2003. Web. [No longer available online].

Treasure, Joe. *The Male Gaze*. London: Picador, 2007. Print.

Trebay, Guy. "Gay Art: A Movement, or at Least a Moment." *New York Times* 6 May 2007. http://www.nytimes.com/2007/05/06/fashion/06gay.html?ex=1336017600&en=6375&_r=0. web.

Trilling, Lionel. *The Liberal Imagination: Essays on Literature and Society*. Garden City, New York: Doubleday/Anchor, 1950. Print.

Trollope, Anthony. *Phineas Finn*. 1869. http://www.gutenberg.org/files/18000/18000-h/18000-h.htm. Web.

Truong, Monique. *Bitter in the Mouth*. New York: Random House, 2010. Print.

"Two Cathedrals." *West Wing*. Episode 44 "Two Cathedrals." NBC. 16 May 2001. Television.

Vanderwees, Chris. "Resisting Remasculinization: Tim O'Brien's 'Sweetheart of the Song Tra Bong.'" *Feminist Studies in English Literature* 17: 2 (2009). http://210.101.116.28/W_files/kiss10/93100391_pv.pdf. Web.

Vendler, Helen. "Modern American Poetry: On *The Dream Songs*." 1995. http://www.english.illinois.edu/maps/poets/a_f/berryman/dreamsongs.htm. Web.

————. "On 'Dream Song 4.'" 1995. http://www.english.illinois.edu/maps/poets/a_f/berryman/song4.htm. Web.

Vida, Vendela. *The Diver's Clothes Lie Empty.* Harper Collins, 2015. Print.

Vinciguerra, Thomas. "The Elusive Girl From Ipanema." *Wall Street Journal.* 29 June 2012. http://www.wsj.com/articles/SB10001424052702303649504577492603567202024. Web.

"Waldorf Stories." Mad Men Season 4, Episode 6. AMC. 29 Aug. 2010. Television.

Waldrop, Rosmarie. "Cut With A Kitchen Knife" *Harpers* June 2016. 68–71. Print.

Walters, Suzanna Danuta. *Material Girls: Making Sense of Feminist Cultural Theory* Berkeley: U of California Press, 1995. Print.

Warner, Jessica. "Saving Feminism from the Hijackers." Rev. Boyd, *Big Sister: How Extreme Feminism Has Betrayed the Fight for Sexual Equality. Toronto Globe and Mail.* 3 July 2004: D7. Print.

Wharton, Edith. *Age of Innocence.* 1920. http://www.gutenberg.org/files/541/541-h/541-h.htm. Web.

———. *Summer.* 1917. http://www.gutenberg.org/files/166/166-h/166-h.htm. Web.

Wheatland, Thomas *The Frankfurt School in Exile.* St. Paul: U Minnesota Press, 2009. Print.

White, Edmund. *City Boy: My Life in New York During the Sixties and Seventies.* New York: Bloomsbury, 2009. Print.

Whitman, Walt. "Song of Myself." 1855. http://bailiwick.lib.uiowa.edu/whitman/1855.html. Web.

Willet, Cynthia & Sherman, Yael. "The Seriously Erotic Politics of Feminist Laughter. *Social Research* 79: 1 (2012). Print.

Williams, Linda. "Introduction." *Viewing Positions: Ways of Seeing Film.* Ed. Linda Williams. 1994. New Brunswick: Rutgers UP, 1997. Pp. 1–20. Print.

Willis, Elizabeth. "Dickinson's Species of Narrative." *Emily Dickinson Journal* 18: 1 (2009). http://muse.jhu.edu.muhlenberg.idm.oclc.org/journals/emily_dickinson_journal/v018/18.1.willis.html. Web.

Winkler, Mary. "Bathsheba." *LITMED.* 25 January 1999. http://medhum.med.nyu.edu/view/10338.Web. Web.

"Winogrand's Women Are Beautiful." Worcester Art Museum. 2013. http://www.worcesterart.org/exhibitions/winogrands-women-are-beautiful/. Web.

Wolosky, Shira. *Emily Dickinson: A Voice of War.* New Haven: Yale UP, 1984.

Woolf, Virginia. "A Room of Her Own." 1929. http://www.haverford.edu/psych/ddavis/psych214/woolf.room.html. Web.

———. *To the Lighthouse.* 1927. New York: Houghton Mifflin Harcourt/Harvest Books, 1989. Print.

Wordsworth, William. *The Prelude, Selected Poems, and Sonnets.* Ed. Carlos Baker. New York: Holt Rinehart, 1954. Print.

Wullschlager, Jackie. "Titian as Master and Muse." *Financial Times* 13 July 2013. http://www.ft.com/intl/cms/s/2/2b9a48c4-cab1-11e1-89be-00144feabdc0. html#axzz2cQEwOEJh. Web.

Yeats, William B. *The Collected Poems: 1889–1939.* http://triggs.djvu.org/ djvu-editions.com/YEATS/POEMS/Download.pdf. Web.

Zink, Nell. *The Wall Creeper.* St. Louis: Dorothy, 2014. Print.

Index

© The Editor(s) (if applicable) and The Author(s) 2017   219
J.D. Bloom, *Reading the Male Gaze in Literature and Culture*, Global
Masculinities, DOI 10.1007/978-3-319-59945-8

Printed by Printforce, the Netherlands